METRICAL VISIONS

A Publication of the Renaissance English Text Society

GC

METRICAL VISIONS

by George Cavendish

Edited by A.S.G. Edwards

Published for
THE NEWBERRY LIBRARY

by the
UNIVERSITY OF SOUTH CAROLINA PRESS

Copyright © University of South Carolina 1980
FIRST EDITION
Published in Columbia, S.C., by the University of South Carolina Press, 1980
Manufactured in the United States of America

Library of Congress Cataloging in Publication Data
Cavendish, George, 1500–1561?
　Metrical visions.
　"A publication of the Renaissance English Text
Society."
　Includes index.
　I. Edwards, Anthony Stockwell Garfield,
　1942–　　II. Newberry Library, Chicago.
III. Renaissance English Text Society.
IV. Title.
PR2233.C26M4　1980　　821'.3　　80–12390
ISBN 0–87249–391–1

CONTENTS

Acknowledgments **vii**
Introduction **3**
Metrical Visions **25**
Preface to the Commentary and List of Abbreviations **147**
Commentary **151**
Appendix: Variant Readings in Ms. Dugdale 28 **229**
Glossary **235**
Index of Names **243**
The Renaissance English Text Society **249**

ACKNOWLEDGMENTS

In the preparation of this work I have incurred many debts that I would like to acknowledge here.

I owe a great debt to Derek Pearsall of the University of York, to Professor Harold F. Brooks of Birkbeck College, University of London, and to V. J. Scattergood of Bristol University. Mr. Pearsall supervised this work in its original form as a University of London Ph.D. thesis; if my work possesses any scholarly merit it is due to his advice and example. Professor Brooks and Mr. Scattergood examined my thesis and I have benefitted from their constructive observations on it. Professor Brooks has, in addition, rendered advice and assistance that materially helped me to bring my work to a successful conclusion.

I also gratefully acknowledge the example and friendship of my earliest mentor, Professor W. F. Bolton of Rutgers University. He has provided encouragement, both spiritual and practical, which I can never adequately acknowledge.

I owe a significant debt to the late Professor Richard S. Sylvester of Yale University. Not only is his edition of Cavendish's *Life and Death of Cardinal Wolsey* an indispensable foundation for any subsequent work on Cavendish, but he also gave me personal encouragement and advice and generously commented on a number of my conclusions. His support substantially eased the difficulties of preparing this edition. Professor David M. Bevington of the University of Chicago and Professor Robert S. Kinsman of the University of California, Los Angeles, also kindly read this edition in draft and made many constructive suggestions.

For generous financial help in the course of my work thanks are due to the Essex County Council, and especially to Dr. A. M. Potter, for a postgraduate award, and to the Canada Council for the award of a doctoral fellowship. The University of Victoria kindly granted me a year's leave of absence to facilitate the completion of this work. I am particularly grateful for the kindness and encouragement of Dr. R. F. Leslie, who was then chairman of the Department of English.

This book has been published with the help of a grant from the Humanities Research Council of Canada, using funds provided by the Canada Council.

Much of this work was undertaken in confusing personal circumstances. The support and encouragement of many friends cannot be acknowledged adequately here. But I am glad to have this opportunity to thank those who for a period of time fed, housed, and sustained me during this work, particularly Donald and Virginia Miller, Katherine and David Brodie, Anthony and Elizabeth England, Michael and Terry Best, Constance and Leon Rooke, Lena and Malcolm Andrew, and Margaret MacGregor. This work owes much to the support of their friendship.

My greatest debt is to my wife, Diane, to whom this work is dedicated and whose belief in it made its completion possible.

INTRODUCTION

INTRODUCTION

George Cavendish and his Metrical Visions

George Cavendish was born circa 1499 and was probably the eldest son of Thomas Cavendish, Clerk of the Pipe under Henry VII. Presumably through his father's influence, possibly in the early 1520s, George began his service to Cardinal Wolsey as a gentleman usher. After Wolsey's death in 1530 Cavendish withdrew from public affairs to Suffolk, where he seems to have disengaged himself from any official duties. During the final period of his life, in the 1550s, Cavendish undertook his literary works, his *Metrical Visions*[1] and the great prose biography of his former patron, *The Life and Death of Cardinal Wolsey*. Cavendish died in the early 1560s.[2]

The *Metrical Visions* have been published only once in their entirety, by Samuel W. Singer in 1825.[3] His edition is marred by a number of serious deficiencies: the punctuation is on occasion misleading and heavily modernized, as is the orthography; there is only perfunctory effort at annotation; and, most seriously, there are over a hundred instances of mistranscription, omission, and silent insertion and emendation, sometimes totally destroying the meaning of Cavendish's original text.[4] All in all, Singer's work has no claim to definitiveness, and indeed he saw the *Metrical Visions* primarily as an appendix to his edition of the *Life of Wolsey*.

Only once subsequently have the *Metrical Visions* been published, and then only in part. In 1927 E. P. Hammond printed approximately six hundred lines in her anthology *English Verse between Chaucer and Surrey*.[5] The text is generally carefully transcribed (although some errors remain) and extensively annotated.

The most recent attempt at an edition is that of M. R. Fisher in an unpublished Columbia University doctoral dissertation in 1967.[6] This is a particularly unsatisfactory piece of work; it contains many errors in transcription and offers only superficial (and at times very misleading) annotation.

Clearly none of these texts can be viewed as a definitive edition. There has been no adequately transcribed, fully annotated text of Cavendish's work, and study of the text has been limited to that preserved in British Library MS. Egerton 2402 (the nature of which has been misunderstood). No previous editor has examined the text of the *Metrical Visions* preserved in Bodleian Library MS. Dugdale 28 and determined its relationship to the Egerton version. This edition seeks to resolve the basic textual problems posed by the manuscripts of the *Metrical Visions*.

This edition is therefore designed to fill the gap left by the limitations of previous editions and to provide an accurate, fully annotated text of Cavendish's poems based on a careful examination of the available manuscripts. With such an edition it may be possible for modern scholarship to arrive at a just assessment of the merits and significance of the *Metrical Visions*.

The Manuscripts

There are three manuscripts of the *Metrical Visions*: British Library MS. Egerton 2402, ff. 94–151 (henceforward *E*); Bodleian Library MS. Dugdale 28, ff. 228ᵛ–64 (henceforward *D*); and British Library MS. Additional 14,410, ff. 100–102 (henceforward *A*).

E is Cavendish's autograph manuscript, containing his *Life of Wolsey* (ff. 4–93) in addition to the *Metrical Visions*. This is a paper manuscript, into which Cavendish probably began transcribing his fair copy sometime after 1556[7] and which he completed (except for a late additional poem on the death of Mary Tudor) by June 24, 1558, according to his own scribal *explicit* (f. 149). One curious feature of the *Metrical Visions* portion of *E* is that the leaves were bound up incorrectly in the original manuscript, the correct order of the text being: ff. 94–112, 128–29, 134–47, 130–31, 114–27, 132–33, 113, 149ᵛ–51, 148ᵛ–49. No convincing explanation for this disorder presents itself.[8] Any attempts to elucidate the problem are impeded substantially by the fact that the original binding of *E* was removed when it was acquired by the British Museum in 1876; hence, its collation cannot now be established.

The history of *E* is unclear after Cavendish completed it. It served as the exemplar for both *D* and *A* (see below). Its first recorded owner after Cavendish was Clement Rossington of Dronfield, Derbyshire, who owned it in the eighteenth century. He may have acquired the manuscript from the family of William Burton, the seventeenth-century antiquary. The next recorded owner is Thomas Lloyd, a nineteenth-century collector of genealogical and heraldic material, who lent it to Singer for the preparation of his edition of Cavendish. *E* was later owned by two famous nineteenth-century bibliophiles, Richard Heber (d. 1835) and Thomas Corser (d. 1875). It passed from the collection of Corser to the British Museum in December 1876.

D is a collection of unrelated items, bound up by Dugdale sometime after 1660, the date of the latest item in the collection. The Cavendish texts constitute item VIII, beginning on f. 220 with a prose summary of the *Life of Wolsey* which ends on f. 228.[9] The *Metrical Visions* begin on f. 228ᵛ and end on f. 264, being interrupted at f. 239ʳ⁻ᵛ by an extract from the *Life*.[10]

The history of *D* is unknown beyond the fact that it was copied from *E*; nor is it known when or where Dugdale acquired it. The manuscript was received into the Ashmolean in 1686, after Dugdale's death, and transferred to Bodleian in 1860 with the rest of Dugdale's collection. It is now no. 6518 in the Summary Catalogue.[11]

A is a miscellaneous collection, mainly of heraldic materials. It contains three leaves (ff. 100–102) of a page-for-page transcript of *E*, comprising vv. 2279–425. The transcript appears to have been made by Thomas Lloyd, who also owned *E*. It appeared in 1843 in the final portion of the sale of Lloyd's library and was acquired there by Thomas Rodd, the bookseller, who sold it to the British Museum.[12]

The Relationship of the Manuscripts

The relationship of the MSS. *E, D,* and *A* is clear and can be set out briefly. *E* is Cavendish's autograph manuscript.[13] Earlier scholars have been doubtful that it represents his final intentions in view of the number of corrections that had been made to the text after initial transcription. But, as I have shown elsewhere, a detailed examination of these corrections leads inescapably to a contrary conclusion.[14] The alterations in *E* seem in the main not to be the product of authorial revision, but corrections of initial transcriptional (i.e. scribal) errors, the errors of an inexperienced copyist. The evidence in support of this view is compelling. For example, over a third of all the alterations made to the text are nonsubstantive ones; that is, they seem prompted by a concern with the palaeographical clarity and correctness in the actual writing of words and phrases, a concern that scarcely would seem necessary at any stage before the transcription of a completed text. And other changes can be shown to be the correction of obvious initial common forms of scribal error, including haplography, dittography, homeography, eye skip, and stock associations. Very few of the alterations made in *E* have any claim to be substantive changes. There seems little reason to doubt that *E* represents Cavendish's final intentions insofar as he was capable of realizing them.

The relationship of *D* to *E* can be clearly established. It is possible to demonstrate through a misplaced cancelled stanza in *D* that it was copied directly from *E,* at one point following the sequence of leaves in that manuscript when it was disordered.[15] Although the source of *D* is clear, there are a large number of substantive changes (over three hundred in all) made to the text. It is conceivable that such changes could derive directly from Cavendish and that the *D* text could have been prepared under his supervision. This is not, however, likely. A detailed examination of the variant readings in *D* suggests that they are the product of a scribal concern to elucidate his exemplar through a process of simplification, modernization, and regularization. It is not necessary to reiterate the evidence here. It is sufficient to observe that the efforts of the *D* scribe indicate a desire to render his exemplar as accessible as possible to his audience by seeking to clarify and render more current the diction and syntax of *E,* and even to adjust what he seems to have felt to be stylistic infelicities. Although his attempt on the whole is intelligent, he does leave sufficient indications (particularly in such ways as his introduction of nonsense readings and disruptions of the rhyme scheme) that the variant readings in *D* have no claim to authority.[16]

The third manuscript of the *Metrical Visions*, MS. *A*, is of no significance. It is a fragmentary text, of three leaves, containing the final 147 lines of the text. The variants are minor ones and have been recorded elsewhere.[17] The manuscript is a late copy; as I have noted, it was probably made by Thomas Lloyd and copied directly from *E*.

An editor has no option but to use *E* as the basis for an edition of the *Metrical Visions*. It is an autograph and seems to be a fair copy embodying Cavendish's final intentions. Nor is there any evidence that the changes in *D* have any authority. Accordingly the text of this edition is based on *E*.

Date

The evidence for the date of the *Metrical Visions* has been set out elsewhere and can be summarized briefly.[18] The *terminus ad quem* for their composition is provided by the *explicit* of *E*: "Ffinis et compile le xxiiii[er] jour de Iunii annus regnorum Philippi Rex et Regine Marie iiii[th] et v[th] per le auctor G.C." (f. 149), i.e. June 24, 1558. But this date is of little help since it is a scribal rather than a compositional one.

The most conclusive evidence for a compositional *terminus a quo* is provided by the lament for the death of Edward VI (vv. 1838–1907), which is followed by a reference to Mary's accession:

> But God that knewe / our lamentable sore.
> Hathe agayn / of hys especyall grace.
> Torned our olde sorrowe / to a newe solace /
> Ffor the losse of a kyng / whiche was a virgyn clean
> He hathe restored vs / a mayden quene / [vv. 1924–28]

The identification of Mary as "mayden quene" places this passage before her marriage to Philip of Spain on July 25, 1554. And since Cavendish interjects both the lament for Edward and his praise of Mary into the middle of another narrative, it seems likely that the event was, for him, one of immediate moment. Since the sequence of Cavendish's groups of tragedies is roughly chronological, and since by the time he reached his reference to Mary, Cavendish had completed nearly five-sixths of his work,[19] the allusion provides the basis for legitimate speculation about the composition of the *Metrical Visions*. It would seem reasonable to place the beginning of the work no earlier than 1552,[20] over a year before Mary's accession, and quite possibly even earlier than that since he had completed so much of it before July 1554.

There is nothing to suggest that the *Visions* were continued after 1554. Of the tragedies recounted after Mary's accession, the latest chronologically is that of the Duke of Suffolk (vv. 2125–87), who died on February 23, 1554. Cavendish seems to have had no wish to continue his work after this point. The beginnings of an addition on f. 113^v are cancelled and the envoy "Thauctor to hys boke" (ff. 148^v–49) follows. There is nothing to indicate that Cavendish worked on the *Visions* (except perhaps for revisions attendant upon the transcription of his fair copy) between mid-1554 and some point after November 17, 1558, when he added a supplementary "Ephitaphe of our late quene Marye" (ff. 149^v–51^r).

In conclusion, some mention must be made of the related problems of the actual circumstances of the composition of the *Metrical Visions*. Hammond has argued that they were not conceived as a unified work but were composed piecemeal at intervals: "It would seem that Cavendish closed off, and then continued his work from time to time; for twice at least in the long series of lamenting personages a 'Finis' has been put and then more material, of later date, added" (p. 369). There is not a great deal that can be usefully said about the process of composition of the work, but such misconceptions need correction. There is little evidence to support Hammond's view. In fact "Ffinis" is used to mark off a section of the work five times (apart from at the end of the work). It is written at the end of the prologue (v. 84), after Wolsey's lament (v. 259), at the end of the epitaph for Henry VIII (v. 1473), to mark off the beginning of the lament for Edward VI (v. 1837), and at the conclusion of the epitaph for Mary Tudor (v. 2383). Such use does not seem to offer much evidence of structural intent on Cavendish's part. "Ffinis" seems to be used to indicate chronological divisions of the work, marking off the reigns of Henry, Edward, and Mary. Its occurrence immediately after the tragedy of Wolsey is puzzling, but may be an indication of the personal importance to Cavendish of his former patron. It is in any case difficult to attach much weight to the use of "Ffinis" at these points since it may have first occurred in the preparation of the fair copy *E*. The manuscript headings shed little light on the composition of the *Metrical Visions*.[21]

There is virtually no basis upon which to draw conclusions about the method of composition of Cavendish's work. It is possible that in transcribing *E* he was working from drafts made nearer the time of the events he describes, but speculation remains fruitless with the available evidence.

To sum up: Cavendish does not seem likely to have commenced the *Metrical Visions* before 1552 and does not seem to have worked on them beyond mid-1554 until after Mary's death. It is unclear why Cavendish would have allowed such a lapse of time between composition and the final transcription of *E*, completed in June 1558. The most likely explanation is that between 1554 and 1558 he was engaged in the composition of the *Life and Death of Cardinal Wolsey* (which Sylvester suggests was begun after November 4, 1554) and wished to delay making a fair copy until he had both texts ready.

Sources of the Metrical Visions

> Of ffortunes fykellnes / hereafter shall I wright
> How greatest estates / she ouerthroweth by myght . . .
> The cause that moved me / to this enterprice.
> Specyally was / that all estates myght se
> What it is to trust to ffortunes mutabylite [vv. 48–49, 54–56]

Cavendish seeks to place his work within the *de casibus* tradition. Indeed, the *Metrical Visions* come near the end of a sequence of attempts to render speculations about Fortune into literary form.[22] In England the most extensive example of tragedy concerned with "ffortunes fykellnes" was undoubtedly John Lydgate's *Fall of Princes* (c. 1432–38), a verse translation of a French prose version of Boccaccio's *De Casibus Virorum Illustrium*. During the fifteenth and sixteenth centuries, when it seems to have been widely read, Lydgate's poem was copied, plundered for exempla of historical tragedy, and plagiarized.[23] For Cavendish to have turned to the *Fall* as a model for his own work would have been natural, but he goes much further than that. The *Metrical Visions* clearly draw upon the *Fall of Princes* not only in form but also in important respects in content. Cavendish's work follows (albeit on a vastly reduced scale of time and chronological scope) Lydgate's own roughly chronological progression of historical figures, loosely linked by a narrator in the framework of a dream or reverie.

That Cavendish was attempting to imitate the *Fall* is also demonstrated clearly by the nature and extent of his *verbal* borrowings from Lydgate's poem, which have not previously been appreciated.[24] Nearly two hundred lines in the *Metrical Visions* are borrowed from Lydgate.[25] Cavendish's knowledge of the *Fall of Princes* appears to have been wide ranging. He drew on at least the first six books (over thirty thousand lines) to find particular lines or stanzas to suit his purposes.

These borrowings also bear testimony to Cavendish's intimacy with Lydgate's work. Thus, at one point (vv. 309–36) four consecutive stanzas are drawn, in order, from Books III, V, III, and IV, and combined into a passage of generalized moral reflection. Cavendish's ability to select stanzas that are widely separated in Lydgate, and to impose upon them a requisite unity of sense and tone for his own purposes, suggests that he possessed an awareness of the texture of the *Fall* which could have come only after careful study. Nor was he content to copy out material uncritically from the *Fall*. A comparison of the relevant portions of the *Visions* with Lydgate indicates the extent to which Cavendish was capable of adapting and reworking his model where necessary. One example of this is the single stanza (IV, 2948–54) incorporated into the lament for Cromwell (vv. 680–86), where Cavendish reworks a felicitous image to give it an additional sting in its final lines.[26] And elsewhere (e.g. vv. 1530ff.) he proves himself capable of skillful adaptation of longer passages. Generally Cavendish's borrowings seem to be governed by a considered sense of their particular contextual appositeness in the *Metrical Visions*, a sense clearly based on a careful reading of Lydgate.

The evidence of what has been justly termed the "pressure of the Lydgatean stereotype"[27] on Cavendish does not end with the indications of his extensive verbal debt to Lydgate. Indeed, the *Metrical Visions* seem to attempt to reproduce the whole apparatus and ethos of the *Fall of Princes*. Cavendish introduced exhortations on Fortune and admonitions on the mutability of human affairs. He added formal envoys, made interpolations in his narrative, and varied the length of his tragedies. In all these respects he followed the example of Lydgate. Such formal and tonal appropriations from the *Fall of Princes* seem unique in their range and degree.[28] Lydgate, then, is the main source for the *Metrical Visions*. One other possible literary influence is discernible in Cavendish's poem. He may have read Skelton's poems, and to some degree his work may reflect this study. The evidence for such a view is not as clear-cut as that for Cavendish's debt to Lydgate. But there are some verbal and situational parallels, as well as some general indications of possible stylistic and even attitudinal indebtedness.[29] The possibility certainly cannot be ruled out, but the evidence is inconclusive.

Other discernible sources of and influences on the *Metrical Visions* are minor. At points Cavendish supplements Lydgate with biblical exempla.[30] And at another point he may echo, in the refrain from his lament on the death of Edward VI, the wording of a contemporary ballad on the same subject.[31] Elsewhere, the most likely sources for his assertions are either personal acquaintance with the subjects of his tragedies or contemporary rumor.[32]

The Significance of the Metrical Visions

The *Metrical Visions* have not been treated kindly by scholars. The comments of S. W. Singer, Cavendish's first editor, have set the tone: "They have little or no merit as verses, being deficient in all the essential points of invention, expression and rhythm, and we cannot but regret that Cavendish, who knew so well how to interest us in his artless narration of facts in prose, should have invoked the muse in vain" (I,xx). E. P. Hammond reached similar conclusions: "[The] 'Visions' are clumsy and stilted, loaded with rhetoric and fettered by formulae; they have indeed their verities, but it is only when we turn to the prose life of Wolsey, that a human voice speaks simply and freely" (p. 369). Derek Pearsall's is the most recent and most dismissive voice: "The extraordinary thing about the *Visions* is that Cavendish should have bothered to write them at all."[33] These are stern judgments, but they are not without some justice. The design of Cavendish's tragedies is often confused and at times contradictory. His grasp of meter is uncertain, while the diction of his work is littered with stock tags and phrases. Cavendish's verse suffers inevitably in comparison with his later, assured prose.

But within their limitations (which are undeniably considerable) the *Metrical Visions* do possess some merit. Some passages of the work achieve a plangent and moving elegiac note. Most striking in this regard is Cavendish's epitaph on Mary Tudor (vv. 2279–383), where his sonorous lament recalls the more successful passages of his model, Lydgate's *Fall of Princes*. Elsewhere, it is tempting to attribute to Cavendish a greater degree of irony in his presentation than has hitherto been accorded him, particularly in his lengthy series of unapt comparisons to Henry VIII (vv. 1434–73). At other times (e.g. vv. 169–72, 222–24, 348–50) he shows some sense, albeit crude, of the possibilities of wordplay. It would be inappropriate to make large claims for Cavendish's poetic abilities. But such areas of evidenced sensibility, together with his capacity for intelligent adaptation must, at least partially, qualify the dismissive tone of previous criticism.

However limited may be the claims of the *Metrical Visions* to intrinsic merit, it is a work of historical importance. There had been, before Cavendish, isolated attempts to interpret the falls of contemporary figures in *de casibus* verse tragedy, but such attempts had dealt only with single figures.[34] The *Metrical Visions* are the first sustained attempt to write verse *de casibus* tragedy that draws its subject matter from contemporary history. This is Cavendish's most significant achievement: he offers, in the *Metrical Visions*, a version of literary tragedy that seeks, on a relatively large scale, to interpret contemporary history. In this regard he anticipates the *Mirror for Magistrates*,[35] an infinitely more wide-ranging and successful attempt to render a poetic tragic vision of British history. And it is tempting to speculate on the relationship between Cavendish's own work and the later, more ambitious *Mirror*. It is conceivable that the *Metrical Visions* could have circulated in manuscript form to one or more of those involved in the later work. Such a connection between the aged, reclusive Cavendish and larger literary circles might have been possible through William Forrest, Mary Tudor's chaplain, who may have been Cavendish's friend, and whose *History of Griseld the Second* seems to bear some relationship to the *Life of Wolsey*.[36] The potential connection between the *Visions* and the *Mirror* is a tantalizing one that cannot be satisfactorily resolved in our present state of knowledge. But enough is clear

INTRODUCTION 13

to suggest that in terms of literary history Cavendish's poem reflects a distinct development in the *de casibus* literature of the period.

Apart from the possible connection with the *Mirror* there is no indication that the *Metrical Visions* had any discernible influence. The work remained in manuscript for nearly three hundred years after its composition, and its manuscript tradition is an attenuated one, suggesting a restricted audience and a limited appeal. But Cavendish is a figure whose verse, particularly for historical reasons, merits more examination than it has hitherto received.

Editorial Principles

This edition is based upon British Museum MS. Egerton 2402, a manuscript that is a holograph attempt at a fair copy. The manuscript does not require a great deal of emendation or correction; but, as I have pointed out, Cavendish was not a meticulous copyist, and he introduced a number of minor errors into his transcription of Egerton. These errors fall into three categories: (1) The omission of single letters (see e.g. vv. 133, 345, 442, 1133, 1164, 1224, 1256, 1410, 1411, 1894, 1956, 2015, 2140, 2237) and the mistranscription of single letters (e.g. vv. 3, 96, 434, 498, 1576). Into this category also fall a number of otiose contraction marks (e.g. vv. 293, 345, 922, 2062, 2334). (2) The omission of whole words (e.g. vv. 1301, 2239) or the seemingly erroneous cancellation of correct readings (e.g. vv. 353, 1694). On one occasion a whole line has been omitted (v. 969, where I have filled in the lacuna from *D*). (3) Points where the text seems defective in additional respects. There are not many such places. They include lines in which the rhyme scheme seems defective: in a number of such cases the intended correct reading seems recoverable (e.g. vv. 715, 1099, 2025). At one point (v. 1904) a confusion between singular and plural forms has been editorially corrected. Corrections falling into this category are discussed in the Commentary at the appropriate points. In all three classes of error, I have made appropriate emendations. No emendations have been made to the text on metrical grounds, since no certain criteria for such emendation present themselves.[37]

Orthography has presented some difficulties. Cavendish's spelling is not consistent, and I have not emended to provide consistency. Thus I have allowed such variant spellings as "worldly" (v. 724) and "wordly" (e.g. vv. 219, 333, 1113) since there is warrant in the *Metrical Visions* and the *Life* for both spellings. I have, however, emended forms that occur uniquely in the *Metrical Visions* and for which there is no other warrant when grounds for an assumption of error are strong. Particular cases (e.g. vv. 498, 1495) are discussed in the Commentary.

In the case of emendations to the copy-text, the following procedures have been adopted: the emended reading is silently introduced into the text; it appears in the textual apparatus at the foot of the appropriate page marked off by a half square bracket; the rejected reading appears after the square bracket preceded by its siglum *E*. Where the emendation has the support of *D* this fact is noted immediately after the half square bracket by the appearance of the siglum *D*; for example: 486. Chaple] D; E Chapleyn. When both sigla *D* and *E* appear before a rejected reading they share a reading to which editorial conjecture has been preferred; e.g. 715. land] DE realme. Where the readings of *D* and *E* vary in providing rejected readings, the reading of *E* appears first; for example: 1472. forthy] E for thyn; D far worthy.

The textual apparatus also includes (where legible) the cancelled readings in *E*. This has been done because the manuscript is an autograph and because the cancellations provide important evidence as to the nature of the text in *E*. Illegible letters have been indicated in the apparatus by a point within parentheses (.); uncertain letters have been placed within round brackets.

Capitalization in *E* is generally inconsistent and capricious. Only occasionally are particular words (e.g. "Royal") consistently capitalized. And it is often difficult to determine whether a letter is capitalized; in such cases I have preferred the lower case form. In general, I have regarded all forms as lower case unless they are unambiguously capital. I have normalized the text by capitalizing all proper names; the initial letter of each has also been capitalized since this seems to have been Cavendish's general, but not invariable, practice.

Punctuation presents greater difficulties. Cavendish uses three main marks of punctuation:

(1) The virgule (/): this is used in a number of different ways. It is used regularly to mark the caesura. It is also used to indicate exclamatory phrases (e.g. vv. 937, 1051, 2129) and on occasion as a comma (e.g. vv. 654, 664). Also such phrases as "he said" and "quod she" are regularly

INTRODUCTION 15

marked off from direct speech by virgules preceding and following the phrase (e.g. vv. 972, 1272, 1637, 1768, 2210). In addition the virgule is employed to mark the end of over half the stanzas in *E* (at a rough count). It is also used frequently to mark the ends of lines. At times a double virgule (//) is used, apparently to denote emphasis (e.g. vv. 91, 735, 1027, 1109, 1273, 1412, 1919, 2418, 2425). On two occasions (vv. 37, 1434) a triple virgule is used. Also on one occasion (v. 751) a double virgule precedes the line. Finally, there are a number of occurrences of the virgule within the line in contexts that do not appear to conform to any of the usages outlined above (e.g. vv. 378, 449, 491, 497, 603, 634, 684, 752, 1047, 1065, 1104).

(2) The point (.), also rarely (..) (e.g. vv. 14,16): this is used in a variety of ways, most of them similar to the functions of the virgule. It is used as a comma (e.g. vv. 90, 356, 660, 1909, 2294) and occasionally to indicate an exclamation (e.g. v. 911) and to mark the caesura (e.g. v. 946). It is also often used to mark the end of lines and sometimes of stanzas. In addition, as with the virgule, it occurs within the body of the line in contexts where its function is not readily apparent (e.g. vv. 388, 466, 567, 644, 1018, 1214, 1627, 1667, 1773, 2007, 2387, 2425).

(3) The combination of these signs (. /) or (/ .) or, very rarely (e.g. vv. 1080, 1122), (: /) or (v. 319), (/ :). Hilary Jenkinson, in noting the use of this sign in the punctuation of medieval archive writers, describes it as a "curious stop."[38] It does not seem to have been used in Cavendish's prose (it is not recorded in Sylvester's edition of the *Life*), and conceivably may have possessed a function in Cavendish's mind that was specifically connected with verse composition. The sign is regularly used to mark the caesura, occurring in only a few cases at the end of the line (e.g. vv. 147, 486, 504, 532, 1423, 1508, 1651, 1718, 1794, 2251, 2252, 2362). I have been unable to determine what (if any) function it serves.

Other marks of punctuation occasionally appear. The colon (:) is used from time to time (e.g. vv. 1370, 1498, 1499, 1646, 1841), invarably at the end of the line. The comma is used very rarely (e.g. v. 379).

All in all Cavendish's punctuation is puzzling in its forms and seemingly inconsistent in its usages. Although certain patterns of usage can be detected, they are by no means regular, nor are they distinctively identified with any individual type of punctuation. The pointing seems neither regularly syntactic, nor rhetorical, nor even physiological,[39] although it fulfills all of these functions at various times. It does much to confirm

McKerrow's rueful conclusion that "so far as punctuation is concerned, there seems very little evidence that many authors [in the sixteenth and seventeenth centuries] exercised any care about it whatever."[40]

This poses problems for the editor. Singer and Fisher have dispensed with the existing punctuation of *E*, preferring to modernize it. Hammond preserves *E*'s punctuation in the parts she edits but offers no discussion of the problems involved.[41] (Sylvester's edition of the *Life* sheds no light on Cavendish's punctuation of his verse.) Ideally, of course, it would be desirable to retain Cavendish's punctuation, emending it where it was demonstrably anomalous. But, as I have shown, his practice is so loose, and the function of various punctuation marks so apparently interchangeable, that it is not possible to establish any norms upon which emendation could be based.

My approach to this problem has been conservative. I have preserved Cavendish's punctuation in my text. There seem to me, ultimately, to be compelling reasons for this, in spite of the difficulties I have outlined. The punctuation *is* authorial, and there are few points where it is positively confusing. Moreover, the punctuation practices of late medieval writers are unlikely to be fully understood without the complete presentation of the evidence available from such autograph texts as *E*.[42] This decision has, as will be apparent, caused me a measure of difficulty. But my decision is based upon a genuine effort to fulfill, rather than evade, the proper responsibilities of an editor toward an autograph manuscript.

All contractions in the text have been silently expanded. The contractions noted below occur most frequently and have been expanded as indicated: (1) The superscript sign for $-au-$ or $-a-$: expanded as $-au-$ when the rhyme scheme or preferred spelling seems to indicate this as most appropriate. Thus v. 557, in which "au*au*nce" is so expanded even though at other points the contraction seems to have the simple value of $-a-$ (e.g. vv. 677, 699, 1105). (2) The superscript sign (mainly in terminal positions in a word) for $-ur$, $-ure$, or $-r$. The various possible interpretations of this sign have necessarily led to some arbitrary decisions. Thus "honor" (vv. 325, 734, 844) is so expanded on the basis of the apparent preferred spellings at vv. 90, 221, 786. The fact that in certain instances the spelling "honoure" occurs (e.g. vv. 2285, 2292) has not affected the consistency of my expansion. "Honoure" occurs in these instances as a rhyme word and in any case occurs in a part of the text written later than the main work. In most other cases this contraction has

INTRODUCTION

been expanded as −*ur* unless rhyme scheme or preferred spelling indicates other possibilities. Again this has not led to absolute consistency. Thus "fauo*r*" (e.g. vv. 35, 99, 194, 450, 509) is so expanded on the basis of apparent spelling preference (cf. e.g. vv. 2028, 2132). Occasionally the contraction is expanded as −*ure* (e.g. v. 872, "pleas*ure*," where such spelling is necessary to the rhyme scheme), or simply as −*u*− (e.g. vv. 793, "endevo*u*r," 1126 "conquero*u*r"). (3) The superscript sign for a nasal: this is expanded as −*m*− or −*n*−. (4) The superscript sign for −*er*−: (e.g. v. 134, "sylu*er*"); when following *p* this sign is expanded as *re*− (e.g. v. 10 "opp*re*ssed"). (5) The suffix sign for −*es* (e.g. v. 17, "thyng*es*"). (6) The suffix sign for −*us* (e.g. vv. 101 "superfluo*us*," 662 "hayno*us*"). (7) The contraction for −*pro*−, indicated by a curled downward stroke through the descender of *p* (e.g. vv. 6 "App*ro*chyng," 160 "P*ro*motyng"). (8) The contraction for −*per*− or −*par*− indicated by a curled upward stroke through the descender of *p* (e.g. vv. 19 "*per*swade," 121 "*per*sonages," 155 "*par*cyall," 172 "*par*de"). (9) The contraction for −*ser*− or −*sur*− indicated by a long *s* with a curled stroke through the descender (e.g. vv. 254 "*ser*uaunt," 1544 "*sur*mysed"). (10) The superscript suffix −*t* expanded as −*ent* (e.g. vv. 15 "advisem*ent*," 1709 "punysshem*ent*").

In addition, the following words regularly occur in a contracted form and have been consistently expanded: w^t as wi*th*; yo^z as yo*ur*; q^d as q*uo*d; m^r as m*aste*r; ma^{tie} as ma*ies*tie (e.g. v. 1382); w$^{ch(e)}$ wh*i*ch(e); spualtie: as spiritualtie (e.g. v. 158). The ampersand also has been regularly expanded.

As will be apparent, superscript letters of simple value have not been distinguished in the case of expanded contractions. Nor has Cavendish's tendency to leave final −*e*'s often incomplete been noted.[43] Barred *l* or *ll* is treated as *l* or *ll*.

The word division of the manuscript has also been preserved.

Notes to the Introduction

1. The title *Metrical Visions* is wholly without authority, being the invention of their first editor, S. W. Singer. None of the manuscripts has a title. I have, for convenience, retained Singer's title throughout, while preferring Dugdale's (MS. Dugdale 28, f. 219^r): "diuers Elegieciall Poems upon sundry persons."

2. Cavendish's biography is detailed with full references in R. S. Sylvester's edition of *The Life and Death of Cardinal Wolsey*, E.E.T.S., o.s. 243 (London: Oxford University Press, 1959), pp. xiii–xxvi. The account in this paragraph derives wholly from this source. This work is cited in the Introduction as *Life*.
3. *The Life of Cardinal Wolsey and Metrical Visions*. 2 vols. (Chiswick, 1825); vol. 2 contains the *Metrical Visions*. This work is cited throughout as Singer.
4. For details see my note, "S. W. Singer's Edition of George Cavendish's *Metrical Visions*," *Book Collector*, 22 (1973), 236–37.
5. (Durham, N.C.: Duke University Press, 1927); Hammond prints vv. 1–273, 1105–95, and 1217–473. This edition is cited throughout as Hammond.
6. For a brief account of this work see *Dissertation Abstracts*, 28 (1968), 5014-A.
7. The evidence for this date is not conclusive. It derives from the paper in *E*, which is watermarked throughout with a *pot a une anse* that appears identical with no. 12739 in C. M. Briquet, *Les Filigranes* (Paris: A. Picard 1907), and is dated there as 1556. But it is difficult to accept this date as authoritative since Briquet uses tracings of the watermarks in his collection which are of uncertain reliability for purposes of dating.
8. Hammond (p. 369) gives an incorrect account of the page order. The lack of catchwords and signatures may have caused confusion. A hand apparently contemporary with the manuscript (but not Cavendish's) has noted the correct sequence of leaves.
9. For a discussion of this summary, see my article "A Tudor Redactor at Work," *Yearbook of English Studies*, 3 (1973), 10–13.
10. This extract is printed and discussed in my article "Thomas Cromwell and Cavendish's *Life of Wolsey*: The Uses of a Tudor Biography," *Revue de l'Université d'Ottawa*, 43 (1973), 292–96.
11. See, F. Madan et al., *A Summary Catalogue of the Western Manuscripts in the Bodleian Library* (Oxford: At the University Press, 1937), II, ii, 1083–84, which contains a general description of *D*.
12. For fuller accounts of all these manuscripts and their provenances, see my article "The Text of George Cavendish's *Metrical Visions*," *Analytical and Enumerative Bibliography*, 2, (1978), 3–62.
13. Cf. *Life*, x: "There can be little doubt that Egerton 2402 is an autograph." The assertion is substantiated there (x–xi) and at greater length in particular relation to the *Metrical Visions* in my article "The Text of George Cavendish's *Metrical Visions*," pp. 4–26.
14. See my article "The Author as Scribe: Cavendish's *Metrical Visions* and MS. Egerton 2402," *The Library*, 5th series, 29 (1974), 446–49.

INTRODUCTION 19

15. For details see my article "The Dugdale Manuscript of George Cavendish's *Metrical Visions*," *Papers of the Bibliographical Society of America*, 68 (1974), 167–70.
16. For full evidence in support of this point see my article "The Text of George Cavendish's *Metrical Visions*," pp. 26–40.
17. For description and full listing of variant readings see my article "A New Manuscript of George Cavendish's *Metrical Visions*," *Papers of the Bibliographical Society of America*, 69 (1975), 388–91.
18. See my article "The Date of George Cavendish's *Metrical Visions*," *Philological Quarterly*, 52 (1974), 129–32.
19. Actually 1921 out of a total of 2320 verses (excluding the epitaph on the death of Mary Tudor, which was added later).
20. Conceivably in June of that year, if the opening line of the work is not conventional in its astrology. The first stanza does not afford the possibility of any precise dating; see Commentary, vv. 1–6.
21. Cavendish several times (e.g. vv. 965–66, 1217–18, 1914) announces his intention of imminently terminating his work. But such announcements do not, of course, provide any evidence as to composition. Rather, they seem intended to place Cavendish in the role of helpless narrator, rendered powerless by the ongoing procession of tragedies that he must narrate. He also appears in this persona at vv. 1637–41 and 1754–60. Cavendish probably adopts this literary device from his study of Lydgate's *Fall of Princes*.
22. These attempts are excellently surveyed in W. Farnham, *The Medieval Heritage of Elizabethan Tragedy* (Berkeley: University of California, 1936).
23. See my article "The Influence of Lydgate's *Fall of Princes*: A Survey," *Mediaeval Studies*, 39 (1977), 424–39.
24. In her selected edition Hammond notes (pp. 368, 528) borrowings and reworkings from Lydgate totalling eleven lines. But she fails to note far more extensive borrowings within the limits of her selections in e.g. vv. 1308–12, 1329–33, 1336–40, 1343–49.
25. See my note "Some Borrowings by Cavendish from Lydgate's *Fall of Princes*," *Notes and Queries*, 216 (1971), 207–9.
26. Cf. v. 686, where *Fall of Princes*, IV, 2954: "Yit euer sum tech mut folwe of his lynage" is changed in Cavendish to read: "Yet wyll the Egles / disdayn hys parentage" sharpening the contemptuous allusion to Cromwell's humble origins.
27. D. Pearsall, "The English Chaucerians," in D. S. Brewer, ed., *Chaucer and Chaucerians* (London: Thomas Nelson, 1966), p. 235.

28. For a further discussion of this point, see my article "The Influence of Lydgate's *Fall of Princes*," cited above.
29. For further details, see Commentary, especially vv. 1–7, 510–11, and 1434–73.
30. Cf. e.g. vv. 708–14, 1000.
31. Cf. v. 1844 and Commentary.
32. Cavendish's acquaintance with Wolsey, Cromwell, Henry VIII, and Anne Bolyen needs no further documentation. In addition it is clear from the *Metrical Visions* that he was acquainted with Catherine Howard (v. 858) and Viscountess Rochford (v. 971) and with Mark Smeaton, a former member of Wolsey's household (vv. 485–86). It is moreover clear from the *Life* that he knew Norris (cf. 93/19ff., 101/34–104/10, 184/4ff.), Brereton (cf. 139/15) and Arundel (104/22; cf. also *Metrical Visions*, vv. 1772–74). It is also well within the realm of probability that during his years at court he encountered others whose fate he narrates. George Boleyn, the Countess of Salisbury, and Mary Tudor are likely cases. See Commentary, vv. 2146–49, for an example of an assertion possibly based on rumor.
33. Derek Pearsall, *John Lydgate* (London: Routledge and Kegan Paul, 1970), p. 252.
34. Cf. e.g. *Of the Death of the Noble Prince, Kyng Edward the Forth* (sometimes attributed to Skelton), *The Lamentation of King James IV* (c. 1513), David Lyndesay's *Tragedye of . . . Father Dauid . . .* (c. 1546) and More's *Rufull Lamentation*. It also seems clear that work had begun on some version of the *Mirror for Magistrates* before 1555; a fragment of a suppressed edition is extant—see W. A. Jackson, "Wayland's Edition of the *Mirror for Magistrates*," *The Library*, 4th series, 13 (1932–33), 155–57. It is not improbable that both Cavendish and the compilers of the *Mirror* were influenced by the appearance of two editions of the *Fall of Princes* (by Tottel and Wayland) c.1554.
35. See further on this point my article "The Date of George Cavendish's *Metrical Visions*," *Philological Quarterly*, 52 (1974), 129–32.
36. See *Life*, pp. 259–62.
37. D. Pearsall has dismissed Cavendish's metrics as "chaotic" ("The English Chaucerians" in Brewer, ed., *Chaucer and Chaucerians*, p. 235). In broad terms an analysis of the verse of the *Metrical Visions* confirms its lack of conformity to any strict metrical norms. Its prosody is most sympathetically viewed as loosely based on some theory of half-line stresses along the lines advanced by C. S. Lewis in "The Fifteenth-Century Heroic Line," *Essays and Studies*, 24

(1938), 28–41. But even if underpinned by any such theoretical position, Cavendish's practice is so loose as to render emendation impossible.
38. Hilary Jenkinson, "Notes on the Study of English Punctuation of the Sixteenth Century," *Review of English Studies*, 2 (1926), 153.
39. For a useful discussion of these aspects of punctuation theory, and the apparent lack of any form of distinction between them in the sixteenth century, see W. J. Ong, "Historical Backgrounds of Elizabethan and Jacobean Punctuation," *PMLA*, 59 (1944), 349–60.
40. R. B. McKerrow, *An Introduction to Bibliography for Literary Students* (Oxford: At the University Press, 1927), p. 250.
41. It is difficult in consequence to be sure whether her divergences from *E* are dictated by policy or error. At several points (e.g. vv. 196, 1260, 1463) she silently omits virgules from *E*.
42. For a recent account stressing the need for greater attention to punctuation in sixteenth-century autograph poetical manuscripts, see J. Daalder's criticism of Muir and Thompson's edition of *Collected Poems of Sir Thomas Wyatt* (Liverpool: Liverpool University Press, 1969) in his "Some Problems of Punctuation and Syntax in Egerton MS. 2711 of Wyatt's Verse," *Notes and Queries*, 218 (1971), 214–16.
43. Except in the special case of v. 1099, where contracted final −*es* has been emended to −*e*.

METRICAL VISIONS

f. 94ʳ]

Prologus / de lauctor G C

In the monyth of Iune / I lyeng sole alon
Vnder the vmber of an Oke / with bowes pendaunt
Whan Phebus in Gemynye / had his course ouergoon
And entred Cancer / a sygne retrogradaunt
In a mean measure / his beames Radyaunt   5
Approchyng Lion / than mused I in mynd
Of ffikkellnes of ffortune / and of the Course of kynd

How some are by ffortune / exalted to Riches
And often suche / as most vnworthy be
And some oppressed / in langor and syknes /   10
Some waylyng lakkyng welthe / by wretched pouertie
Some in bayle and bondage / and some at libertie
With other moo gyftes / of ffortune Varyable.
Some pleasaunt / Somme mean / and some onprofitable..

But after dewe serche / and better advisement   15
I knewe by Reason / that oonly God above..
Rewlithe thos thynges / as is most convenyent
The same devydyng / to man for his behove.
Wherfore dame Reason / did me perswade and move /
To be content / with this my small estat   20
And in this matter no more to vestigate /

1. of *interl*.
3. Gemynye] D; E Gemynys; cou *canc. before* course
5. mean *interl*.
6. in *interl*.
7. cous *canc. before* Course
11. of *canc. before* welthe

f. 94ᵛ]

Whan I had debated / all thyng in my mynd
I well considered / myn obscure blyndnes
So that non excuse could I se or fynd
But that my tyme / I spend in idelnes   25
Ffor this me thought / and treu it is doughtles
That sence I ame / a reasonable creature.
I owght my reason and wyt / to put in vre /

Than of what matter / myght I devise to wright
To vse my tyme / and wytte to excercyse.   30
Sythe most men haue / no pleasure or delight
In any history. / without it sownd to vice /
Alas shold I than / that ame not yong attise.
With lewed ballattes / faynt hartes to synne
Or flatter estates / some fauor of them to wynne /   35

What than shall I wright /// the noble doughtynes
Of estates. / that vsed is now a dayes.
I shall than lake iust matter / ffor gredy Couetousnes
Of vayn Ryches / whiche hathe stopt all the wayes.
Of worthy Chyvallry. / that now dayly sore dekayes.   40
And yet thoughe some behaue them nobly.
Yet many ther be / that dayly dothe the contrarye

22. all *interl*.
25. tymes *canc. before* tyme
41. some *interl*.
42. dothe *canc. before* dayly *and interl. before* the

f. 95ʳ]

Ffor some lovyth meate fynne and delicious
And some baudye brothes. / as ther educasion hathe be.
So some lovethe vertue / and some tales vicious   45
Sewerly suche tales / gett ye non of me
But to eschewe all Ociosite
Of ffortunes fykellnes / hereafter shall I wright
Howe greatest estates / she ouerthrowyth by myght

Thoughe I onworthe / this tragedy do begyne   50
Of pardon I pray / the reders in meke wyse
And to correct / where they se fault therin.
Reputyng it for lake / of connyng exercyse.
The cause that moved me / to this enterprice.
Specyally was / that all estates myght se   55
What it is to trust to ffortunes mutabylite

With pen and ynke I toke this worke in hand
Redy to wright the deadly dole / and whofull playnt
Of them whos fall the world dothe vnderstand
Whiche for feare made my hart to faynt /   60
I must wright playn / colours haue I none to paynt
But termes rude / ther dolours to compile
An wofull playnt must haue an wofull style /

44. hath *canc. before* hathe
50. onworthely *canc. before* onworthe; onworthe *interl.*
57. y(k) *canc. before* ynke

f. 95ᵛ]

To whome therfore / for helpe shall I nowe call
Alas Caliope my callyng wyll vtterly refuse /   65
Ffor mornyng dities / and woo of fortunes falle
Caliopie dyd neuer. / in hir dyties vse.
Wherfore to hir I myght my self abuse
Also the musis that on Parnasus syng
Suche warblyng dole / did neuer tempor stryng   70

Nowe to that lord / whos power is celestiall
And gwydyth all thyng of sadnes and of blysse
With humble voyce. / to the I crie and call
That thou woldest direct / my sely pen in this
Ffor wantyng of thy helpe / no mervell thoughe I mysse   75
And by thy grace / thoughe my style be rude
In sentence playn / I may full well conclude

Nowe by thy helpe / this hystory I wyll begyn
And frome theffect varie nothyng at all
Ffor if I shold / it ware to me great Synne   80
To take vppon me a matter so substancyall
So waytie so necessarie of ffame perpetuall
And thus to be short / oon began to speke /
With deadly voyce / as thoughe his hart wold breke /
    Ffinis Quod G. C.

64. call *canc. before* call
66. who *canc. before* woo
75. want of *canc. before* wantyng
76. Ffor *canc. before* And; And *interl.*

Le Historye / Cardinalis Eboracensis

O ffortune / quod he / shold I on the complayn 85
Or of my necligence that I susteyn this smart
Thy doble visage hathe led me to this trayn
Ffor at my begynnyng / thou dydest ay take my part
Vntill ambysion had puffed vppe my hart
With vaynglory . honor . and vsurped dignyte. 90
Fforgettyng cleane my naturall mendycitie //

Ffrome pouertie to plentie whiche nowe I se is vayn
A Cardynall I was / and legate de latere
A bysshope and archebysshope / the more to crease my gayn
Chauncelor of Englond / fortune by hir falce flatere 95
Dyd me avaunce / and gave me suche auctorytie
That of hyghe and lowe / I toke on me the charge
All Englond to rewle / my power extendyd large

Whan ffortune with fauor / had sett me thus alofte
I gathered me Riches / suffisaunce cowld not content 100
My fare was superfluous / my bed was fynne and softe
To haue my desiers / I past not what I spent
In yerthe such aboundaunce / ffortune had me lent
Yt was not in the world / that I cowld well requyer
But fortune strayt wayes / dyd graunt me my desier 105

---

96. avaunce] D advance; E avaumced
96. s *canc. before* me

f. 96ᵛ]

My byldynges somptious / the Roffes with gold and byse
Shone lyke the Sone / in the myd day spere
Craftely entaylled / as connyng cowld devyse
With images embossed. / most lyvely did appere
Expertest artificers / that ware bothe farre and nere   110
To beatyfie my howssys / I had them at my wyll
Thus I wanted nought / my pleasures to fullfyll /

My Galleryes ware fayer / bothe large and long
To walke in theme / whan that it lyked me best
My Gardens swett / enclosed with walles strong   115
Enbanked with benches / to sytt and take my rest
The knottes so enknotted / it cannot be exprest
With arbors and alyes / so pleasaunt and so dulce
The pestylent ayers / with flauours to repulce /

My chambers garnysht / with arras fynne.   120
Importyng personages. / of the lyvelyest kynd
And whan I was disposed / in them to dynne
My clothe of estate / there redy did I fynd
Ffurnysshed complett accordyng to my mynd
The subtill perfumes / of muske and swett amber.   125
There wanted non / to perfume all my chamber.

107. the *canc. before* the myd

f. 97ʳ]

Plate of all sortes / most curiously wrought
Of facions newe / I past not of the old
No vessell but Syluer / byfore me was brought
Ffull of dayntes vyaundes / the Some cannot be told 130
I dranke my wynne alwayes in syluer and in gold.
And daylye to serue me / attendyng on my table
Seruauntes I had / bothe worshipfull and honorable

My crossis twayn / of siluer long and greate
That dayly byfore me / ware Caried hyghe. 135
Vppon great horses / opynly in the strett
And masse pillers / gloryouse to the eye
With pollaxes gylt / that no man durst come nyghe
My presence / I was so pryncely to behold
Ridyng on my mule / trapped in siluer and in gold. 140

My legantyn prerogatyve / was myche to myn avayle
By vertue wherof. / I had thys highe preemynence /
All vacant benefices. / I dyd them strayt retaylle
Presentyng than my Clarke / asson as I had intellygence
I preventid the patron / ther vaylled no resistence. 145
All bysshoppes and prelattes / durst not oons denay.
They doughtyd / so my power / they myght not dysobey. /

128. old *canc. before* old
133. worshipfull] D; E worshpfull
134. large *canc. before* long; long *interl*.
135. f *canc. before* byfore
135. cared *canc. before* Caried
136. the *interl*.
140. in² *interl*.

f. 97ᵛ]

Thus may yow se / howe I to riches did attayn
And with suffisaunce / my mynd was not content
Whan I had most / I rathest wold complayn 150
Ffor lake of good / alas howe I was blent
Where shall my gatheryng / and good be spent
Somme oon perchaunce / shall me therof discharge /
Whome I most hate. / and spend it owt at large

Syttyng in iugement / parcyall ware my domes 155
I spared non estate / of hyghe or lowe degree.
I preferred whome me lyst / exaltyng symple gromes
Above the nobles / I spared myche the spiritualtie
Not passyng myche / on the temperaltie /
Promotyng suche / to so hyghe estate 160
As vnto prynces / wold boldly say chekmate /

Oon to subdewe / that did me allwayes fauor
And in that place an other to auaunce.
Ayenst all trewthe / I did my busy labor.
And whilest I was workyng / witty whiles in Fraunce 165
I was at home supplanted / where I thought most assuraunce
Thus who by fraud / ffraudelent is found
Ffraude to the defrauder / wyll aye rebound

f. 98ʳ]

Who workyth fraude / often is disceyved
As in a myrror / ye may behold in /. me.   170
Ffor by disceyt / or I had it perceyved
I was. dissayved / a guerdon met parde
Ffor hyme that wold. / ayenst all equyte
Dysseyve the innocent / that innocent was in deade /
Therfore iustice of iustice / ayenst me must procede   175

Ffor bye my subtill dealyng / thus it came to passe.
Cheafely disdayned. / ffor whome I toke the payn
And than to repent / it was to late alas
My purpose . I wold than haue chaynged fayn
But it wold not be / I was perceyved playn   180
Thus Venus the goddesse / that called is of love
Spared not with spight / to bryng me frome above /

Alas my souerayn lord / thou didest me avaunce
And settest me vppe in thys great pompe and pryde
And gavest to me thy realme in gouernaunce   185
Thy pryncely will / why did I sett a side
And folowed myn owen / consideryng not the tyde
Howe after a floode / an Ebbe commythe on a pace
That to consider / in my tryhumphe / I lakked grace /

---

182. (..e) *canc. before* to; to *interl.*
188. an] D; E and
188. pase *canc. before* pace

f. 98ᵛ]

Nowe fykkell fortune / torned hathe hir whele 190
Or I it wyst all sodenly / and down she dyd me cast
Down was my hed / and vpward went my heale.
My hold faylled me / that I thought suer and fast
I se by experyence / hir fauor dothe not last
Ffor she full lowe nowe hathe brought me vnder 195
Thoughe I on hir complayn / alas it is no wonder.

I lost myn honor . my treasure was me berafte
Ffayn to avoyd / and quykly to geve place
Symply to depart / for me no thyng was lafte
Without penny or pound / I lyved a certyn space / 200
Vntill my souerayn lord / extendyd to me his grace
Who restored me sufficient / if I had byn content
To mayntayn myn estate / bothe of . lond and rent

Yet notwithstandyng / my corage was so hault
Dispight of myn ennemyes. / Rubbed me on the gall 205
Who conspired together. / to take me with a fault.
They travelled without triall / to geve me a fall /
I therfore entendyd / to trie my frendes all
to fforrayn potentates wrott my letters playn
Desireng ther ayd / to restore me to fauor agayn 210

209. prynces *canc. before* potentates

f. 99ʳ]

Myn ennemyes perceyvyng / caught therof dysdayn
Doughtyng the daynger / dreamed on the dought
In Councell consultyng. / my sewte to restrayn
Accused me of treason / and brought it so abought
That travellyng to my triall / or I could trie it owte   215
Deathe with his dart / strake me for the nons
In Leycester full lowe / where nowe lyethe my boons

Loo nowe may you se / what it is to trust
In wordly vanytes / that voydyth with the wynd
Ffor deathe in a moment / consumyth all to dust   220
No honor . no glory. / that euer man cowld fynd
But tyme with hys tyme / puttythe all owt of mynd
Ffor tyme in breafe tyme / duskyth the hystory
Of them that long tyme / lyved in glory

Where is my Tombe / that I made for the nons.   225
Wrought of ffynne Cooper. / that cost many a pound
To couche in my Carion / and my Rotten boons.
All is but vaynglory / nowe haue I found
And small to the purpose / whan I ame in the ground
What dothe it avaylle me / all that I haue /   230
Seyng I ame deade / and layed in my grave /

---

214. it *interl*.
217. f(.) *canc. before* full; now *canc. before* where; nowe *interl*.
220. wᵗ *canc. before* in
222. memory *canc. before* mynd; mynd *interl*.
229. whan *canc. before* I; whan *interl*.; layed *canc. before* in
231. the g *canc. before* my

f. 99ᵛ]

Ffarewell Hampton Court / whos ffounder I was
Ffarewell Westmynster Place / nowe a palace Royall
Ffarewell the Moore / lett Tynnynainger passe.
Ffarewell in Oxford / my Colege Cardynall   235
Ffarewell in Ipsewiche / my Scole gramaticall
Yet oons . ffarewell I say / I shall you neuer se
Your Somptious byldyng / what nowe avayllethe me /

What avayllyth / my great aboundaunce
What is nowe laft / to helpe me in thys case.   240
Nothyng at all / but dompe in the daunce /
Among deade men / to tryppe on the trace /
And for my gay howsis / nowe haue I this place
To lay in my karcas / wrapt in a shette.
Knytt with a knott / att my hed and my feete   245

What avayllyth nowe / my ffetherbeddes soft
Shettes of Raynes. / long large and wyde /
And dyuers devysis / of clothes chaynged oft
Or vicious chapleyns / walkyng by my syd
Voyde of all vertue / fulfilled with pryde /   250
Whiche hathe caused me / by report of suche fame /
Ffor ther myslyvyng / to haue an yll name /

237. se *canc. before* se

METRICAL VISIONS

f. 100ʳ]

This is my last complaynt / I can say you no moore.
But farewell my seruaunt / that faythefull hathe be.
Note well thes wordes / quod he / I pray the therfore   255
And wright them thus playn / as I haue told them the
All whiche is trewe. / thou knowest it well parde /
Thou faylledest me not / vntill that I dyed.
And nowe I must depart / I may no lenger byde /
Ffinis

Thauctor G.C.

Whan he his tale had told / thus in sentence.   260
His dolorous playnt / strake me to the hart
Pytie also moved me / to bewayll his offence /
And with hyme to wepe / whan I did aduert
In hys aduersyte / howe I did not departe
Tyll mortall deathe / had gevyn hyme his wond.   265
With whome I was present / and layed hyme in the ground.

Whan I had wepte / and lamentyd my ffyll
With Reason perswaded / to hold me content
I aspied certyn persons / commyng me tyll
Strayngely disgwysed / that grettly did lament   270
And as me semed / this was ther entent
On ffortune to complayn / ther cause not slender.
And me to requyer ther ffall to remember.

256. playn *canc. before* playn
258. dyd *canc. before* dyed
270. strayngely *interl.* r

f. 100ᵛ]

Vycount / Rocheford

Alas / quod the first / with a full hevy chere
And Countenaunce sad / pitiouse and lamentable 275
George Bulleyn I ame / that nowe dothe appere
Some tyme of Rocheford / vicount honorable
And nowe a vile wretche / most myserable
That ame constrayned / with dole in my visage
Even to resemble / a very deadly image / 280

God gave me graces / dame . nature did hir part
Endewed me with gyftes / of naturall qualities
Dame Eloquence also / taught me the arte
In meter and prose / to make plesaunt dities
And ffortune preferred me / to highe dignytes 285
In suche aboundaunce / that combred was my wytt
To render God thankes / that gave me eche whitt

Yt hath not byn knowen / nor seldeme seen
That any of my yeres / byfore thys day
In to the prevy councell / preferred hathe byn 290
My souerayn lord / in his chamber did me assay
Or yeres thryes nyne / my lyfe had past a way
A rare thyng swer / seldome or neuer hard
So yong a man / so highely to be preferred

283. th(e) *canc. before* taught
293. thyng] D; E thynges

METRICAL VISIONS

f. 101ʳ]

In this my welthe / I hade God clean forgott 295
And my sensuall apetyte / I did allwayes ensewe
Estcmyng in my self / the thyng that I had not
Sufficyent grace / this chaunce for to eschewe.
The contrary I perceyve / causithe me nowe to Rewe.
My ffolly was suche / that vertue I sett a syde 300
And forsoke God / that shold haue byn my gwyde /

My lyfe not chast / my lyvyng bestyall
I fforced wydowes / maydens I did deflower
All was oon to me / I spared non at all
My appetit was / all women to devoure 305
My study was bothe day and hower.
My onleafull lecherey. / howe I myght it fulfill
Sparyng no woman / to haue on hyr my wyll

Allthoughe I before / hathe bothe seen and Rede
The word of Godd / and scriptures of auctorytie 310
Yet cowld not I resist / this onlefull deade
Nor dreade the domes of God / in my prosperitie
Lett myn estate therfore / a myrror to you be /
And in your myndes / my dolors comprehend
Ffor myn offences / howe God hathe made dissend 315

302. chast *canc. before* chast
305. to *interl.*
311. I re *canc. before* not
314. (..) *canc. before* comprehend

f. 101ᵛ]

Se how ffortune can alter and chaynge hir tyde
That to me but late / cowld be so good and ffauorable /
And at thys present / to frowne / and sett me thus aside.
Whiche thought hyr whele /: to . stand bothe firme and stable.
Nowe have I found hyr / very froward and mutable   320
Where she was frendly / nowe is she at dyscord
As by experyence / of me vicount Rocheford

Ffor where God lyst to punyshe / a man of Right
By mortall sword / farewell all resistence.
Whan grace fayllyth / honor hathe no force or myght   325
Of nobilitie also / it defacyth the highe preemynence
And chayngythe ther power / to feoble impotence /
Than tornyth ffortune / hir whele most spedely.
Example tak of me / for my lewde avoultrie

All noble men therfor / with stedfast hart intyer   330
Lyft vppe your corages. / and thynke this is no fable
Thoughe ye syt highe / conceyve yt in your chere
That no wordly prynce / in yerthe is perdurable
And synce that ye be / of nature reasonable
Remember in your welthe / as thyng most necessary   335
That all standythe on ffortune / whan she listithe to vary.

321 disco(r)d *canc. before* dyscord
331. vppe *interl.*
334. ye be be *canc. before* that

f. 102ʳ]

Alas to declare / my lyfe in euery effecte /
Shame restreynyth me / the playnes to confesse
Lest the abhomynacion / wold all the worl enfect
Yt is so vyle / so detestable / in wordes to expresse / 340
Ffor whiche by the lawe / condempned I ame doughtlesse
And for my desert iustly iuged to be deade /
Behold here my body / but I have lost my hed /

Thauctor / G C

An other was there Redy to complayn
Of his evyll chaunce / crying owt alas 345
And sayd of all grace / no man more barayn
Than he was / that in his tyme so happie was
And nowe onhappie / fortune hathe brought to passe
That where most happiest / he was but of late.
Nowe most onhappiest / ffortune hathe torned hir date / 350

Norres

With welthe.worshipe / and houge aboundaunce
My souerayn lord / extendyd his benygnytie.
To be Grome of his stoole / he dyd highly avaunce
Of all his prevye chamber / I had the souerayntie.
Offices and Romes / he gave me great plentie. 355
Horsys . hawkes . and houndes / I had of eche sort
I wanted no thyng / that was for my disport /

---

339. enfect *canc. before* enfect
345. chaunce] D; E chauance; crying] D; E cryng
353. be] DE me; be *canc. before* Grome; me *interl*.; me *canc. before* highly; highly *interl*.

f. 102ᵛ]

Of welthy lyf / I dought it neuer a wytt
Thou knewest well / I had / and therof no man more.
All thynges of pleasure . vnto my ffantzis ffitt 360
Till ambyssion blyndyd me that I forthynke soore.
Ffrome the myddes of the streme / drevyn to the shore.
Ffrome welthe I say / alas to wretchednes and waylyng
Ffor my mysdemenor / to God and to the kyng.

My chaunce was suche / I had all thyng at wyll 365
And in my welthe / I was to hyme onkynd
That thus to me / did all my mynd fulfyll
All his benyvolence / was clean owt of mynd
Oh alas / alas / in my hart howe cowld I fynd
Ayenst my souerayn / so secrettly to conspier. 370
That so gently gave me all that I desier.

His most nobyll hart / lamented so my chaunce.
That of his Clemencye / he graunted me my lyfe.
In case I wold / without dissimulaunce.
The trouthe declare / of his onchast wyfe. 375
The spotted quene / causer of all this stryfe.
But I most obstynate with hart as hard as stone
Denyed his grace / good cause therfore to / mone

---

361. forthynk sore *canc. before* forthynke soore
362. the² *interl.*
364. dismen(or) *canc. before* to¹; mysdemenor *interl.*
366. to *canc. before* in
369. fynd *canc. before* fynd

f. 103ʳ]

To sighe, to sobbe / it ware but wast
To wepe to waylle / or to lament   380
Yt woll not prevaylle / the tyme is past.
Alas in tyme / why did I not prevent.
The Rage and fury / of ffortuns male intent
But than I did. / as nowe all other do.
In tyme of welthe / lett all thos thoughtes goo /   385

Who is more wyllfull / than he that is in welthe
Who ys more folyshe / than he that shold be wyse
Who syknes soner . dothe forgett / than he that hathe his helthe
Or who is more blynd / than he that hathe ii eyes.
Who most hathe welthe / doth fortune most dispies   390
Evyn so dyd I / for whant of Goddes grace
What nowe remaynyth / but sorowe in thys case.

Somtyme in trust / and nowe a traytor found
Sometyme full nyghe / but nowe I stand affare
Sometyme at libertie / and nowe in preson bound   395
Sometyme in office / and nowe led to the barre.
The Rigor of the lawe. / iustice wyll not deferre
But for myn offences / sythe nedes that I must die /
Ffarewell my frendes / loo hedlesse here I lye /

382. did *canc. before* not
386. in *interl.*
387. whoo *final* -o *canc.*
399. lye *canc. before* lye

f. 103ᵛ]

Thauctor / G.C.

Next hyme folowed an other / that was of that band   400
With teares bespraynt / and color pale as leade.
Yt was Weston the wanton / ye shall vnderstand
That wantonly lyved without feare or dreade /
Ffor wyll without wytt / dyd ay his brydell leade.
Ffolowyng his ffantzy / and his wanton lust /   405
Havyng of mysfortune / no maner mystrust /

Weston

Ffortune / quod he / not so but not fearyng God above /
Whiche knowyth the depthe of euery mans mynd
Whome I forgott to serue / in dread and in love.
By wanton wyll / for that I was so blynd.   410
Whiche caused my welthe / full sone to be ontwynd
And cheafe of all and most to be abhorred
Ffor my onkyndnes / ayenst my souerayn lord.

Beyng but yong / and skant owt of the shell
I was dayntely norysshed / vnder the kynges wyng   415
Who highly fauored me / and loved me so well
That I had all my wyll and lust / in euery thyng
Myndyng no thyng lesse. / than chaunce of my endyng
And for my dethe / that present is nowe here /
I loked not for / this ffyvetie or threscore yere /   420

---

407. but *interl. and canc. before* not so; but *interl.*
415. fed *canc. before* norysshed

f. 104ʳ]

My lust and my wyll / ware knytt in alyaunce.
And my wyll folowed lust. / in all his desier.
When luste was lusty. / wyll dyd hyme avaunce
To tangle me with lust / where my lust did requyer.
Thus wyll and hot lust / kyndeled me the fier   425
Of ffilthy concupicence. / my youthe yet but grean
Spared not my lust / presumed to the quene /

And for my lewed lust / my wyll is nowe shent
By whome I was ruled / in euery mocion
Nowe wyll and lust / makythe me sore to repent   430
That wyll was my gwyd / and not sad discression
Therfore ayenst wyll / I ame brought to correccion
Who folowyth lust / his wyll to obeye
May chaunce to repent / as I do this day.

Lust than gave cause / why wyll did consent   435
Willfully to Rage / where wytt shold restrayn
So highly to presume / to furnyshe his entent
Will was to sawcy. / and wold not refrayn
Hauyng no regard to pryncely disdayn /
Wherfore by iustice / nowe hether am I led   440
To satysfie the Cryme / with the losse of my hed.

---

422. lus(..) *canc. before* lust
423. a(v)ance *canc. before* avaunce
428. lewed *additional* -nes *canc.*
434. chaunce] D; E chamce
441. with] D; E wᵗi

f. 104ᵛ]

Thauctor / GC

Than approched an other / his chaunce to declare
And sayd that fortune hathe gevyn hyme a fall
Whiche sowced hyme in sorowe / and combred hyme with kare
Yt avayllyth hyme nothyng / to crie and to call   445
Ffor frendes hathe he none / ther helpe is but small
To socoure hyme nowe / loo what it is to trust.
To fykkyll ffortune / whan she doth chaynge hir lust /

Breerton

But late / I was in welthe / the world can it record
Fflorysshyng in ffauor / ffreshely besen   450
Gentilman of the Chamber / . with my souerayn lord
Tyll fortune onwares / hathe disseyved me clen
Whiche pynchethe my hart / and Rubbyth me on the splene
To thynke on my fall / remembryng myn estate.
Renewyth my sorowe. / my repentaunce commythe to late   455

Ffurnysshed with Romes / I was by the kyng
The best I ame sewer / he had in my Contre
Steward of the Holt / a rome of great wynnyng
In the marches of Wales the / whiche he gave me
Where of tall men / . I had sewer great plentie   460
The kyng for to serue / bothe in town and feld
Redely furnysshed / with horsse spere and sheld /

---

442. approched] D; E approced
448. l *canc. before* lust
452. well *canc. before* clen
455. commythe] D; E commiythe
459. the² *interl.*

f. 105ʳ]

God of his iustice / forseyng my malice
Ffor my Rusty Rigor. / wold punysshe me of right
Mynestred vnto / Eton / by Color of iustice   465
A . shame to speke / more shame it is to wright
A gentilman borne / that thorowghe my myght
So shamfully was hanged. / vppon a gallowe tree
Oonly of old Rankor / that Roted was in me

Nowe the law hathe taught me / iustyce to knowe   470
By dyvyn dome / Goddes wordes to be trewe
Who strykythe with the sword / the sword wyll ouerthrowe
No man shall be able / the daynger to eschewe.
Thexperyence in me / shall geve you a vewe
That rigor by Rigor / hathe quyt me my mede.   475
Ffor the Rigor of iustice / dothe cause me to blede.

Loo here is thend of murder and tyranny.
Loo here is thend / of envious affeccion
Loo here is thend of ffalce conspiracye.
Loo here is thend of falce detection   480
Don to the innocent / by cruell correccion
Allthoughe in office / I thought my self strong
Yet here ys myn end / for mynestryng wrong /

465. ius *canc. before* iustice
476. blede *canc. before* blede

f. 105ᵛ]

Thauctor / G C

Than came an other / whiche hade lyttill ioye
Sayeng that sometyme / I did hyme knowe 485
In the Cardynalles Chaple / a syngyng boy. /
Who humbly requered me / and lowted full lowe.
To wright his dekay. / as last of this Rowe /
And that his desier. / I wold not refuse.
Ffor by his conffession he dyd them all accuse 490

Marke alias / Smeton

My ffather / a Carpynter / . and labored with hys hand
With the swett of his face / he purchast hys lyvyng.
Ffor small was hys rent / muche lesse was hys land
My mother in Cottage / vsed dayly spynnyng /
Loo in what mysery. / was my begynnyng 495
Tyll that Gentill prynce / kyng of this realme
Toke me / de stercore / et erigens pauperem

And beyng but a boy / clame vppe the hyghe stage
That bred was of naught / and brought to felicyte
Knewe not myself / waxt prowd in my Corage / 500
Dysdayned my ffather / and wold not hyme se
Wherfore now ffortune / by hir mutabylitie.
Hathe made so cruelly / hir power for to stretche.
Ffor my presumpcion / to dye lyke a wretche /.

486. Chaple] D; E Chapleyn
493. was¹ *interl.*
498. hyghe] D; E hyght
503. stretche *canc. before* stretche
504. (......) *interl. and canc. before* to; to *interl.*

f. 106ʳ]

Loo what it is / fraylle youthe to avaunce 505
And to sett hyme vppe / in welthy estate.
Or sad discression / had taken hym in gouernaunce
To bridell his lust whiche nowe comes to late.
And thoughe by great fauor / I lease but my pate.
Yet deserued haue I / cruelly to be martred. 510
As I ame iuged / to be hanged drawn and quartered.

Thauctor / G C

In the myddys of my labor / entendyng to take rest
Beyng fortossed / in thys my long traveyll
Disposed to pawse / I made me therto prest
But as I satt musyng / on fortune so frayll 515
A lady I sawe sobbyng / that happe made to wayll
Wryngyng of her handes / hir voyce she owt brayd
Complaynyng on fortune / thes wordes to me she sayd /

Quen / Anne

Alas wredched woman / what shall I do or say.
And why alas was I borne / this woo to susteyn 520
Oh howe infortunat / I ame at this day.
That Raygned in ioy / and nowe in endles payn
The world vnyuersall / hathe me in dysdayn
The slaunder of my name / woll aye be grean
And called of eche man / the most vicious quen 525

---

517. his *canc. before* handes; her *interl.*

f. 106ᵛ]

What nedythe me my name / for to reherce
Ffor my fall I thynke / is yet freshe in thy mynd
I dread my faultes / shall thy paper perce
That thus haue lyved / and byn to God onkynd
Vices preferryng / settyng vertue behynd 530
Hatfull to God / to most men contrarye
Spotted with pride / viciousnes and cruelte / .

Oh sorowfull woman / my body and my sowle.
Shall euer be burdened / with slaunder detestable.
Ffame in hir regester / my defame woll enroll 535
And to race owt of the same / no man shall be able
My lyfe of late / hathe byn so abhomynable.
Therfore my frayltie / I may bothe Curse and ban.
Whissyng to God / I had neuer knowen man /

Who was more happier / if I had byn gracious 540
Than I of late / and had moore my wyll
Ffor my souerayn lord / of me was so amorous
That all my desires / he gladly did fulfyll
My hosbond and souerayn / thought in me non ill
He loved me so well / hauyng in me great trust 545
I turned trust to treason / and he chaynged all his lust

539. had *interl.*; had *canc. before* knowen
546. I *followed by* I he *the latter interl. and both canc.*; he *interl.*; to *canc. and replaced by* his *interl.*

METRICAL VISIONS

f. 107ʳ]

The noblest prynce / that raygned on the ground
I had to my hosbond / he toke me to his wyfe /
At home with my ffather / a mayden he me ffound
And for my sake / of pryncely prerogatyfe   550
To an Erele he auaunced / my father in his lyfe
And preferred all them / that ware of my bloode /
The most willyngest prynce / to do them all good.

Whan ffortune had displayed / abrode my freshe sayle
Also had arryved me / in the most ioyfull port   555
I thought that ffortune / wold me neuer faylle
She was so redy / to auaunce all to my comfort
But nowe alas / she is as redy / my vice to transport
Chayngyng my / ioy to grat indignacion
Leavyng me in the stormes / of depe desperacion   560

I may be compared / in euery circumstaunce
To Gatholia / that distroyed Davythes lynne
Spared not the blood / by cruell vengaunce
Of Goddes prophettes / but brought them to Rewyn
Murder askythe murder / by murder she did fyne   565
So in lyke wyse / resistyng my quarell
How many . haue dyed / and endyd in parell /

---

548. hsbond *canc. before* hosbond
558. to *canc. before* my
559. ioy *interl.*
564. rewen *canc. before* Rewyn

f. 107ᵛ]

I was the auctier / why lawes ware made
Ffor spekeng ayenst me / to daynger the innocent
And with great Othes / I found owt the trade   570
To burden mens concyence / thus I did invent
My sede to auaunce / it was my full entent
Lynnyally to succed / in this Emperyall crown
But howe sone hathe God / brought my purpose down

Who that woll presume / a purpose to achyve.   575
Without Goddes helpe . ther matters for to frame
At thend they shall / but skarsly thryve
And for ther enterprice / receyve grett blame.
At Goddes handes / presumyng to the same /
Thexperyence in me / wantyng Goddes ayed   580
Wold mount aloft / howe sone ame I dekayd

Yt had byn better / for myn assuraunce
To haue led my lyfe / in meke symplyssitie
Owt of all daynger / of ffortunes dissemblaunce
Vsyng my lyfe / in wyfely chastitie /   585
As other women / regardyng myn honestie
Oh howe myche prayse is gevyn to thos
That wold in no case / ther chastitie loos.

571. burden *final* -s *canc.*
573. in *interl.*

f. 108ʳ]

But well a way / euermore the spott
Of my default / shall aye spryng and be grean 590
Ffor who alas . can beare a greatter blott
Than of suche lyfe / to heare the name onclean
My Epetaphe shall be. / the vicious quen
Lyethe here of late / that iustly lost hir hed
By cause that she / did spott the kynges bed 595

But God that dyd abhorre / this lothesome deade
Ffor that I was a quen / and lyved not chast
Hathe spotted me / alas / and all my sede
Oon for a pledge. / here left behynd for bast
Thus after swett sawce / folowed an egere tast 600
A payment fyt / full well as it apperes
Dewe vnto me / for myn oniust desiers

Howe happye art thou / quen Iane / the kinges next wyfe.
Whose fame frome ferre / dayly dothe rebound
Ffor vsyng of thy chast / and sober lyfe 605
All thoughe thou art deade / and layed in the ground
Yet deathe wantithe power / . thy fame to confound
Ffor of thy chast sides / . perpetually to record
Sprong kyng Edward / that swete and loyall lord

---

590. ay *canc. before* aye; aye *interl.*
591. alas *canc. before* alas
596. Ffor *canc. before* But
600. sawce *canc. before* sawce
604. rebound *canc. before* rebound
609. and *interl.*

f. 108ᵛ]

O lady . most excellent / by vertue stellefied 610
Assendyng the hevyns / where thou raynest aye
Among the goddes eternall / there to be deified
Perpetually to endure vnto the last daye.
And I most wredched / . what shall I do or saye
But humbly beseche the / O Lord for thy passion 615
That my worthy deathe / may be my Crymes purgacion /

Nowe must I depart / there is non other boote
Ffayer welle fayer lades / . ffarewell all noble dames
That sometyme ware obedyent / and kneled at my foote
Eschewe detracion / preserue your honest names 620
Geve non occasion / a sparke to kyndell flames
Remember this sentence / that is bothe old and trewe
Who wyll haue no smoke. / the fier must nedes eschewe /

Ffarewell most gentill kyng / ffarewell my lovyng make /
Ffarewell the pieusaunt prynce / fflower of all regally 625
Ffarewell most pityfull / and pitie on me take.
Regard my dolorous woo / mercyfully with your eye /
Howe for myn offences / most mekely here I dye /
Marcy noble prynce / I crave for myn offence /
The sharped sword / hathe made my recompense / 630

621. occasion *final* (.) *canc.*
627. who *canc. before* woo

f. 109ʳ]

Thauctor / G.C.

Ffynysshyng hyr dole / . and wofull complaynt
Concludyng the same / with a sorowfull conclusion
My hart lamentid / by carefull constraynt
To se ffortune / conceyve / suche an occasion
A quene to ouerthrowe / frome hyr Royall mancion   635
Hauyng no respect to hyr hyghe renown
But frome hyr estate / thus cruelly to throwe down

Thus beyng astonyed / with ffortunes mutabylitie
Who no man fauoryth / of hyghe or lowe estate
Hir assuraunce standyth not / in any sewer tranquylitie /   640
But at a soden blast / she saythe to them chekmate
Then hir to resyst / alas it is to late /
Syttyng in thys muse / for sorowe lakkyng brethe
A nomber . dyd appere / that suffred paynnes of dethe /

Of parsons lamentable / whome ffortune dyd forsake   645
And left them in daynger . / of deathe / and wordly shame
Whome she byfore encorraged / boldly to vndertake
As traytors to rebell / deseruyng that fowlle name
There fame detestable / blowen a brode by fame
And for as myche as ther offences / ware not all of oon effecte   650
I leave therfore the circumstaunce / ther names to you detecte /

---

631. playnt *canc. before* complaynt

f. 109ᵛ]

Ffirst I will ther names / playn to you resite
Kepyng non order / but as they come to mynd
As lord Husy / lord Darcy / and Constable the knyght
Lord Hungerford also / that wrought ayenst kynd   655
And lord Leonard Gray / accused as I fynd
Wrongfully in Irelond / evyn of very spight
God send his accusers as they deserued of right

Aske of the northe / ther Captyn onkouthe
Bygott . and Bulmer . Percy . and Nevell.   660
Lumly the yong / Lord Dacres of the southe
And Tempest also / that haynous rebell
Ffortescue / Dyngley / Roydon / Froudes / and Mantell
Also Carowe and Moore / than knyghtes bothe twayn
Ffor ther offences / whome iustice hathe slayn   665

Many moo there ware / that stode in a rowte
Of prestes . and prelattes / a bysshope them among
Ffor old custumes / that than ware sought owt
With wepyng and waylyng / they tewned ther song
Ffor certyn abusis / sayd they vsed long   670
To tell yow ther names / I cannot at this season
But lett them alon / defamed with treason /

---

652. playn *interl*.
664. Moore *canc. before* Moore
665. whome *canc. before* ther
666. May *canc. before* Many
668. accustumes *canc. before* that; custumes *interl*.; brought *canc. before* owt; sought *interl*.
670. whiche was *canc. before* sayd they

f. 110ʳ]

The Auctor / G.C.

An other there was / of whome I nedes must tell.
Crumwell / all men hyme knewe as well as I
Whiche in my mynd / all other dyd excell /   675
In extort power / and insacyat tyrannye
Ffirst auaunced to be / the kynges secretarye
And next sett vppe / on the toppe of the whele.
Made Erle of Essex / and lord prevye seale /

Cromwell / Erle of Essex

Than began he to speke / suche was myn adventure   680
To be placed / quod he / in highe dignyte.
Wenyng my auctorytie / euer to endure
And neuer to be trobled / with non aduersitie
But I perceyve / with Royall egles / a kight may not flee.
All thoughe a iay may chatter / in a golden cage   685
Yet wyll the Egles / disdayn hys parentage

I Rayned and Ruled / in highe estymacion
Ffrome office to office / assendyng the degrees
Ffirst in the prevye councell was my foundacion
And cheafe secretory / with all vauntages and ffees   690
Then folowed me Sewters / lyke a swarme of bees
Thus began ffortune / on me for to smyle
I trusted hir so myche / that she did me begyle /

689. chamber *canc. before* was; councell *interl.*
692. for (.) *canc. before* ffortune

f. 110ᵛ]

The title of vicegerent / I had in my stile.
Gouernor of the prelacye / and of the lawes devyne.   695
Also master of the Rolles / I was in short while
Thus began my glory / to floryshe and to shyne /
As thoughe ffortune wold / hyr whele to me resigne
Vnto thestate of Baron / she did me than auaunce
And next to an Erle / thus was ffortunes chaunce   700

In this hyghe estate / I myght not long endure
Ffortune did so chaynge / . hir ffauorable chere
She slipte a way all sodenly / as it hathe byn hir vre
Hir Couert countenaunce / dyd then to me appere
I trusted hyr to myche / . I bought hir trust to dere   705
She promysed me so fayer / that I could not beware
Of hir disceytfull bayte / till I was in hir snare /

To Aman the Agagite / I may be compared
That invented lawes / Goddes people to confound
And for Mardocheus / a Galhowsse he prepared   710
To hang hyme theron / if he myght be found
Whiche he erected fyvetye Cubyttes frome the ground
Wheron Mardocheus to hang / was all his trust
Yet was hyme self hanged on theme furst /

695. (..) *canc. before* of the prelacye
713. ther *canc. before* his

f. 111ʳ]

So wrought I alas / with the lawes of this land. 715
Devised a law ayenst the accused
Condempnyng without answere / or he could vnderstand
The ground of hys offence / it myght not be refused
Thus straytly the lawes / my subtill wytt abvsed
Therfore oon of the first I ame / tastyng on the payn 720
Suche measure I mesured / is measured me agayn

I may therfore conclude. / experyence hathe me taught
All is but vayn / that man doth here invent
Ther worldly wytt / god bryngyth oft to naught
And with ther workes / he is not well content 725
Behold my deades. / then may you se it evydent
That for my presumpcion / wantyng Goddes grace /
My lyfe consumed is / within a short space /

This is thend of my complaynt / I must therfore departe.
Ffarewell my frendes / ffarewell my foos all 730
Take of me ensample / and plant it in your hart
That suche lyke fortune / may geve you a lyke fall
Consider well therfore / that here ye be mortall
All thyng hathe end / whye do ye honor crave /
Whan ye shall as I ame / be couered with your grave // 735

---

715. land] DE realme
719. abused *canc. before* abvsed
723. here *canc. before* but; subtilly *canc. before* here; here *interl.*
728. within *final in interl.*

[f. 111ᵛ]

Thauctor / G C.

Thys late lord Cromwell / may warne you all
That formost ride / a loft in the chayer.
Not to trust ffortune / that tomblethe as a ball
Ffor chaunces vncerteyn / that often fall onware
To God se first / your hartes ye repayer.   740
And next after that / in all your doyng
Obserue your faythe / and allegyaunce to the kyng /

Pawsyng a whyle / reformyng of my penne /
Ffordulled with writyng / and feobled was my brayn
Thus sittyng in a muse / I saw too noble men   745
Present byfore me / redy to complayn
Desiryng me bothe / to take on me the payn
Ther fall to remember. / dissendyd of oon Race
Whome to behold it was a pityous case.

Markes of Exeter / Lord Montagewe

What gretter / prerogatyfe / quod they. / haue we   750
// Of our lyves / or stand in more sykkernes
Allthoughe of the lynne / imperyall / dissendyd we be
Than hathe the mean sort / of ffortunes ffykkilnes
Yf she lyst to swerve / than is it remedylesse /
We must ffortune abyde / and suffer all with pacience. / 755
Ffor hir to resist / there botythe no violence /

---

738. tomble *canc. before* tomblethe

f. 112ʳ]

I was quod thoon / a marques / of late creacion
Called of Exetor. / and lynyally dissended
To the Erldome of Devonshyre / by dewe generacion
Alas all this haue I lost / it cannot be amendyd   760
Ffor we be accused. / of purpose pretendyd
Our souerayn to offend / in suche an offence
As nothyng but our heddes can make therfore recompence /

That is trewe / quod thother. / I must it nedes confesse.
Ffor I haue felt the smart / whome ye knowe full well   765
Sometyme lord Mountagu / and nowe in great distresse
Suche is my chaunce / I can it not refell
But with my Cosyn here / suffer euery dell
Of ffortunes lott / and take it in good part
Gevyng God thankes therfore / with all my hart /   770

The blast of our Cryme / is greatter shame
Than is the losse / of all our bryttell glorye
That we / alas / shold bere the slaunderous name
Of traytors falce / in any boke or storye
What is he of our bloode /./ that wold not be sory   775
To here our names. / with vile ffame so detected
Wherwith our posteritie / shall allwayes be suspected

f. 112ᵛ]

What cause shold we haue / to be onkynd
Vnto our souerayn lord / of highe magnyficence
Whiche with his regall benyfittes / did vs hyghly bynd   780
To bere to hyme our love / and dewe obedyence.
Wherof all the world / had intelligence /
That we of all other / bothe of blood and otherwyse.
Had least cause / his maiestie to dispise.

But the Evyll spirytt / that of Canckard malygnytie   785
Malygned our honor. / and hyghe renowne
Disdayned our blood / and auncyent dignytie
Intendyng our ouerthrowe. / and to bryng vs down
Accused vs of conspyracye / ayenst the Royall crown
Whos falce accusacions / ware than regarded more.   790
Than euer was our trouthe / vsed allwayes byfore.

Accused by hyme / that shold rather excuse.
And defend our treuthes / with all his trewe endevour
Oh how onkyndly did he / vs abuse.
The fact onnaturall / purged woll be neuer.   795
But allwayes freshe / contynuyng still for euer.
Who ayenst nature / condempned hathe his brother
To cruell deathe / so hathe he don his mother /

---

782. wol *canc. before* world

f. 128ʳ]

To the great slaunder / and blott of hys name /
His credytt is lost / and so is his estymacion   800
And he confused / alas / he was to blame
Hymeself to ouerthrowe / and all his generacion
Ayenst God nowe / howe can he make purgacion
That so agaynst nature / onnaturally hathe wrought
Distroyeng all his blood / and brought hymeself to nought   805

O cruell accuser. / thy malyce was too strong
Our fall to conspyer / by falshod brought abought
Ayenst all nature / thou hast don vs great wrong
Therfore frome shame / we put the owt of dought
Thou shall neuer escape. / it is so ferre blowen owt   810
Ffor of all kynd of vices. / shortly to conclude.
The worst ayenst God / is ingratitude /

Thoughe thy necligence / bryngythe vs to this end
Yet that thou mayst haue therof remembraunce
We / God humbly beseche / suche grace to the send   815
That thou mayst repent / or he on the take vengaunce
Ffor thy great ingratitude / take this for thy penaunce
Allwayes in thy hart / call to thy memory.
That by thy oonly meane hedles here we lye /

799. of *canc. before* and
804. wrought *canc. before* wrought
813. vs to *interl.*
816. vengaunce *canc. before* vengaunce

f. 128ᵛ]

Lenvoy de / lauctor G.C.

Synce ffortune sparith non / of highe lynnage.   820
All men therfore / be ye not recheles
Prewdently to forsee / the daynger of this pilgrymage
Syth ffortune waytithe / onwarely you to oppresse.
Be circumspect I advise you / in all your busynes
And with vertewe ay / preserue your noble pieusaunce   825
Byfore fortune / extendyth hir cruell vengaunce

Ffor it is not your estates / ffortune can defend
Your dyligent travell / or noble behavor
Whan flykkeryng fortune / dothe hir self entend
To cast you owte / of your prynces fauor   830
Ffor if a prynce hathe caught / a deadly sauor
Of indygnacion / ffarewell all treuthe and noblenes
To the blokke ye must / it is remedyles

There is no consideracion / with prynces in ther ire
And most in especyall / ayenst an highe estate   835
Ffor where dread and disdayn / hathe sett the hart on fier
Of a wilfull prynce / with mercy not socyatt
Also where pitie and clemency. / cannot his ire abate /
There you myghty peers must take ffortuns chaunce /
To trype on the trace / as some hathe led the daunce /   840

---

820. degree *canc. before* lynnage
836. his *canc. before* hart; the *interl.*
839. peese *canc. before* peers

f. 129ʳ]

To be a lord / of Royall bloode and dygnytie
Sometyme ye se / dothe but small avaylle
Ffor better it ware / to be of basse and lowe degree
Than in suche honor / for a while to prevaylle
A ragyng wynd may tourne your brittell sayle   845
And dryve ye bake agayn / and roue you on some Rocke
Where your noble pattes / may happe to catche a knocke /

Thauctor / G. C.

Therfor thou salved smert / for ay shallt be sore
The great losse / most worthy to be playned
The onware chaunce / that passed but of yore   850
Wherof the greaffe / so depe in me is grayned
That frome myn eyen / the teares skantly be refrayned
Ffor the great dekay / that still commyth me toward
Of the late quen / whos name was Katheren Haward

Thus as I sat the teares in myn eyen   855
Of hir the wrake / whiles I did debate
Byfore my face / me thought I sawe this quen /
No wytt as I hir last / God wott of late
But all bewepte / in blake and poore estate /
Whiche prayed me / that I ne wold forgett   860
The fall of hyr / within my boke to sett /

---

842. it *canc. before* dothe
848. shalt *canc. before* for
854. is *canc. before* was; was *interl.*
858. hir *interl.*; lete *canc. before* late

f. 129ᵛ]

Quene Katheren / called Kateren Howard /

O cruell destiny / quod she / O fortune insacyable /
O waveryng world. / Rollyng lyke a ball /
You are so wayward / and so vnstable
That neuer any assuraunce / can be in you at all   865
To all estates / you are ennemyes mortall
Who list of you / to haue experyence /
My fall may geve them intelligence /

To be a quen / ffortune dyd me preferre /
Fflorysshyng in youthe. / with beawtie ffresshe and pure /   870
Whome nature made shyne / equall with the sterre /
And to Reyng in ffelicitie / with ioy and pleasure
Wantyng no thyng / that love myght procure /
So hyghly beloved ffare beyond the Rest
With my Souerayn lord / who lodged in his nest /   875

But well away. / howe dredfull is the ioyell
Of bryttill beawtie / that grace dothe not concerve.
Yf dread of shame / do not attend it well
Howe lyke is lust / to make them for to swerve /
With wanton provokyng / whan reason dothe not preserue.   880
Ffrome onleafull licence / whiche causithe youthe parde
To breke the ffetters. / of ffame and chastitie /

---

869. *following this line 877 deleted*
877. do(th)e *canc. before* dothe

f. 134ʳ]

O tender youthe / ffrayle for to resist
The wanton appetites / of carnall delight
Whan love with lust / dothe in youthe consist 885
Than hard for youthe / ayenst vice to fight
Ffor youthe is blynd / and hathe no sighte
The trade to consider / of honest wyfehod
Tyll shame / hathe beten them with her rode

Alas dame Nature / who hathe in euery vayn 890
Endewed me with gyftes / as to hir propirtie she thought mete.
Beawtie alas also. / thou gevest me cause to playn
Why fflorysshest thou my youthe / with thy licoure swette
Excellyng all other / ffrome toppe vnto the feete
My blasyng beawtie / is greatly to reprefe / 895
Chefe cause and ground of all my myschefe

Who wysshythe beawtie / or wanton youthe desier
They covett that thyng / they shold no wyse do so
The brond I nowe repent / that late was sett on fier
Within my brest / whiche workythe me all this woo / 900
What daynger in Cupydes fier / I playnly nowe do knowe
Beware all ye therfore / that nature hathe you lent
Lyke graces / vse theme well / lest after ye repent

889. her] DE ther
892. com *canc. before* playn

f. 134ᵛ]

Culpeper yong / and I God wott but fraylle
We bothe to feoble / our lustes for to resist 905
Whan shamfastnes in me began to faylle
Of chastitie / than dyd I breke the twyst
With Dereham first / that my maydenhed possyst
Death was ther mede / I with shame defaced
Who shamly dothe / of long wyll not be raced 910

O . vessell of vice / O thou fraylle youthe
In whome no vertue / can take roote
Onles that grace / have on the rewthe
To plant in the / some vertue sote
Vice to resist / there can be no boote 915
Where grace wantithe / and hathe of youthe no cure
There vertue in youthe / hathe syldeme byn in vre

Nowe I knowe well / quod she / among my frendes all
That here I laft / the day of my dekaye
That I ne gett / no pompes ffunerall 920
Nor of my blake / no man my charge shall paye
Save that some oon / perchaunce may happe to sey
Suche oon there was / alas / and that was ruthe
That she hir self distayned / with suche ontreuthe /

907. vppe *canc. before* the
913. dothe *canc. before* have
915. can *canc. before* can
922. perchaunce] D; E perchauance; say *canc. before* happe

f. 135ʳ]

Ffarewell my Bretherne / and frendes all arowe 925
Ffor all your harmes / I oonly ame to blame
That thus haue fallen / as all men knowe
To your dekay / and my great shame
Thoughe I ame well worthy / of the same
Yet pray ye to God / allthoughe that I haue swerved 930
That my sowlle may haue better than my body deserued

Epitaphe

By preve of me / non can denye
That beawtie and lust / ennemyes to chastitie
Have byn the tweyn / that hathe dekayed me
And hathe brought me / to thys end ontoward 935
Some tyme a quen / and nowe hedlesse Haward

Culpeper

And I Culpeper / alas / borne in Kent
Admyttyd ffrome a boy / to be the kynges page.
Prowde owt of measure / whiche I may repent
Drowned in the depthe / of myn own owtrage 940
Ouermyche wenyng / put God owt of knowlege.
Ffor by myn abusion / of prid and viciousnes
My lyfe is endyd with shame and wredchednes

---

930. swerved *canc. before* swerved
931. haue *interl.*; sowle *canc. before* deserued; body *interl.*
937. alas *canc. before* Culpeper
939. of *canc. before* owt

f. 135ᵛ]

Take example of me / I desire you yong men all
That ragithe in youthe / and tradyth the Courtly lyfe /   945
All is but vanytie . your lyves be but bestiall
Bytwen wyll and deade / lett vertue breake the stryffe
And suffer vyce to asswage / whiche hathe in you prerogatyfe
So contynewe ye may / and lyve in your degree
Ffor if ye folowed vice / dought it woll not be   950

I folowed my pleasure / of God I had no feare
Thynkyng my self but idell / and my labour vayn spent
In dyvyn seruyce / the tyme that I was there
Ffor my devocion / and my hole entent
Was gevyn all to pleasure / suche as I did invent   955
Nowe I repent therfore / my necgligence to God
Who hathe me Corrected / with his dyvyn Rod.

Besechyng you my frendes / whome I haue left behynd
To pray that lord / whome I most haue offendyd
That he of his mercy / wyll to me be kynd   960
Ffor nowe to late / my lyfe to be amendyd
Wherfore mercy good lord / that for me dissendyd /
To shed his precious blode / hangyng on a tree.
Nowe yet mercy good lord / I hartely byseche thee /

---

959. hathe *canc. before* haue
960. be *canc. before* to

METRICAL VISIONS

f. 136ʳ]

Thauctor / G.C.

As I drewe towardes thend of my boke. 965
Purposyng to ffynysshe / that I had begon
By chaunce a syde / as I cast my loke
I aspied a wydowe / in blake full woo begon
Who praid me in most lamentable mone
That I wold hyr / a place here aford 970
Whome I oons knewe / Iane vicountes Rocheford

Vicountes / Rocheford

My grave father / quod she / of the Morlas lynne
My mother of the Seynt Iohns / this was my parentage
And I alas / that dyd my self inclyne
To spot them all / by this my owltrage 975
Brought vppe in the Court / all my yong age.
Withoutten bridell of honest measure
Ffolowyng my lust / and filthy pleasure

Without respect / of any wyfely truthe
Dredles of God / ffrome grace also exempte. 980
Viciously consumyng / the tyme of thys my youthe
And whan my beawtie / began for to be spent
Not with myn owen harme / sufficed or content
Contrary to God / I must it nedes confesse
Other I entised / by ensample of my wredchednes / 985

969.] D; E *omits*
976. the *interl.*

f. 136ᵛ]

Of Right me thynkyth I owght / to be a glasse
To all the rest of great estates and dames
Seyng me nowe / consideryng what I was.
Without any blott / to kepe ther honest names
Seyng that vice / ne endyth without flames   990
And thoughe that shame / may be waylled all day
Therof the blott / will not be washt away

Howe bryght among vs / yet dothe shyn the starre.
Of them that ride / within the chayer of ffame /
Above all thynges. / whiche oonly did preferre   995
The brewte to kepe / of ther onbroken name
As auctors ryght well. / dothe testefie the same /
Ayenst suche vices / that wan the victory
And beare the palme / to ther eternall glorye /

As vertuous Sara. / Rebecca / and Racell /   1000
Iudythe / Hester / and chast Pennolopie /
And Cornelia / that onbroken kept the shell
And bare the lampe / of onquenched chastitie.
Ffleeyng excesse / or superfluyte
Where carnall lust / for all his violence   1005
Ne made them breke / chastitie / or obedyence /

986. me thynkyth *interl.*
991. alldiay *canc. before* all day

f. 137ʳ]

Where sturdy Silla / to nature Contrarious
Enforced by lust / hir fathers heare to pull
With Cleopatra / concubyn to Anthonyous
With vicious Pasiua / that deled with the bull   1010
And Messalyn insacyat / that neuer was full
But euer thes wretches. / vicious and discommendable
To God and nature / they lyved / abhomynable /

Wold to God that I / in my flowryng Age.
Whan I did trade / the Courtly lyffe   1015
Had fosterd byn / in a symple village.
Beryng the name of an honest and chast wyfe
Where nowe my slaunder. / for euer shall be . ryfe
In euery matter. / bothe early and late
Called the woman / of vice insaciatt   1020

The tyme is past / and I haue nowe receyved
The dewe dett / of my oniust desiers
Prayeng to God / my fall may be conceyved
With in ther hartes / that bourne in vicious fiers
The iust God / as right allwayes requyers   1025
That hathe me punysshed / for my mysgouernaunce
Ne take of me / a greatter vengaunce //

1008. here *canc. before* heare
1018. shalle *canc. before* shall
1020. insa(cia)tt *canc. before* insaciatt

f. 137ᵛ]

Thauctor / G. C.

Endynge thus hir playnt / an other was commyng.
Of Corage impotent / and depe worne in age.
Whos pitious dekay / if that I had Connyng   1030
I wold expresse / hir grevous dammage
Althoughe she ware / a lady of excellent parentage
Of the blood Royall / lynyally dissendyd
Yet by Cruell ffortune / at myschefe she endyd

Ffor ffortune ye knowe / regardyth non estate   1035
All estates to hir is oon / whan that she list to ffrown
Wherfore ye nobles / beware of hir cruell hate
Non hathe more nede / than ye of great renown
Ffor whan ye are most hyghest / than dothe she throwe you down
And tomblyth you hedlesse / frome your hyghe stages   1040
Who wyll not be retayned / with nowther fees or wages.

Countes of / Salesburye

Thys matron hir playnt / began in thys wyse
Alas / quod she / age hathe no more assuraunce
Of ffortunes / sewertie / whome she dothe dispise
Than hathe lusty youthe / all hangyth in hir ballaunce   1045
Disposyng as she wyll / to fauor or to myschaunce
Whiche I haue felt / as well thoon / as the other
Allthoughe I was the doughter of a kynges brother /

1032. hyghe *canc. before* excellent
1045. h *canc. before* all

f. 138ʳ]

My ffather a duke / of Claraunce was hys stille
And brother to kyng Edward / the iiiith of that name   1050
Who was condempned also / alas / alas the whyle
By subtill accusacion / and he no thyng to blame
Ffor a prophane prophecye / of whome than ran the ffame /
Condempned therfore to dye / and drowned in a butt of wynne
Thus by Crewell ffortune / brought he was to Rewyn /   1055

A brother than I hade / who also was hys heyer
Yong and tender / and I God wott not old
Laft in the handes / of worldly dispayer
Whos lyfe thoroughe daynger / was bothe bought and sold
And so I here remayned / in sorowes manyfold   1060
Vntill my souereyn lord / of hys Royall Clemencye
Restored me agayn / to the Erledome of Salesbury

Ledyng thus my lyfe / accordyng to myn estate
I was the more estemed / for my grave demeanour.
I banysshed allwayes / the cause / of Ryott and debate /   1065
Owt of my hall / my chamber and my bower
With whome I had non acquayntaunce / day ne hower
So that my souerayn / for my sad disposicyon
Assigned me the gouernaunce / and prudent direccion

1053. fr *canc. before* ffame
1060. may *canc. before* manyfold

f. 138ᵛ]

Of his oonly doughter / than prynces of this land 1070
Of ffemynyn vertues / the very souerayn flower.
The Caier than of whome / I gladly toke in hand
To gouerne and Rewle / as lady gouernor
Of that swett lady / I did my best endevoure
Ffor whome God / I did beseche and pray 1075
That he wold preserue hir / long and many a day

Thus passed I my lyfe / not wyllyng to offend
But did my self / employ / with all my dyligence
That whiche was amyse / to se it well amendyd
In all thos my places: / wherof I had preemynence 1080
In mynestryng of iustice / I neuer vsed vyolence
But with pacyence / and charitie / asswaged my affeccion
Beryng in my hart / no malice after correccion /

Yet at the last / for all my sober lyfe
The chaunce of ffortune / I cowld no wyse resist 1085
Whos crueltie / . myn honor . Cruellye did depryfe
And gave me an ouerthrowe / or euer I it wyst.
With a ffrownyng Countenaunce / she shoke at me hir fyst
As thoughe she had sayd / in wordes expresse.
Thou shalt not escape / this hand of Cruelnes. 1090

1071. ffemynyn *final* (.) *canc.*
1072. toke *canc. before* toke

f. 139ʳ]

I sawe no remedy for deathe with hys mace /
Gave me chekmate / led to execucyon
Ther boted no excuse / I cowld fynd no grace.
I was condempned / withowt examynacion
Of the Plantagynettes last of that generacion   1095
Whiche bare that name / of old and noble ffame
Some tyme estemed / and nowe in worldly shame

O ye matrons / that be of noble race /
A myrror make of me / trust not your estate
Beware of ffortune / with hir dissimuled face   1100
Allthoughe she smyle / as she did on me but late /
With face benyng / yet nowe she dothe me hate
And will no more spare. / for all my highe degre
I warne you all / example / take of me /

1094. execucion *canc. before* examynacion
1099. estate] E estates; D estats
1101. did *interl.*; but *interl*; of *canc. before* late
1102. nowe *interl. and canc. before* dothe; nowe *interl.*
1103. sa(.)e *canc. before* for; spare *interl.*; highe *interl.*

f. 139ᵛ]

The Erle of / Surrey

What advauntage had I to be a dukes heyer   1105
Endowed with suche qualities / as fewe in my tyme
Lakkyng nothyng / that nature myght repayer
In dewe proporcyon / she wrought hathe euery lyme.
Assendyng ffortunes whele // made lyke to clyme
Syttyng in myn above / supposyng to sitt fast   1110
With a sodeyn tourne made me dissend as fast

Whoo trustith in honor / and settythe all hys lust
In wordly Riches / hauyng of theme aboundaunce
Lett hyme beware / and take good hede he must
Of subtill ffortune / with dissemblyng countenaunce   1115
Ffor whan she smylyth / than hathe she least assuraunce
Ffor the fflatteryng world / dothe often them begyle
With suche vayn vanyties. / alas / alas / the whyle /

I haue not only / my self nowe ouerthrowen
But also my ffather / with heares old and hoore   1120
Allthough his actes marsheall be right welle knowen
Yet was myn offence: / taken so passyng sore.
That I nedes must dye / and he in preson for euermore
Shall still remayn / ffor it wyll not avaylle
All his great conquestes / wherin he did prevayle /   1125

1111. tourne *canc. before* tourne; she *canc. before* made
1116. she *interl.*
1121. mercyall *canc. before* marsheall

METRICAL VISIONS

f. 140ʳ]

O Iulyus Cesare / O thou myghty conquerour /
What myght thy conquestes and all thy victorye
The prevayle / that of Rome was Emperoure.
Whos prowes yet remaynyth / in memorye
Whan Brewtus Casseus / with ffalce conspyracye   1130
Ayenst the in the Capitoll / did contend
Than all thy worthynes / could the not defend

Also Scipio of Affrican / that for the comen wele
Of Rome the empier / the Citie beyng in distresse
Lykly to be subdewed / than euery dele   1135
By Anyballes / valyaunt hardynes
And dyuers noble victoryes / as the history dothe expresse
That he atchyved / to the honor of the town
Cowld not hyme prevaylle / whan ffortune lyst to frown

Thes myghty Champions / thes valyaunt men   1140
Who for the publyke whele / travelled all ther lyfe
Regarded not ther ease / nowther where or when
But most valyauntly / with corage intentyfe
Defendyd the wele publyke / frome all myschyfe
Yet was ther nobles / put in oblyvion   1145
And by matters conspired / brought to confusion /

1133. comen] D; E coen; whele *canc. before* wele
1134. the *canc. before* Rome

f. 140ᵛ]

Loo the Reward / alas that somme men shall haue
Ffor all ther travelles / in ther dayes old
With a small spot / ther honor to deprave
Alas it causithe full often / mens hartes to be cold   1150
Whan suche chaunces / they do behold
Howe for oon offence / a thousaund conquestes valyaunte
Can haue no place / ther lyves make warraunt /

Therfor noble ffather / hold your self content
And with your Captyfe lyve / be ye nothyng dysmayd   1155
Ffor you may se / in historys playn and evydent
That many noble persons / as ye are hathe byn dekayed
The chaunce therfore of ffortune / nedes must be obeyed
And perpetuall presonment / here shalbe your Gwerdon
And dethe for my desertes / without remyse and pardon   1160

Ffor all my knowlege / . wysdome and science.
That God hathe me endowed / all other to precell
Gave me here / but small preemynence /
All thoughe some ware aduaunced in the comen wele /
Ffrome basse estate / as experience dothe tell   1165
Ffor suche vertues / as vices in me accompted were.
Caused me to be doughted / and in great feare /

1151. behold *canc. before* behold
1164. comen] D; E coen
1167. (f..) (fr) *canc. before* feare

f. 141ʳ]

That thyng whiche in some / deseruyth commendacion
And hyghly to be praysed / as verteus commendable.
Beyng estemed therfore / worthy exaltacion   1170
And to be auaunced / to dygnyties honorable
I assure you ware to me / nothyng profetable /
Ffor suche some tyme / as are but vayn and idell
Disdaynythe all them / that awght to rewle the bridell

Therfor ffarewell / my peers / of the noble sect   1175
Desiryng you all / my fall for to behold
Lett it a myrror be / that ye be not enfecte
With ffolyshe wytte / wherof be not to bold
My warnyng / to you / is more worthe than gold
An old prouerbe there is / whiche trewe is at thys day.   1180
The warned is half armed / thus I hard men saye /

I thought of no suche chaunce / as nowe to me is chaunced
I trusted so my wytt / my power and myn estate
Thynkyng more rather / highly to be auaunced
Than to be deposed / as I haue byn but late /   1185
Be it right or wrong / loo I haue lost my pate
Ye se thend / of many noble estates
Take a vewe of me / and of some your late mattes

1170. w *canc. before* worthy
1177. enfect *canc. before* enfecte
1181. say *canc. before* saye

Thauctor / G C

With that he vanysshed / I wyst not whether
But a way he went / and I was left alone 1190
Whos wordes and talk I gathered them together /
And in this sentence rewde / wrott them euerychone.
Yet was my hart / with sorowe full woo begon
So noble a yong man / of wyt and excellence /
To be condempned / for so small offence 1195

Lenvoy de / le auctor

But nowe behold the busynes / that some hathe to ouerthrowe.
Some suche whiche after cowld hurt them but a small
Marke them well / howe they ffolowe on a rowe.
Stumblyng at the bloke / they doughted not at all
But as they measure / that same to them shall falle 1200
Thexperyence is seen / dayly byfore ther eyes.
But will woll not suffer them / ffrome folye to arise /

Hope of long lyfe / causithe all this desier.
With ambycious honor / that ther wittes defaces
Yt makethe them so poore blynd / they cannot se the fier. 1205
Whiche them consumyth / playn byfore ther faces
But to be short / it is for lake of graces.
Whiche they myght haue / if they wold call to God
But they be so stoute / they feare not his iust rod

1190. (O) *canc. before* way
1193. with sorowe *interl.*
1197. theme *canc. before* hurt
1204. deffaces *canc. before* defaces

f. 142ʳ]

Evyn so did he. / but nowe he ffelythe the smert 1210
Trustyng than as they do nowe / in his tong and wytt
To prevent all suche . myschefes / wherof he had his part
Perceyvyng what wytt is / whan frome God it dothe flytt
Trust in hyme therfore / whiche eternally . above dothe sytt
Beholdyng your madenes. / whiche ye so myche esteme / 1215
Laughyng thereat / and for ffoly dothe it deme /

Lauctor / G C

Intendyng here to end / this my symple work
And no further to wade / in this onsavery lake
My penne was fordulled / my wyttes began to lurke /
I sodenly trembled / as oon ware in a brake 1220
The cause I knewe not / that I shold tremble and shake.
Vntill dame fame I hard / blowe hir trembleng trompe.
Whiche woofull blaste brought me / in a soden dompe /

Dame ffame I asked / why blowe ye your trompe so shyrll
In so deadly a Sownd / ye make my hart full sary 1225
She answerd me agayn / and sayd / sir so I wyll
Deade is that Royall prynce / the late viii[th] Harry.
Wherfor adewe / I may no lenger tarry.
Ffor thorowghe the world I must / to blowe this deadly blast
Alas thes woofull newes / made my hart agaste / 1230

1210. so *interl.*; fethy *canc. before* ffelythe
1212. myschefes *canc. before* myschefes
1224. ffame *interl*; trompe] D; E trome
1230. agaste *canc. before* agaste

142ᵛ]

I went my wayes / and drewe my self aside
Alon to lament the deathe of this Royall kyng
Perceyvyng right well / dethe wyll stope no tyde
With kyng or kaysier / therfore a wonderouse thyng
To se howe will in them dothe raygn makyng ther ryconyng   1235
Euer to lyve / as thoughe deathe ware of them afeard
To byd them chekmate / and pluke them by the berd /

To ffynysshe thys worke / I did myself dispose
And to conclude the same / as ye byfore haue red
I leaned to my chayer / entendyng to repose   1240
In a slepie slomber I fille / so hevy was my hed
Morpheus to me appered / and sayd he wold me lede
My spyrittes to revyve / and my labor to degest
With whome ffantzy was redy / and stayed in my brest /

Ffantzy by and bye led me as I thought   1245
To a palice Royall / of pryncely Edyfice
Plentyfully furnysshed / of riches it lacked nought
Astonyed not a littill / of the wofull cries
Whiche I hard there / with many wepyng eyes
Euer as we passed / frome place to place /   1250
I behild many a pityfull bedropped face.

1246. place *canc.* before Royall; palice *interl.*

METRICAL VISIONS

f. 143ʳ]

So that at the last / to tell you playn and right
We entred a chamber / without light of the day
To whome wax candelles gave myche light
Wherin I perceyved a bed of Royall array   1255
To the whiche I approched / makyng no delay /
Wherin a prynce lay syke / with a deadly face
And Cruell Attrophos standyng in that place /

Clotho / I aspied also / that in hyr hand did support
A distaffe / wherof the stuffe / was well nyghe spent   1260
Whiche Lacheses dothe spynne / as poettes dothe report
Drawyng the lyvely thred / tyll Attrophos had brent
Hir sharped sheres / with a full consent /
To shere the thred / supporter of hys lyfe
Ayenst whome ther botyth / no prerogatyfe   1265

Attendyng on his person / was many a worthy grome
Where he lay syke / to whome syknes sayd chekmate /
Allthoughe he ware a prynce / of highe renome.
Yet syknes regardyd not hys Emperyall estate
Tyme approched / of his lyfe the fynall date /   1270
And Attrophos was prest / his lyves thred to devyde
Hold thy hand / quod he / and lett thy stroke abyde /

1255. Where I s(aw) perceived a bed / of Royall array: perceived *interl. and whole line canc. and rewritten in margin*
1256. approched] D; E approced
1264. lyffe *canc. before* lyfe
1269. p *canc. before* Emperyall

Henricus Rex / loquens ad mortem

Geve me leve Attrophos // my self for to lament
Spare me a littyll / for nature makes me sewe
The ffleshe is frayle / and lothe for to Relent   1275
Ffor deathe with lyfe cannot be shett in mewe
They be contrariaunt / there is nothyng more trewe
Ffor lyfe ayenst dethe / allwayes dothe rebell
Eche man by experience / naturally this can tell /

Ffrome Clothos distafe / my lyvely stuffe is spent   1280
Whiche Lachesis / the slender thred hathe sponne
Of my lyfe Emperyall / and thou Attrophos hast brent
The sharped sheres / to shere my feoble throme
That the warbeled spendell / no more abought shold ronne /
And of my Regall lyfe / thus hast thou great disdayn   1285
So slender a thred / so long shold it susteyn

But leave of Attrophos / thou nedes not make suche hast
My symple lyfe / with vigor to confound
Thy sheryng sheres / thou shalt but spend in wast
Ffor the spyndelles end / alredy is at the ground.   1290
The thred ontwynned cannot more be twound
Great folly in the / that takes suche idell paynne
To slee that thyng / that is all redy slayn /

1281. hathe sponne *canc. before* the
1284. abo *canc. before* abought

Wherfore leave of Attrophos / for end of lyfe is deathe
And deathe I se / is end of worldes payn   1295
What shalt thou wyn than / to stope my faynted brethe
Sythe well thou knowest / whan that thou hast me slayn
To welle or woo / I shall oons rise agayn
Thoughe in thy fury / my lyfe nowe thou devoure
To sle me agayn / it shall not lie in thy power.   1300

Slee me not Attrophos / but lett the spyndell ronne
Whiche long hathe hanged / by a feoble lynne /
Ffor whan Lachesis / hir fyned fflees hathe sponne
The Spyndell woll fall / thou seest well with thyn eyen
No stuffe is laft / agayn the thredes to twyn   1305
So slender it is / that with oon blast of wynd
The thred will breke / it is so slakley twynd.

But nowe alas / that euer it shold befall
So famous a prynce / of ffame so notable
That ffame with defame / shold the same appall   1310
Or cause my concyence / to be so onstable
Whiche for to here / is wonderous lamentable
Howe for the love / and fond affeccion
Of a symple woman / to worke all by collusion

1298. who woo (..) *canc. before* shall; woo / I *interl.*
1301. the] DE *om.*

f. 144ᵛ]

I brake the bond of mariage / and did my self inclyne.   1315
To the love of oon / in whome was all my felicitie
By means wherof / this Realme is brought in Rewyn
Yet notwithstandyng / I nedes wold serue my ffantzye
So that all my lust / in hir was ffyxt assuredly.
Whiche for to coloure / I colored than my case   1320
Makyng newe lawes / the old I did deface /

With coloure of Concience / I colored my pretence.
Entendyng therby. / to sett my bond at lybertie.
My lustes to frequent / and haue of them experience.
Sekyng but my lust / of onlefull lecherye   1325
Wherof the slaunder / Remaynythe still in me
So that my wilfullnes / and my shamfull trespace.
Dothe all my maiestie / and noblnes deface /

Whan Venus Veneryall / of me had domynacion
And blynd Cupydo. / my purpose did auaunce   1330
Than willfull lust / thoroughe indiscression
Was chosyn iuge to hold my ballaunce
Of onlefull choyse / by whos onhappie chaunce
Yt hathe darked my honor / spotted fame and glory
Whiche causithe my Concience / oft to be full sory: 1335

f. 145ʳ]

Alake therfore / greatly I ame ashamed
That thus the world / shold knowe my pretence
Wherwith my maiestie / is slaundred and defamed.
Thoroughe this poysoned / lecherous offence
Whiche hathe constrayned / by mortall violence   1340
So many to dye / my purpose to attayn
That nowe more grevous / suerly is my payn /

Thoughe I ware myghty / and Royall in pieusaunce
Havyng all thyng / in myn owen demayn
Yet was my reason / vnder the obeysaunce   1345
Of ffleshely lustes. / fetered in Venus chayn
Ffor of my lust / will was my souerayn
My reason was bridelled / so by sensualite
That wyll rewled all / without lawe and equyte /

After I forsoke / my first most lawfull wyfe   1350
And toke an other / my pleasure to fullfill
I chaynged often / so inconstant was my lyfe
Deathe was the meade / of some that did non ill
Whiche oonly was / to satisfie / my wyll
I was so desirous / of / newe to haue my lust   1355
Yet could I fynd / non lyke vnto the furst /

f. 145ᵛ]

In excellent vertues / and wyfely trouthe /
In pryncely prudence / and whomanly port
Whiche fflorysshed in hir / evyn frome hyr youthe
So well disposed / and of so sad a sort /   1360
To all men it was / no small comfort
And synce the tyme / that I did hir devorse /
All Englond lamentithe / and hathe therof remorse

Hir to commend and prayse / evyn at the ffull
As she was worthy / it lyethe not in my myght   1365
My wytt and connyng / is to grosse and dull
Hir worthynes / in so rude a stile to wright /
Ffor she may be compared / evyn of very right
Vnto pacient Greseld / if euer there ware any.
Ffor lyke hyr pacience / there hathe not regned many: 1370

What inconvenyence / haue I nowe brought to passe
Thoroughe my wilfullnes / of willfull necligence
Within thys realme / fare frome the welthe it was
Yt nedes not therfore / to geve you intelligence.
Ffor you haue fillt the smart / and the indygence /   1375
Wherfore to make / any ferther declaracion
Yt ware to me / but an idell occupacion /

1361. conf *canc. before* comfort
1363. men *canc. before* Englond
1366. to grosse and dull *canc. before* connyng

f. 146ʳ]

Ffor all my conquestes / and my Royall powers
My plesunt tryhumphes / and my bankettyng chere
My pryncely port / and my youthefull powers   1380
My great liberalites / vnto my darlynges dere
My Emperyall maiestie / what ame I the nere
Ffor all my great aboundaunce / nothyng can me defend
Ffrome mortall dethe / all fleshe must haue an end

Who had more ioyes / who had more pleasure   1385
Who had more Riches / who had more abondaunce
Who had more ioyelles / who had more treasure
Who had more pastyme / who had more dalyaunce
Who had more ayed / who had more allyaunce
Who had more howsis / of pleasure and disport   1390
Who had suche places as I. / for my comfort.

All thyng to reherce / wherin I toke delight
A long tyme I assure you / wold not suffice /
What avayllythe nowe / my power and my myght
Synce I must dye / and shall no more aryse   1395
To raygn in this world / nor seen with bodely eyes
But as a clott of claye / consume I must to dust
Whome you haue seen / to raygn in welthe and lust /

1378. Royall *interl.*

f. 146ᵛ]

Ffarewell my nobles / ffarewell my prelattes pasturall
Ffarwell noble dames / ffarewell you pieuselles fayer   1400
Ffarewell my Citezens / ffarewell my comens all /
Ffarewell my howsses / where I was wont repayer.
Ffarewell my gardens / ffarewell the pleasaunt ayer.
Ffarewell the world / ffarewell eche creature.
Ffarewell my ffrendes / my lyfe may no more endure /   1405

Adewe myn impe / adewe my Relyke here.
Adewe my Sonne Edward / sprong of the Royall race /
Of the wight roose and the rede / as it may well appere
Lord God I beseche the / to send hyme of thy grace
Prosperously to Raygne / and long to enioy my place /   1410
To thy will and pleasure / and the Comen welthe /
Iustly here to gouerne / in great ioy and helthe //

Lauctor / G C

With that I sawe his brethe / fast consume away.
And lyfe also. / allthoughe he ware a kyng /
Whan deathe was come / nedes he must obeye   1415
Ffor dethe is indyfferent / to eche creature lyvyng
He sparithe none / all is to hyme / oon rykconyng /
All estates by deathe must end / there is none other bootte.
Loo here nowe I lie / quod he / vnder nethe your foote /

1400. my *canc. before* noble
1401. co *canc. before* comens
1402. howsse *canc. before* howsses
1405. Ffarewell *final* -es *canc.*
1410. Prosperously] D; E Properously
1411. Comen] D; E Coen
1417. oon *canc. before* to

f. 147ʳ]

Makyng thus an end / of his most dolorouse talke /　　　　1420
I strayt awoke / owt of my sobbyng slomber.
Morpheus than forsoke me / and forthe began to walke
But ffantzy with me abode / who did me myche encomber / .
Puttyng me in remembraunce / of the lamentable nomber
Whiche in my slepe I sawe / with euery circumstaunce /　　1425
Yt was no small greave / to my dull remembraunce /

And whan I degested / eche thyng as it was
I cowld but lament / in my faythfull hart
To se the want / of our wonted Solas
With whome I nedes must take / suche equall part　　　　1430
And than to my remembraunce / I dyd agayn reuert
Recountyng his noblenes / shortly to conclude.
Wrott than thus his Epitaphe / in sentence brefe and rude /

Epytaphe

Victoryously . didest Rayn ///
The viii^th Herrye　　　　　　　　　　　　　　　　　　1435
Worthy most souerayn
Tenthe worthy / worthy. /

A Iupiter of providence /
A strengthe of Herculus
A Mars of excellence /　　　　　　　　　　　　　　　　1440
A paynfull Pirrus

1421. slombryng *canc. before* sobbyng
1434–73. *written in 3 parallel columns: col. 2 beg.* 1446, *col. 3 beg.* 1460.

f. 147ʳ]

A Ceser of clemencye
A Corage of Hector.
A Salomon in sapience.
An armez of Arthore.   1445

A Cicero in eloquence /
A hardy Anyball /
A Davyd in prudence /
An Allexander liberall

A Plato in peace.   1450
Of beawtie an Absolon
An Achilles in presse
In gouernaunce Agamemnon

A force of Sampson
A Charlmayn in myght   1455
A Godfroy of Bulloyn
A Rowlond in fyght /

An holy Phocion /
A contynent Ffabricyus
An intier Caton.   1460
A pieusaunt Pompeyous

f. 147ʳ]

A Marcus Marcellus
A Cipio Affrican /
A Ceaser Iulius
An other Octauyon   1465

This beawtie of Britayn
Reyned prosperously
Of progeny Troiean
Dissendyd lynyally

Whos honor to magnefie   1470
The myghty power dyvyn
Hathe chosyn hyme forthy
Above the sterres to shyn
    Ffinis / G / C /

1472. forthy] E for thyn; D far worthy
1473. shyne *canc. before* shyn

f. 147ᵛ]

Lauctor / G C

Thus havyng / iust cause / on dyuers thynges to wonder.
Wayeng within my self the soden chaunce and fall   1475
Of pryncely maiestrates / whome ffortune hathe brought vnder
Chayngyng ther swetnes / vnto bitter gall
Hauyng no respect / to great / ne yet to small /
Thys all men knowyth / that hathe both wytt and reason
That ffortunes ffayned ffauor / lastithe but a season   1480

Thus syttyng in a dombpe / sodenly came in /
Oon with visage sade / and pale as any leade /
Inwardly pensyve / complaynyng of his kynne /
Who was condempned / for to loose his hed
Hymself to defend / he knewe non other stede   1485
But paciently to suffer. / as ffortune shold provyde /
The Crueltie of theme / that shold haue byn his gwyde /

Lord Seymor

Sometyme lord Seymor I was and vncle to a kyng /
Allthoughe / quod he / onworthy to so highe a name /
Yet did hys grace / encrease so my lyvyng   1490
To my highe honor / and perpetuall fame /
I maried the Quene / by means of the same
Who was wyfe to Kyng Herre / my souerayn lord
Whereat some disdayned / and greatly did remord

1475. so *canc. before* soden
1483. kynne *canc. before* kynne
1494. Whereat *medial* -re- *interl.*; (d) *canc. before* did

METRICAL VISIONS

f. 130ʳ]

They grudged they groned / and frett very soore.　　　　1495
They fumed they fomed / ffantazyng what way
They myght me dispatche / . and distroy for euermore
Ther purpose cloos wrought / whiche they did delay:
Vntill they brought abought / my vtter dekay:
Procured by a woman / as all the world saythe　　　　1500
No malice lyke thers / who it iustly wayethe /

Oh ingrat / quod he / O kyn onkynd alas
Ayenst all nature / thus to be vnkynd.
All the world abhorrethe / to se it brought to passe
Nature to repugne / that often is full blynd　　　　1505
Yt grudgyth myche more / euery honest mynd
Than it did the Romans / whan Nero slewe his mother
A fact as onnaturall / oon brother to slee another / .

Nature alas / to disdayn / ayenst natures newe estate /
Where nature shold reioyce / there nature to repyne.　　　　1510
Yt nedes must cause nature / to thynk it onnaturat.
To cause his owen nature / frome nature to declyne /
Thorowghe ambycyous disdayn / so myserably to synne
Alas that brother ayenst brother / suche vengaunce shold procure
Can there be more vengaunce / no I make you sewere /　　　　1515

1495. groned] DE goned
1514. procure *canc. before* procure

f. 130ᵛ]

I allwayes ment iustly / lord / be thow my iuge.
Entendyng no man hurt / nother in word or deade.
My souerayn lord / who was my chefe refuge
I loved and obeyed / as nature did me leade /
Yet that notwithstandyng / ayenst me they did proced.   1520
Not hauyng to iustice / or nature / any respecte
But oniustly ayenst nature / dyd me thus detecte /

I deamed all treuthe / to be in my brother.
Supposyng that he / had byn so to me /
Perceyvyng non occasyon / I sawe in hyme non other.   1525
But brotherly lvoe / voyed of all duplicite /
But who . alas / did euer here or se
Or who did euer in any story fynd
Blood vnto blood / to be more onkynd.

As a brother shold / I put in hyme my trust.   1530
And trusted hyme euer / in hart wyll and thought
Ffor by hys countenaunce / non other cause I wyst
And of any malice / I mystrusted hyme nought
That euer he cowld / so falce a thyng hathe wrought
But who may soner / another man dissayve.   1535
Than he in whome / no malice men conseyve /

1519. lede *canc. before* leade
1528. euer *interl.*
1534. hathe] E *adds* a; D haue

f. 131ʳ]

My brother surmysed / and toke a wrong occasion
To condempn me of treason / oniustly for to fayn
A matter / ayenst right / to bryng me confusion
The whiche he conceyved of hatred and disdayn   1540
Ayenst me affirmyng / in very certeyn
That I ayenst trouthe / and myn allegeaunce
Wold of my souerayn / haue the hole gouernaunce /

The whiche was surmysed / of pretenced malice
Hyme self well knowyng / it was not so   1545
Yet ayenst concyence / he dyd my deathe devyse
Not lyke a brother. / but lyke a Cruell foo.
And to thencrease / of my mortall woo.
In short processe / by crafty invencion
He imagyned my deathe / and my distruccion   1550

Whos oonly purpose / kyndeled was by couetise.
Thys Realme to rewle. / cheafe cause of hys disdayn
And yet myght the gouernaunce / truly to devyse
Haue byn gouerned / by vs bretherne twayne
The better for our sewerties / and lesse to our payn 1555
Howbeit he dispatched me / and brought to distruccion
Hymeself allonly. / to haue therof proteccion

1538. (..) *canc. before* for
1545. wel *canc. before* well

f. 131ᵛ]

This falce conspiracy. / was not wrought alon
Of my oonly brother / without the helpe of other
Whiche in my way / hathe cast this mortall bone   1560
Yt was the Erle of Warwyke it was non other
That to my deathe / procured hathe my brother.
By whos consent / hathe brought me to thys end
Whiche at his most nede / myght haue byn his ffrend

The very ground and cause / was of my distres   1565
The sayd Erle of Warwyke / thoonly sours and well
And cheafe inventor / of all this falcenes.
Who in Craft and falshod / all other did precell.
As all the world / can beare me wytnes well
Whome I supposed. / of my deathe to be innocent /   1570
But suerly it was he / and that he may repent

This whyly beare / that entendyd to devoure
My sely lambe / onprovided for defence /
Not sekyng any helpe / my self for to socoure
I was so innocent / to make any resistence /   1575
Mysdemyng no falcehod / mystrustyng non offence
What wonder was it / the frawde not conceyved.
Thoughe I beyng innocent / onwarely was dyssayved

1562. brother *canc. before* deathe
1576. no *final* -n *canc.*; mystrustyng] D; E mystruttyng; offence *canc. before* offence
1578. dyssayved *canc. before* dyssayved

METRICAL VISIONS

f. 114ʳ]

Allthoughe my greafe. / be great / as nedes it must.
Yet some thyng it is released. / whan I inwardly / remember.   1580
The deathe of the quen / that nowe lyeth in the dust.
Ffor if in this world. / she myght haue lyved lenger
Hir deadly sorowes / shold haue byn not full slender.
Whos deyntie dolower. / wold myche encrease my payn
Whan I the teeres shold se / ffrome hir face derayn /   1585

But blessed is she. / that thus is nowe depryved
The paynfull cares / of thys tempestious see
Whos alterasion / the Orygynall is deryved
Ffrome onstedfastnes. / and sodayn mutabylitie.
Therfor I nedes must say. / that blessed nowe is she /   1590
Synce she is delyuerd / of this my desolacion
Whiche wold haue chaynged / hir ioy to lamentacion /

I thought to myn answere / I shold be forthe brought
Where that my trouthe / myght iustly haue byn tried
And proved all thyng vayn / whiche ayenst me was wrought   1595
But whan they consulted / and had well espied
That ther accusacions / myght lawfully byn denyed.
Than without answare / condempned I was to dye.
Yf the lawe be suche / than iustice I defie /

1592. our *canc. before* hir
1594. t *canc. before* trouthe
1596. well *canc. before* had; espyed wele espied: wele *interl. and all canc. before* well espied

f. 114ᵛ]

But whan ther purpose / was ffully resolued 1600
Be it right or wrong / malice wold geve no place /
Ffor right was sett aside / and treu iustice desolved
Sey what I wold / and still defend my case.
My deathe was determyned / byfore any trespace /
That nedes I must dye / do what I can 1605
Yt boted me not / to requyer iustice than

Ther malice was great / yt apperithe by ther factes
After dethe to slaunder me / and cause falce report
Ye may se it playn / in ther parliament actes
And yet not content / but a precher they did exhort 1610
Opynly in a pulpett. / byfore a noble sort /
To accuse me of thynges / to all men onknowen
Whas it mete for a precher / suche slaunder / to be blown /

O precher what moved the / me to defame /
Was it thyn office / or was it thy profession 1615
To applie Goddes scrypture / to the slaunder of my name /
Are not ye therfore / brought to confusion
You may se / howe God wyll in conclusion.
All suche punyshe / that slaunder inventes.
Therefore preche no slaunder / of innocentes 1620

1620. sh *canc. before* slaunder

f, 115ʳ]

Innocent I was / of any cryme or offence /
That myn ennemyes / ayenst me cowld prove
Therfore deathe here I take / vppon that pretence /
And to that iust iuge / syttyng in hevyn above /
I commytt my cause / that for the tender love /   1625
He bare to mankynd / when he suffred passion
Haue mercy . vppon me / and graunt me clean remyssion /

Lauctor / G C

With that / I stept vppe / and wold haue gon my wayes
Nay not so soone / to me than sayd another
Ffor I ame come to commplayn / my fall and my dekayes   1630
He that last departed hence / was my very brother
Ower father sir Iohn Semore. / and borne of oon mother.
Alas I was the causer of his dethe / craftely surmysed
An act as onnaturall / as cowld be devysed /

Wherfore I pray the / wright my complaynt   1635
And spare me not / ffor I woll tell the duly
Alas / quod I / my hart nowe / waxith faynt
With sittyng so long. / I tell the truly.
Heryng complayntes / of men so onruly.
Wherfore be short I pray you / and goo your way   1640
I will wright all thynges / what so euer you say /

1622. ennemy *canc. before* ennemyes
1631. that *interl.*
1632. Semor *canc. before* and; Semore *interl.*

f. 115ᵛ]

The Duke / of Somersett

Howe to complayn / or what sorowes for to make /
Or howe to lament / quod he / my woofull chaunce
I lake teeres sufficient / ffortune hathe me forsake
Whome she heretofore / highly did auaunce   1645
And traced me forthe / in the pleasaunt daunce:
Of wordly honors / and hyghe dignytie /
Hauyng no regard / to hir mutabilitie /

O mortall lyfe / O momentany estate
O deathe oncertayn / and yet no thyng more suer.   1650
O honor and renome / whos suertie hathe no date. /
So that in this world / nothyng may endure
The prove in me / ye may playnly se the vre
Ffor late I was a duke / of highe renown
Whome ffortune / hathe full lowe brought down   1655

I Clame aloft / and mounted vppe the stage.
Of honourouse estate / to be a noble peere.
But ffikkyll ffortune / in hir cruell rage /
Of very dispight / hathe thrust me frome hir speere
She is nowe fleed / and will no more come neere   1660
Thus ame I left alone / in an woofull case.
In wordly ffelicitie / I fynd but littill grace /

1651. whos *canc. before* whos; (.) *canc. before* date
1653. se *canc. before* playnly ; se *interl.*

METRICAL VISIONS

f. 116ʳ]

With great presumcion / whan the noble kyng was gon.
And passed the passage of this oncertyn lyfe.
To be than the protector / I presumed to it anon   1665
And banysshed all theme / that had prerogatyfe.
By his pryncely . will / to avoyd all stryfe /
And the lawes of this realme whiche he made of equytie
I chaynged and made newe / with great extremytie /

I thought for my wytt / mete to be a iuge   1670
All other to precell in wysdome and discression /
Yet by comparison / in wytt I was a druge.
Ffor if wysdome had had / of me any possession
I shold haue considered / for to reule a region
Was a greatter matter / than my wyt cowld comprehend   1675
I was but a foole / and so it proved at thend

Yf Reason had rewled me / or wysdome had place /
I wold not haue meddeled / not mete for my capacitie /
But ordered all thynges / by the wyll of the kynges grace /
As he left them in writyng / for a perfect / memorye   1680
And to preserue thes lawes / whiche ware of auctorytie
That the kyng had made / for the preseruacion
Of this hys Realme / and his Sonnes educasion /

1663. gon *canc. before* gon
1667. prynly *canc. before* pryncely
1668. I ch *canc. before* whiche

f. 116ᵛ]

Alas yong prynce / thou reygnedst lyke a kyng
Thou barest the name / but I rewled all by wyll   1685
And bare a kyngly port / in euery maner thyng
I presumed on thy name / whan I wold fulfill
My couetous appetyte. / owther in good or yll
Thoughe he ware kyng / and bare therof the name /
I had the gaynes / wherin I was to blame /   1690

Sewrly a protector / shold in euery thyng
Defend the Realme / ffrome warre and debate /
And mantayn thos ffortes / whiche Herre our kyng
Whan in his owen persone / in his Royall estate.
Leavyng them to his Sonne / after that rate /   1695
Whiche I suffred to be lost / for lake of defence.
That owght to be defendyd / with my personall presence /

I mynysshed his howshold. / and his regall port
I consumed hys treasure / I abated hys possessions.
I banysshed all men / that ware not of my sort   1700
I estemed no gentilmen / of auncient condicions
I mayntened the comens / to make insurreccions.
I thought in the comens / to haue suere ayd
But at my most ned. / I was of them denayed /

1689. bare *canc. before* therof ; bare *interl.*
1694. in¹] E *canc.*; D *om.*
1697. (ow) *canc. before* owght

f. 117ʳ]

The plage of God / must iustly on me lyght   1705
Ffor shedyng of my brothers blood / by cruell assent
Whome I caused to dye / of malice and dispight
Alas I was to blame / to his deathe for to concent
Therfore I ame well worthy / of thys punysshement /
Ffor suche ontruthe / with lyke ontruthe agayn /   1710
God will punysshe / the shame shall still remayn

Of all my greves / nothyng more grevous.
Than to remember / my cruell deade /
Whiche ayenst nature / was mere contrarious
O brother forgeve me / for I stand in great dreade /   1715
Of Goddes indignacion / nowe at my neade
Fforgeve me good God / my fact onnaturall
Ffor mercy and pitie / to the I crie and call. /

A kyng and hys realme / I presumed to defend.
That at my most ned / cowld not myself preserue /   1720
O blynd Asse / wye wold I than pretend
A prynce and his realme / royally to conserue /
Supposyng for my / worthynes / honor to deserue.
Of an auncyent dukdome / to beare the highe style.
Twyse I was subdued / I enioyed but a whyle /   1725

1720. (.) *canc. before* preserue
1723. for *interl.*; wyttes / *canc. before* worthynes

f. 117ᵛ]

At last lyke a traytor / led to the barre.
There of highe treason / for to be raygned
And tried by my peers / to mak or to marre
Whome. they of iustice / without fauor fayned
Quyt me therof / whereat some disdayned   1730
And rayned me agayn of ffellony conspired
Yt was but my deathe / that they desired /

Well. / I was condempned / and iuged for to dye /
To hang lyke a Thefe / suche was than my iugement
Who hathe hard the lyke or seen with hys eye /   1735
A duke condempned / for a ffellonous entent
Where was no hurt don / that they cowld invent
Howbeit I ame the first / that shall in this case
Ffor others ensample / dye without trespase /

My tyme is come / and I must nedes suffer.   1740
The rigor of the lawes / there is no remedye
And for my lyfe / it boted not to proferre
Gold ne syluer. / but dye I must assuredly
And yet God wott / there is no cause whye
Howbeit my hed is lost / and I ame goon byfore   1745
My ennemyes may ensewe / and repent therfore /

1742. boke *canc. before* lyfe

f. 118ʳ]

Le Auctor / G.C.

Thend of hys / complaynt / made me for to muse
More than the rest / of all his tale byfore
A duke most shamfully / with crueltie to abuse.
And a kynges vncle / whome they shold haue forbore   1750
But howe they durst presume / it wonders me therfore
Howbeit I se Goddes workes / whiche be knowen to none /
Ffor his iugementes be secrett / tyll they be past and goon /

As I loked abought / and cast my hed aside
Beyng faynt with travell / in thys wofull playnt   1755
Ffower knyghtes / on a rowe / bye me I aspied
Desiryng me / vouchesalue / for to consent
To wright ther myshappe / whilest they ware present
Goo to than / quod I / and say what ye lyst /
Your sayenges I woll wright / or I desist   1760

With that I hard a sound / and a wonderous noyce.
As thoughe they wold haue spoken / all at oons.
Whos speches semed me / to be but oon voyce /
They shevered for cold / with bare and naked boons
Ffull lamentable / was ther woofull moons.   1765
They agreed / at last / and oon spake first of all
Thes ware hys wordes / of whome I make rehersall /

1748. next *canc. before* rest
1752. to *interl.*
1759. they *canc. before* I; what *canc. before* ye; what *interl.*
1760. desyst *canc. before* desist

f. 118ᵛ]

Sir Thomas / Aroundell

Alas / quod he / sometyme I was a knyght
Beyng in my Contre of great estimacion
By my father Aroundell / evyn so my name hight   1770
A yonger brother / I was by dewe generacion
And with the Cardynall / . Wollsey was my educasion
Whos fauor . brought me / first to aboundaunce
Of Riches and possessions. / of great enheritaunce

Chauncylor I was / also / onworthy thought I ware   1775
To Katheren Haward / that sometyme was quene /
Suche fayned fauor / than fortune me bare
That worthy of dignytie / she did me esteme /
As I than thought / she vsed me so cleane
But the quen is dekayd / and past this vyle passage   1780
Whiche by wanton youthe / was brought in dottage /

Yet it was of trouthe / I must nedes confesse /
Se of prevye malice / howe God nowe plagethe me
Evyn for his cause / whos cause causeles
I was cheafe cause to bryng to Calamytie   1785
Yea God / in his iugementes / a right wyse iuge woll be
Ffor thoughe I offendyd not / wherin found Gyltie /
Yet hathe God punysshed me / for my prevye envye /

1768. kyng *canc. before* knyght
1775. of *canc. before* I
1788. enu(..) *canc. before* envye

METRICAL VISIONS

f. 119ʳ]

But wyll you se a wonderous thyng /
That God hathe wrought / by dyvyn operacion   1790
Marke nowe and ye shall here / shortly concludyng
With the duke of Northumberland / I was in consultacion
Who bare the duke of Somersett / highe indignacion
I was cheafe councellor. / in the first ouerthrowe / .
Of the Duke of Somersett / whiche fewe men dyd knowe /   1795

Thynke not to escape / ye that do offend
The punysshement of God / ffor your offence.
He knowyth the secrettes / that you do pretend
Thoughe it be wrought with a secrett pretence
Ye cannot blynd his dyvyn intellygence /   1800
Therfore ame I punysshed / for my conspiracye
Ayenst the innocent / with my deadly ennemye /

To be hanged / thoughe my iugement ware
Yet to do me honor / they chaynged ther sentence
And to leese but my hed / to ease me of my care /   1805
But deathe was the thyng of all ther pretence /
Whiche they desired / suche was ther concyence
Here I make an end / and I without redresse
As here ye may se / me / a symple body hedlesse /

1789. se *interl.*
1793. indygnacion *canc. before* indignacion
1796. to *interl.*
1799. Thoughe] D; E Thought
1805. (.) *canc. before* care

Sir Michell / Stannope

Than came forthe another. / makyng lyke complaynt 1810
And sayed he was / a knyght dobbyed by the kyng
That worthy / prynce / that worthy innocent
Edward the syxt / vertuous in lyvyng
As it appered / in all his procedyng
Of whos prevye chamber / I was without dought / 1815
And nowe condempned / and clean cast owt

Our deathes ware conspyred / to satisfie and content
Some persons that thought / we stode in ther waye.
In suche matters / whiche after did repent
They studyed to compas / both nyght and day 1820
Ther purpose howe they myght / by pollecy conveye.
To bryng that to passe / whiche they long loked for
That oons knowen / did all honest hartes abhorre /

Nowe we be deade / and passed thes stormy showers
Lett theme alone / whiche wrought vs all this woo / 1825
The day wyll come / whan they woll the deathe of owers
Repent full soore / ffortune may tourne hyr purpose soo.
Ffor fortunes whele / tornythe often to and froo.
Thexperyence ye may behold / whan we begon
Ffarewell my frendes / hedlesse I leve you alon / 1830

1812. tha *canc. before* prynce
1814. lyvyng *canc. before* procedyng
1820. compas *canc. before* compas
1822. loked long loked for: loked² *interl. and all canc. before* long
1828. whe *canc. before* whele
1830. leave *canc. before* leve

f. 120ʳ]

Sir Rafe a Vane and / Sir Myles Parteryg

Too other knyghtes / that ware of that band
Complayned them soore / of ffortunes chaunce /
Whome she had taught / for to vnderstand
Howe to knyghthod / she did theme lately auaunce
And gate them possessions / of great enheritaunce /   1835
But at last she fauored so ther highe degree
That they ware bothe hanged / vppon a Gallowetree /
      Ffinis

Le Auctor in / mortem Regis Edwardi vith

I lake teares to lament / and Connyng to compile
Matter sufficient / of ffame most worthye /
My wytt ys to dull / ffor so lamentable a stile   1840
And my penne is to blount / to put in memory:
Of Edward the vith / the woofull tragedye /
Whiche hathe here passed / the paynfull passage
Of thes mondayn stormes / in his tender age /

He was a kyng Royall / of byrthe and of port   1845
In vertue surmountyng / garnysshed with grace /
In vice he had no ioye / ne any disport
Sober in Countenaunce / no lyghtnes in his face /
All was don with gravitie / in tyme and in place /
Yong he was of yeres / but in maners sage /   1850
Yet deathe devoured hyme / in his tender age /

1833. th(a)ught *canc. before* taught
1836. dignytie *canc. before* degree
1845. (.) *canc. before* and

f. 120ᵛ]

Ah deathe most cruell / thy self to revenge /
On so tender an impe / of vertue the flower.
Oh deathe / thy bytt was bytter in tarenge
Alas I say / that euer / we sawe that hower: 1855
That thou sholdest so cruelly / this prynce devoure
Regardyng hyme no more / than a poore page
Thou sholdest haue spared hym / in hys tender age /

In Connyng and wysdome / Salomons right heyer
His wytt was so excellent / his sentence so profound 1860
Absolon / in beawtie / his visage was so fayer.
Yf he myght haue lyved / there shold not haue byn found
A prynce more excellent / Raynyng on the ground
Yet for all his vertues / and noble parentage /
Deathe hathe hyme devoured / in his tender age / 1865

Noble Alexander / whome Clarkes call Severe.
That was of Rome / Emperoure by eleccion
Who rewled his Empier / in love and in feare /
Duryng all his lyve / by clemency and correccion
To whome this yong kyng / myght make comparison 1870
Yf deathe wold haue spared / in his cruell rage /
Hyme to devoure / in his yong and tender age /

1853. the *canc. before* vertue

f. 121ʳ]

Wanton youthe raygned in hyme nothyng at all
But wysdome . Connyng / and Sober gravytie /
Ffor all his care / and study pryncypall   1875
Was to consider hys charge / knytt to his dignytie /
And to gouerne his subiectes / in iustice and equytie
And nobly to raygne / without any owtrage
This was his disport / in his tender age /

A virgyn prynce / a mayden kyng   1880
Neuer corrupte / with thought oncleane /
So chast he was / in all hys lyvyng
Suche grace in hyme / was daylye seen
That all men dyd / bothe iuge and deme /
Deathe to be to blame / in hir fond rage /   1885
Thys prynce to devoure / in his tender age /

Ffrome hyme all vice / banysshed was by grace /
That no Rote of onclennes / cowld take hold
Vertue had so ffurnysshed / fully in the place
Whiche made vice in hyme / so fyble and cold   1890
And vertue so famylier / that made hyme so bold
With discression to rewle / hys realme and baronage
Tyll deathe devoured hym in his tender age /

1878. rage *canc. before* owtrage

f. 121ᵛ]

With pride he neuer entendyd / to stryve.
Of Couetous also / he had non acquayntaunce   1895
Nor had indignacion / to any man alyve
And to be revenged / he neuer knewe vengaunce
Gloteny cowld not prevayle / for temperaunce
Idelnes was banysshed / his commyn vsage
Discression / so rewld his tender age /   1900

My stile to dyrect / with treu dyligence
This Royall prynce / to commend evyn at the full
Of connyng Clarkes / I want the eloquence /
My experyence / in suche matters is very dull
And wysdome is banysshed / my old grosse skull   1905
Therfore I beseche the lord / whiche is eternall
That in hevyn this prynce / may raygn immortall

Lauctor / G C

Musyng of this world / and of the incertentie
Where nother prynce . kyng / ne any other estate
In lusty youthe fflorysshyng in ffelicitie   1910
Can haue of deathe / any sewer date
Ffor whan deathe saythe oons / to them chekemate
Geve ouer the playe / for ye haue lost the game /
This was my last studye / musyng on the same /

1894. stryve] D; E styve
1904. is] D; E are
1905. this *canc. before* my
1906. the *interl.*

f. 122ʳ]

Perceyvyng at the last / it ware great folly 1915
Fferther to muse / of thynges in experyence
Whiche daylie is seen / bothe of symple and iolly.
That departithe thys lyfe / where can be no resistence /
Ffor all must desolve // and depart frome hence /
Therfore to be sorrye. / it ware but a madnes 1920
Ffor after old sorrowes / commyth newe gladnes

The wether brake vppe / that clowdy was byfore
And the Sonne gave lyght / whome mystis did deface /
But God that knewe / our lamentable sore.
Hathe agayn / of hys especyall grace. 1925
Torned our old sorrowe / to a newe solace /
Ffor the losse of a kyng / whiche was a virgyn clean
He hathe restored vs / a mayden quene /

In laudem / regine Marie

Whome our Lord / of his benygne goodnes
Hathe preserued / ffrome many stormye showers 1930
Or elles had she perysshed / in great distresse /
But nowe hathe he made hyr / a quen of owers
Whome Ihesu defend / all tymes and howers /
And geve hyr grace / to rewle thys realme in peace
To the honor of God / our welthe and quyet ease 1935

f. 122ᵛ]

Lett vs love hir / with faythfull hartes
Ffor she is our lawfull quen / borne by iust dissent
We be hir subiectes / it is therfore our partes
To be to hir obedyent / with a good entent
And lett vs not dought / that euer we shall repent   1940
Yf we do otherwyse / our wyttes be to blunt
Quia Corda regum in manu Dei sunt /

God hathe ordened hyr / to reygn in this regally
Therfore lyke trewe subiectes / lett vs be content
To grudge ayenst God / it ware a great folly   1945
Ffor he is lord / that workyth his dyvyn entent
Secretly and cloos / ayenst all mens intendement
His workes be not knowen / vntill theye come to passe
Therfore hyme to prevent / thou art a very asse

Yf thou pretend / Goddes holy word to knowe /   1950
Wye dost thou rebell / ayenst hyr grace
Maliciously abrode / Scedycion to sowe /
To slaunder hir honor / hir vertue to deface /
With any falce / reportes / as some of late hase
Mayntayn non suche / lett them not be releved   1955
Ffor frome the Comen welthe / they owght to be remeved

1946. wyll *canc. before* entent
1948. be *canc. before* come
1956. Comen] D; E Coen; be *canc. before* owght

METRICAL VISIONS

f. 123ʳ]

To travell any further / hir vertues to commend
My . tyme I shold / spend with insufficyence /
Thoughe my will be good / my wytt can not comprehend
All hyr nobles / and hyghe magnyficence /   1960
Worthely to prayse / as I awght of congruence
Therfore lest my rude stile / shold them deface /
I hir commyt to the proteccion of Goddes grace /

Leavyng hyr with God / whome she lovyth best
She is his seruaunt / he will not hir dissceyve   1965
Nor leave hir with ennemyes / cruelly to be opprest
Ffrome whos malyce / he wyll hir receyve /
Into his proteccion / as we of late perceyve /
Howe he hathe preserued hyr / this Royall quen
Defend hir good Lord / from ennemyes / yet not seen   1970

Le auctor / G C

Nowe let me retourne / to the fower knyghtes
That late suffred dethe / I knowe not the cause.
But the wyll to fullfill / of a man of myght
Whiche caused theme to dye / by colour of the lawes.
Wherin was found / a certyn defuse clause   1975
Wrested by craft / to a male intent
To cause them to dye / that therin ware innocent /

1959. will *canc. before* not; can *interl.*
1965. h *canc. before* not
1967. Ayenst *canc. before* whos; Ffrome *interl.*
1970. enneis *canc. before* ennemyes
1976. cla *canc. before* craft

f. 123ᵛ]

As I sat / complaynyng / in my study alon
The deathe / of thes knyghtes / and of ther wofull fall.
My hart was so greved / I could no wyse but mon   1980
Rebukyng fortune / most in especyall /
Whiche is of nature / bothe cruell and mutall
Without all pitie / and will no mercy haue.
Of non estate / ther honors to deprave /

Thes Clarkes old / that wrott wofull tragedies   1985
I pray you / ware not ther playntes / of hyghe estates
Recordyng ther onware falles / and dayngerous ieoperdies
Ther sodeyn chaynges / and ther wofull fattes
Ther disdaynous dispyghtes. / and onnaturall debattes
Allwayes concludyng / who lyst to take heade.   1990
Howe highe estates / are allwayes in most dreade /

With that in blakke / I sawe oon come and goo /
Whos countenaunce was sade / nowe standyng in a staye.
His looke down cast / in token of sorowe and woo /
The salt teeres / in droppes / on hys bare chekes laye   1995
Whiche bare record / of his woo / and deadly affray.
Wherfore he prayed me / my penne for to redresse
And therwith to discryve / hys playnt / and hevynes /

1984. deprave *canc. before* deprave
1986. I *canc. before* I
1990. hede *canc. before* heade
1994. token of *interl.*

f. 124ʳ]

Duke of / Northumberland

The grownd / quod he / and begynnyng of my distruccion
I shall to you reherce / shortly in sentence /   2000
Yt was covetous / pryde / and hyghe presumpcion
Disdaynyng all men / of Royall excellence /
Covetyng by Ravyn / to haue the preemynence /
And whome I suspectyd / that stade in my way
I shortly by falshod / invented ther dekay /   2005

Ffirst I Caused a duke / wrongfully to dye
By Rigor of the lawes / purposly . invented
Yt hathe not byn hard / in my symple ffantzy.
A duke for ffellony. / to be convented
Without any acte / wherby that he offendyd   2010
But of cankard malice / my crueltie to fullfyll
Cawsed hyme and knyghtes fower / to dye on Tower Hyll

Ffroward ambycyon / sett so my hart on fier.
To assend vppe / the imperyall see
And to possesse / the gouernaunce / of this Empier   2015
I did the best / that lay in me /
To reule thys realme / and haue the souerayntie /
This was my purpose / by Couetous and pride /
Whan I sawe tyme / the iust titile to sett aside /

2010. ar *canc. before* acte
2015. gouernaunce] D; E gouernnce

f. 124ᵛ]

Ffor lyke a Subiecte to lyve / I was not content /　　　　2020
But this Realme / to gouerne / most lykest a kyng /
Whiche caused me / to study / what meanes to invent
My desier to attayn / and to my purpose bryng /
I revolved in my brayn / imagynyng euery thyng
Howe to gouerne and Rewle / still in this lond　　　　　2025
Till at the last / this subtiltie I fond.

I hade a Sonne / that tender was of age /
Whiche greatly stode / in my conceyt and fauor
Whome I entendyd than / to ioyn in mariage
To the doughter / of Suffolk / the dukes enheritor　　　2030
And so in possibilitie / myght be successor.
Vnto the Emperiall Crown / by the lawes of this land
As by the statutes. / ye may well vnderstand /

Thus I presumed. / by falce vsurpacion
In all Englond / to quenche the cleare light　　　　　　2035
And troble the lynne / of iust succession /
Whiche I entendyd by force / and not of right
Contrary to the order / of a loyall knyght
To subdue the lawfull quene / I falcely did ordeyn
That I in this Regyon the quyeter myght rayn　　　　　2040

2025. lond] DE land
2029. (..) *canc. before* Whome
2030. duke *canc. before* doughter
2033. well *interl.*
2038. to *interl.*
2040. queter *canc. before* quyeter

METRICAL VISIONS

f. 125ʳ]

I assembled to ayd me / shortly to conclude /
A great number of people / in euery degree
Avauncyng thus forward / with a confuse multitude.
Without any title / but grounded on sotiltie /
Wherfore the gentilmen / and comens of the Contre /   2045
All of oon assent / and in / oon oppynyon /
Assembled theme together / brought me to confusion /

Thus can the lord / the meke enhaunce
And frome ther seattes / the proude thrust down /
Specyally them / that haue no remembraunce /   2050
To remember by wysdome / or by reasown
To knowe the lord / most myghty of renown
The lord of lordes / playnly to compile
Who sufferyth tyrauntes to raygn but a wyle /

Ffor Cruell murder / and falce oppression   2055
Caused me to stand / in great hatred
What avaylled me / my highe domynacion
Without love of the people / whan I had most ned
Whome for a wyle / they did honor and dreede
But nowe love and dreade / are quenched and goon   2060
I am but a wretche left all alone /

2044. a *canc. before* title; any *interl.*
2045. of *canc. before* and
2053. lord *final* -es *canc.*

f. 125ᵛ]

Take an example / howe Mallios of Cartage /
Ffor all his towers / and castelles made of stones
Ffor his oppression / tyranny and owtrage /
The people of Affrike / fill on hyme all at oons / 2065
Cuttyng hys fflesshe / and hewghe all hys bones
Entendyng on hyme / they ware so wood
Vnto ther goddes / to offer vppe his blood /

Evyn so was I brought / to myschefe and to dreade
Ffor all my great power / where in I than stode 2070
Here may you se / who lyst to take heade /
Howe gery fortune / furious and wood
Will not spare / for power nor for good /
Myghty prynces / whiche lyst not God to knowe /
Ffrome ther estates to bryng them down full lowe / 2075

What myght avaylle / the conquest of great price
Done by kyng Zerses / in his estate royall /
Whiche ouercame in battayll / as Clarkes dothe devise
Ten hondreth thousand / the nomber was not small /
But yet for all that / he had a cruell fall 2080
Whan he was / as in storyes is remembred
In peces small / petyously dismembred /

2062. of *canc. before* howe; Mallios] D; E Mallions
2068. vppe *interl.*
2071. hede *canc. before* heade
2081. in *interl.*

f. 126ʳ]

My seade / my succession / and all my bloode /
By my default / are brought to distruccion /
Thus Cruell ffortune / most froward and wood 2085
Ffor my great pride / and falce vsurpacion
Hathe thrown me down / and all my generacion /
Thus can ffortune with twynklyng of an eye
Bryng hyme full lowe / that somtyme sat full hye /

Of myn end / what nede yt / any more to wright 2090
Or of my deathe / make ferther degression
God may his vengaunce / a while respight
But murder wyll owte / and all suche treason
And thoughe it ware my disposicion
Ffalcely to murder / to you I must be playn 2095
Nedes must murder / by my Gwerdon agayn /

Therfore I beseche you / that be here alyve
Pray for my sowle / to that lord above
To pardon my conspyracye / that I did late contryve
Whiche ambycious honor therto did me move / 2100
What madnes is to conspire / myself dothe well prove /
Beware by me therfore / thynke not to opteyn
By rebellious conspiracye / ayenst your souerayn /

2097. above alyve alyfe: alyve *interl. and all canc. before* alyve
2100. move *canc. before* move
2101. is *interl.*

f. 126ᵛ]

And here I make an end / of this my complaynt
Repentyng me full soore / of my Corrupt mynd.   2105
My lyffe is consumed / my purpose hathe me attaynt
Therfore ye my frendes. / whome I haue left behynd
That loved my body / to my sowle be not onkynd
Remember me I beseche you / shortly to conclude /
This world and fantzy / did me thus delude /   2110

Lauctor / G C

Whan thys / stowt duke / had endyd thus hys playnt
Ihesu thought I / what did this man entend
To mount the seage Royall / by forceble constraynt /
He was ferre ouerseen / so madly to offend /
Yt was no loyalltie / thus to assend   2115
Therby to enioye / the crown Emperyall
His fond enterprice / requyrethe a iust fall

Beyng discontent / partly in my mynd
To se a man / of honor / and of highe discression
With ambycion to be / so betyll blynd   2120
That he cowld not se / the sequell progression
Whiche dothe ensewe / suche haynous transgression /
With that I hard oon crie / makyng a rewfull mone /
That late was in honor / and nowe left alone /

f. 127ʳ]

Duke of Suffolk

Somtyme / a duke / quod he / of highe estymacion   2125
Of Suffolke / that bare the name and stile /
Whiche hathe nowe corrupted / my hole Generacion /
Yt was ffortune and fantzy / dyd me thus begyle /
And brought me to Ruyn / alas / alas / the while /
I lakked wytt / I lakked also Reason /   2130
Ayenst my souerayn whan I commytted treason /

What nedyd me conspire that was so ferre in fauor
With the quene grace / whome she called cosyn
I myght at lengethe / with my sewte and labor
Delyuerd my doughter / ffrome the daynger she was in   2135
But wenyng made my thynke / all wayes to wyne
All that I went abought / with a corrupt mynd
Hopyng to attayn / that yet I cowld not fynd /

And whan I remember / the fond enterprice /
Whiche I toke in hand / to compasse / and to bryng abought   2140
Yt was the greattest folly. / that I cowld devyse /
Supposyng to assemble / so great a rowte /
To take my part / and to beare theme owte
Ther wittes ware better / than I at that tyme had.
To folowe me / they ware not so ffrantyke made /   2145

2131. I co *canc. before* whan
2132. reason *canc. before* fauor
2140. bryng] D; E byng
2142. rowt *canc. before* rowte

f. 127ᵛ]

I Claymed and proclaymed. / frome place to place /
The title to be iust / of my doughter Iane /
In Citie and town / I travelled than a pase
To declare hyr title iust / but all was prophane /
Ffor I sawe my trust / dayly decrease and wane /   2150
Than was I fayn / to flee / and hide my hed
Ffor if I ware taken / shortly I shold be dede /

Than was I pursewed / and sought for round abought
There was no place / wherin I myght be suer
At the last I was aspied / taken and brought owte   2155
Ffor in whome I put my trust / did me first discure /
My presumcion / no lenger myght endure.
Than was I taken / with shame and dishonor.
And led away / lyke an errant traytor.

And brought to the barre / tried by my peers   2160
Who found me Giltie / wherin I did offend
My offence / was evydent / as playnly yt appeers
My Colours of trowthe / cowld me not defend.
Allthoughe I excused me / howe truly I did entend
Yet wold not myn excuse / so symple be taken /   2165
And whan I sawe that / I knewe I was forsaken /

2147. Iane *final -e canc.*
2162. evidence *canc. before* offence

f. 132ʳ]

Non other remedy / than sawe I none /
But to make me redye / in Charitie to dye /
Yt boted me not / to make fferther mone /
I thought it best / therfore myself to mortefie /   2170
And to receyve my deathe / most paciently
Down to the bloke / to bowe my hed a lowe /
This is the sede that / disloyaltie dothe sowe

Ffarewell lady Ffraunces / my most lovyng wyfe
Lynyally dissendyd / of the blood Royall   2175
Thoughe I be gon / and chaynged hathe my lyfe
Whiche myght haue lyved still / if I had byn loyall /
But presumpcion / hathe now distroyed all
Therfore comfort your self / with sober pacience /
And thynke that nothyng hathe here permanence /   2180

Ffarewell my bretherne / for I ame your dekay.
This is my last farewell / God send you of his grace
To escape the paiaunt / that I must nedes play
Ffor I ame cheafe causer / of your offence and trespace /
Ffarewell all ye also / dissendyd of that race.   2185
Pray God for his mercy / my sowle may be saved
And my hedlesse body / vouchesave to se it graved /

2172. downe *canc. before* a
2173. is *interl.*; s *canc. before* sede; dish *canc. before* disloyaltie
2174. make *canc. before* wyfe
2182. dek *canc. before* farewell; his *initial* t- *canc.*

f. 132ᵛ]

Lauctor / G C

O lord God / yt is to me / a mervelous thyng
To se the ffollye / the madnes / and the pride /
That nowe among states / is dayly raynyng 2190
Yt is for lake of grace / to be ther chefe gwyde
Ffor vertue and wysdome / they are clean sett aside
Alas that you shold / your honors so defile
With fowle disloyaltie / to put all in exile /

O ye honorables / of noble and highe degrees 2195
Whan will ye be content / with suffisaunce
What meane ye so wylfully / so madly to leese
Your highe honors / and riche enheritaunce /
Thorowghe necligence and your myssegouernaunce
Amend your lyves consider well your callyng 2200
Lyve iustly vppright / and forse your fallyng

Than sawe I a ladye. / that tender was of age /
Sodenly appeere / with an hedlesse body.
The sight was straynge / it abated my Corage
To se so yong a thyng to chaunce on suche folly 2205
Hir hed to loose / that mygh haue lyved full iolly
By signes without wordes / she made me vnderstand
To wright hyr doole / that I shold take in hand /

2192. are *interl*.
2195. noble *final* -s *canc.*
2206. ioylly *canc. before* iolly

f. 133ʳ]

Lady Ianne Gray

By sygnes / she taught me / thus to wright
As thoughe / quod she / why did ye me disseyve.　　　　2210
With ffaynyng ffantzes / ayenst all equytie and right
The Regall power / oniustly to receyve
To serue your tornes / I do right well perceyve /
Ffor I was your instrument / to worke your purpose by
All was but falshed / to bleere withall myn eye　　　　2215

O ye councellors / why did ye me avaunce
To a quens estate / full soore ayenst my mynd
Assuryng me / it was my iust enherytaunce
Nowe contrarye to your suggestion / I perceyve and fynd
All was in vayn / your wittes ware to blynd　　　　2220
Me to delude / ayenst the forme of lawe
Fforsothe you ware to blame / and all not worthe a strawe

Your crepyng and knelyng / to me poore innocent /
Browght me to wenyng / with your perswasions /
That all was trewthe / whiche ye ontruly ment　　　　2225
Suche ware your argumentes / suche ware your reasons /
Made to me at Sondrye tymes and seasons /
Your subtill dealyng / dissayved hathe / bothe you and me /
Dissimulacion woll not serue / nowe may you se /

2215. your but falcehed *canc. before* but; eye *final* -s *canc.*
2217. my *interl.*
2220. was *interl.*
2222. you] E yoᶻ; D ye

f. 133ᵛ]

Cowld none experyence / force you to knowe 2230
Howe dissimulacion / and Couert craftynes /
Hathe byn the occasion / of the ouerthrowe /
Of many a person / beyng in welthynes
And suche as vsed / the face of dublenes
Wherfore dissimulacion / and Crafty dealyng 2235
Hathe brought you and me / to vtter vndoyng /

Ffor your pryncely powers / and hault dygnyties
Assured me / with suche perfeccion
To haue establysshed me . in the hyest degrees
Vntill ffortune hathe brought / vs into subieccion 2240
Of the lawes to abyde / the publyke correccion
Nowe accuse we ffortune / as cheafe ground of our falle
And yet is she not giltie / no thyng at all

Yt is your pride / and pevyshe presumpcion /
That hathe vs led / to this myschaunce 2245
By means wherof all is in consumpcion /
Where be nowe your promysis / and your assuraunce
Where is your ayed / where is your mayntenaunce
Be they not abated / and layed full lowe /
Yf ye wold denye / yet all the world dothe knowe / 2250

2234. As *canc. before* suche; And *interl.*
2237. dygnyties] D; E dynyties
2239. haue] D; E *omits*; que *canc. before* me
2241. by *canc. before* the publyke
2246. wherof *interl.*

f. 113ʳ]

My sorowes are treble / and full of doble woo. /
To remember the tragedy / and wofull case. /
That to my father / my hosbond / and me also
Ys happened / thoroughe folly / and lake of grace /
Yt causithe the teeres / to ron down my face /   2255
And to lament your mysfortune and myn
By suche blynd folly to fall into rwyn

Wherfore the lord / that is lord of lordes all /
And sittyth in heven / above the ihearcheyes
Behold and consider / our whofull fall   2260
We the beseche / with thy mercyfull eyes /
And geve thy holy eares / to our lamentable cries
As thou art mercyfull / of thyn owen natures
So haue mercye on vs / thy poore creatures

Ffarewell madame / ffarewell lady mother   2265
Ffarewell my systers / ffarewell my frendes all /
Helpe vs with your prayers / our prayers to ffurther.
Vnto God allmyght / the Lord supernall /
That he of his grace / will vnto hyme call /
The sowles of his creatures / that nowe lyeth deade /   2270
Whiche by the lawes / hathe receyved our meade /

2253. to *canc. before* my; to *interl.*
2262. eares *initial* t- *canc.*
2269. h(.) *canc. before* vnto

f. 113ᵛ]

Lauctor / G. C.

To answere hir complaynt / I wyst not what to say.
Wherfore I thought / to pawse and rest a while /
Entendyng here / to haue made a stay.
No more to wright / of this woofull stile /   2275
Supposyng that ffortune / cowld no more begile
Men so well warned / of hir ffayned fflatery.
Thexperyence beyng so late / had in memorye /

2272. s *canc. before* to
2277. his *canc. before* hir
After 2278 in E two cancelled stanzas occur; these stanzas do not occur in D, although a space has been left between vv. 2278–79.
 These stanzas are given below:

Yet some ther be / that wantyth Goddes grace /
Whos wyttes be [*canc.* so] oppressed / so with vice /
Thoughe ffortune / dothe still them manace /
Yet of suche precedentes / they set small price /
But Runyng hedlonges / without any advice /
Vnto all myschefe / and vtter distruccion
Lyke men geven / to all evyll dysposicion /

That sentence is trewe / yt cannot be denyed.
Quod oon / to me / for I haue [*canc.* the] ffelt the smart
Thexperience in me / is evydently aspied
Whiche causythe me to lament / with a carefull hart
With that I cast myn eye aside / where I did aduerte /
A rowt with sorowe / wofully arayed.
And oon most rewfully to me / thes wordes he sayd. /

f. 149ᵛ]

An Ephitaphe of our / late quene Marye

Discend frome hevyn / O muse Melpomene.
Thou mornfull goddesse / with thye Systers all.   2280
Passe in your playntes / the wofull Niobe
Torne musyke to mone / with teeres eternall
Blake be your habettes / dyme and ffunerall
Ffor deathe hathe bereft / to our great doloure
Mary our mastres / our quene of honoure.   2285

Our quene of honor / compared aptly.
To veritas victrix / doughter of tyme
By God assisted / amased in armye.
When she a virgyn cleare / without cryme
By ryght without myght / dyd happely clyme   2290
To the stage Royall / iust onheretoure
Proclaymed Mary / our quene of honoure

And as a victryx / valerus endewed
With iustice . prudence / hyghe mercy and force /
Dredles of daynger / with sword subdued   2295
Hir vasselles rebelles. / yet havyng remorce
With losse of fewe / she saved the corsse
Suche was thy mercye / surmountyng rigoure
O Marye mystres O quene of honoure /

2283. funerall *canc. before* ffunerall
2284. our *interl.*
2285. our *canc. before* our quene
2286. quere *canc. before* quene
2287. tyme *canc. before* tyme
2288. armye *canc. before* armye
2291. right *canc. before* ryght
2295. sword *canc. before* sword

f. 149ᵛ]

To a virgyns lyfe / whiche lyked the best 2300
Profest was thyn hart / when moved with zele /
And teeres of Subiectes / expressyng request
Ffor no lust but love for the comen weale
Virginites vowe / thou diddest repelle
Knytt with a kyng Coequall in valoure 2305
Thyn estate to conserue / as quene of honoure /

2301. moved *canc. before* with; moved *interl.*
2302. request *canc. before* request
2303. welle *canc. before* weale
2305. knyght *canc. before* Knytt

f. 150ʳ]

The Roos and pomgranatt / ioyned in oon
England and Spayn / by spousall allyed
Yet of thes branches / blossomes came none.
Wherbye ther kyngdoms / myght be supplied						2310
Ffor this coniuncion / a Comyt envied
Influence castyng / of mortall vapoure
On Marye the Roose / our quene of honoure /

2311. a comytt comyt envied: comyt *interl. and all canc. before* a
2313. honor *canc. before* honoure

f. 150ʳ]

Then faded the fflower. / that whyllome was ffresshe
Ffor Boreas blastes / dyd wether awaye   2315
The spirett and lyfe / frome the tender flesshe
Of that impe Royall / that pryme Roos gaye
Equall in odor / to Flora in Maye
The vertue vanysshed / with vitall vigoure
Ffrome our fayer Marye / our quene of honoure /   2320

Thoughe vertue vitall / did vanysshe awaye.
Hir vertues inward / remayn immortall.
Eterne and . exempte. / ffrome deathe and dekaye
As fountayns flowyng / with course contynuall
As vere in verdure / and grene perpetuall   2325
Or lampes euer lyght / supplied with licoure
Enduryng endles / to Maries honoure /

Add than to vertue / bloode and parentage
In all Europa. / no prynces equall
So noble of byrthe / discent and lynnage.   2330
As no man can nomber / the ioyntes legall
Of Emperours old / and howsis regall.
No harauld hewked / in kynges Coote armoure
Sufficyth to blase. / our Maris honoure

2317. prymros *canc. before* pryme
2320. honore *canc. before* honoure
2323. dekay *canc. before* dekaye
2331. legall *canc. before* legall
2333. armure *canc. before* armoure
2334. honoure] D; E honououre

f. 150ᵛ]

Lament ye lordes / and ladys of estate   2335
You pieusaunt prynces / and dukes of degree.
Lett neuer nobles / appere so ingrate
As to forgett the great gratuyte
Of graces grauntyd / and benefittes fre
Gevyn and restored / oonly by fauoure   2340
Of noble Marye / your quene of honoure

Hyghe preste of Rome. / O Paule appostolike
And College conscripte. / of Cardynalles all
And ye that confesse / the ffaythe Catholyke.
Of Cristes chirche in yerthe vnyuersall   2345
O clarkes and religious / to you I call
Pray for your patrone. / your frend and founder.
Mary our mastres / our quene of honoure

2345. chirche *canc. before* chirche
2346. call *canc. before* call
2348. our quene quene and ffoundeure *canc. before* our quene; quene *canc. before* of; quene *interl.*

f. 150ᵛ]

Whiche late restored / the right Religion
And faythe of ffathers. / obserued of old.   2350
Subdewed Sectes / and all dyvision
Reducyng the fflokke / to the former fold.
A piller most ferme / the churche to vphold.
Loo where she lyeth / treu ffaythes defendoure
Mary our mastres / our quene of honoure /   2355

Whan Sacred aulters / ware all defaced
Images of Sayntes / with outrage burned
In stede of prestes / apostatas placed
Holy sacramentes / with spight down sporned
Whan spoylle and Ravyn / hade all ouertorned   2360
This Chaos confuse. / thys hepe of horroure
Dissoluethe Marie / as quene of honoure. /

2351. sectes *canc. before* Sectes
2361. (..) *canc. before* Chaos

f. 151ʳ]

Elizabethe excellent / of God elect
With Cepture to sytt / in Seate Imperyall
In throne thrihumphant / where thou art erecte   2365
Haue deathe allway / in thy memoryall
Deathe is thend / of fflesshe vnyuersall
The world is but vayn / make for your myrror
Mary thye sister / late quene of honor

So shall the Allmyghty. / stablysshe thye throne   2370
In quyet concord / and dewe obeysaunce
And send the a prynce / to appeas our mone /
With happye Reygne / of long contynaunce
This thyng reposed / in depe remembraunce.
Say and pray all / O Crist / O Savyoure   2375
Haue mercy on Marie / our quene of honoure /

O virgyn Marye / mother of Ihesu
O spouse onspotted / and quene Eternall
As our quene Marye / was hand mayd trewe
To the O Lady / in thys lyfe mortall   2380
So of thy grace / and bountie specyall
To the kyng on hyghe / be intercessor
In hevyn to crown hyr / a quene of honor
               Ffiat. / fiat. / ffinis / .

2365. (.) hone *canc. before* throne
2368. world *canc. before* world
2371. concord *canc. before* concord
2373. Reyng *canc. before* Reygne
2375. O *canc. before* O Crist; O¹ *interl.*
2379. mayd *canc. before* mayd
2383. (.) *canc. before* crown

f. 148ᵛ]

Thauctor to / hys boke

Crepe forthe my boke / vnder the proteccion
Of suche as haue / bothe learnyng and eloquence. 2385
Humbly submyttyng the / to the correccion
Of worthy . writers / of vertuous excellence /
Besechyng all them / of ther benyng pacience /
To take the meanyng. / howe euer the matter frame /
Of this thyn auctor / abasshed of his name / 2390

Ffor first of all / whan I do behold
Of ffamous writers / the goodly circumstaunce /
My quakyng hand / my penne vnnethe can hold
So dombe I ame of doctryn / lame of experyence /
Stakeryng in stile / onsavery of sentence. 2395
Save oonly hope / that saiethe withowten fayll
That my well meanyng / shall quytt my travayll

Thus not presumyng / of learnyng ne eloquence /
Hope made me shove / the boote frome the shoore /
Desiryng nothyng / for my farre or expence / 2400
But oonly good wyll / I aske no moore.
And for the hurt of Envy. / that myght roore.
I shall set my shrowd / for my defence /
Vnder the mantell / of well wyllyng audyence /

2396. saiethe] D; E sathe
2399. shove *canc. before* shove
2401. ooly *canc. before* good; oonly *interl.*
2402. (..) *canc. before* Envy

f. 149ʳ]

And pryncypally / this my worke for to assist   2405
I humbly beseche that lord that is eternall
To defend my penne / that wrot this with my / fyst
To be my . savegard / my stafe and my wall
And consequently . for feare / least I shold fall
In the daynger of the learned / and honorable sort   2410
I pray theme all / my lamenes to support /

Least perchaunce / the pleasaunt flode do faylle
Of witty wrytyng / or sugred eloquence /
Ffolowe therfore good wyll / at the bootes tayle
Me to preserue / in the waves of ignoraunce   2415
Socoured by hope / of gentill sufferaunce
Nowe hale vppe Skuller / God graunt me wynd
And Ihesu defend me / to my lyves / end //

Whan thou my boke / commest in to the prease.
Bothe of the wyse / and learned multitude /   2420
To Excuse thyn auctor / thou canst do no lesse
Wantyng learnyng / and of vtteraunce rude
Whiche dyd neuer / thys enterprise entrude
Trustyng other of wytt or learnyng. /
But for an . excersice / and non other thyng //   2425

Ffinis et compile le xxiiiiᵉʳ jour de / Iunii
annus regnorum Philippi Rex et Regine Marie / iiiith and vth
per le auctor G. C.

Added in different ink in same hand at the bottom of the leaf:
Nouus Rex / nova lex / Noua sola Regina probz peur Ruina

COMMENTARY

Preface to the Commentary

This Commentary seeks to elucidate Cavendish's text by appropriate literary, historical, and linguistic discussion. I have sought to make my elucidations contextually apposite. Thus, for example, I have at a number of points drawn attention to parallels between Cavendish's historical allusions (e.g. vv. 1001–11) and Lydgate's *Fall of Princes* rather than citing other more obvious historical sources. This is because Cavendish's extensive indebtedness to Lydgate renders it most likely that he would have gone to him for such information.

With respect to historical matters, I have given biographical data generally in inverse relation to the historical status of the figure being discussed; hence there is more biographical discussion of Henry Norris than there is of Anne Boleyn. All dates given without supporting documentation either rely on the authority of the *Dictionary of National Biography* or have sufficient general currency (e.g. regnal obits.) not to require documentation.

The following abbreviations are used in the commentary:

APC: *Acts of the Privy Council*. Ed. J. R. Dasent. 3 vols. London, 1890.
Arundel/Harington MS.: *The Arundel-Harington Manuscript of Tudor Poetry*. Ed. R. Hughey. Columbus: Ohio State University Press, 1960.
Ballads from MSS.: *Ballads from Manuscripts*. Ed. F. J. Furnivall and W. R. Morfill. 2 vols. London, 1868–73.
Bapst: E. Bapst, *Deux Gentil hommes-poètes de la cour de Henri VIII*. Paris, 1891.

Casady: E. Casady, *Henry Howard, Earl of Surrey*. New York: Modern Language Association, 1938.
Chronicle of Queen Jane: *The Chronicle of Queen Jane and of Two Years of Queen Mary*. Ed. J. G. Nichols. Camden Society. London, 1850.
Cobbett, *State Trials*: W. Cobbett, *Cobbett's Complete Collection of State Trials and Proceedings for High Treason and other Crimes.* . . . 33 vols. London, 1809–26.
Constantyne: George Constantyne, "Memorial to Thomas, Lord Cromwell." *Archaeologia*, 23 (1831), 62–68.
Cooper's *Chronicle*: T. Cooper, *Cooper's Chronicle*. London, 1560.
DNB: *Dictionary of National Biography*. Ed. Leslie Stephen and Sidney Lee. 63 vols. London, 1885–1900.
Dodds: M. H. Dodds and R. Dodds, *The Pilgrimage of Grace, 1536–37, and the Exeter Conspiracy, 1539*. 2 vols. Cambridge: Cambridge University Press, 1915.
Edward's *Chronicle*: Edward VI, *The Chronicle and Political Papers of Edward VI*. Ed. W. K. Jordan. Ithaca: Cornell University Press, 1966.
FP: John Lydgate, *Fall of Princes*. 4 vols. E.E.T.S., e.s. 121–24. London: Oxford University Press, 1924–27.
Grafton's *Chronicle*: R. Grafton, *Grafton's Chronicle*. 2 vols. London, 1809.
Grey Friars Chronicle: *Grey Friars Chronicle*. Ed. J. G. Nichols. Camden Society. London, 1852.
Hall: Edward Hall, *The Vnion of the Two Noble and Illustre Famelies of Lancastre & Yorke*. Reprinted, London, 1809.
Hammond: *English Verse between Chaucer and Surrey*. Ed. E. P. Hammond. Durham, N.C.: Duke University Press, 1927.
Hawes, *Pastime of Pleasure*: Stephen Hawes, *Pastime of Pleasure*. Ed. W. E. Mead. E.E.T.S., o.s. 173. London: Oxford University Press, 1928.
Haynes: S. Haynes and W. Murdin, eds. *Collection of State Papers*. 2 vols. London, 1740–59.
"Histoire de Anne Boleyn": *Lettres de Henri VIII à Anne Boleyn*. Paris, [1826].
Holinshed: R. Holinshed, *The first volume of the chronicle of England, Scotlande, and Irelande*. 3 vols. London, 1577.
Jordan: W. K. Jordan, *Edward VI*. 2 vols. London: Allen & Unwin, 1968–70.

Law: E. Law, *History of Hampton Court Palace*. 3 vols. London, 1885–91.
L&P: *Letters and Papers Foreign and Domestic of the Reign of Henry VIII*. Ed. J. S. Brewer, J. Gairdner, and R. Brodie. 21 vols. London, 1862–1910.
Literary Remains: Jane Grey, *Memories and Literary Remains of Lady Jane Grey*. Ed. N. H. Nicolas. London, 1832.
Loades: D. M. Loades, *Two Tudor Conspiracies*. Cambridge: Cambridge University Press, 1965.
LW: George Cavendish, *The Life and Death of Cardinal Wolsey*. Ed. R. S. Sylvester. E.E.T.S., 243. London: Oxford University Press, 1959.
Machyn: Henry Machyn, *The Diary of Henry Machyn*. Ed. J. G. Nichols. Camden Society. London, 1848.
MED: *Middle English Dictionary*. Ed. H. Kurath. Ann Arbor: University of Michigan Press, 1954–.
Mirror for Magistrates: *Mirror for Magistrates*. Ed. L. B. Campbell. Cambridge, 1938.
MV: *Metrical Visions*
Nichols, *Remains*: *Literary Remains of King Edward the Sixth*. Ed. J. G. Nichols. 2 vols. London, 1857.
OED: *Oxford English Dictionary*. Ed. J. A. H. Murray et al. 12 vols. and Supplement. Oxford, 1888–1933.
Pollard: A. F. Pollard, *Wolsey*. London: Longmans, Green, 1929.
Scarisbrick: J. J. Scarisbrick, *Henry VIII*. London: Eyre & Spottiswoode, 1968.
Singer: George Cavendish, *The Life of Cardinal Wolsey and Metrical Visions*. Ed. S. W. Singer. Vol. 11. Chiswick, 1825.
Skelton: John Skelton, *Works*. Ed. A. Dyce. 2 vols. London, 1843.
Smith: L. B. Smith, *A Tudor Tragedy: The Life and Times of Catherine Howard*. London: Jonathan Cape, 1961.
Spanish Chronicle: *Chronicle of King Henry VIII of England*. Ed. and trans. M. A. S. Hume. London, 1889.
Stow, *Annales*: John Stow, *Annales of England*. London, 1592.
Throckmorton: Nicholas Throckmorton, *Legend of Sir Nicholas Throckmorton*. Ed. J. G. Nichols. London, 1874.
Tilley: *A Dictionary of the Proverbs in England in the Sixteenth and Seventeenth Centuries*. Ed. M. P. Tilley. Ann Arbor: University of Michigan Press, 1950.

Tottel's Miscellany: *Tottel's Miscellany*. Ed. H. E. Rollins. 2 vols. Cambridge, Mass.: Harvard University Press, 1965.
Tytler: P. F. Tytler, *England under the Reigns of Edward V and Mary*. 2 vols. London, 1839.
Whiting: *Proverbs and Proverbial Phrases from English Writings mainly before 1500*. B. J. Whiting and H. Whiting. Cambridge, Mass.: Belknap Press, 1968.
Wriothesley: Charles Wriothesley, *A Chronicle of England*. Ed. W. Hamilton. 2 vols. Camden Society. London, 1875–77.
Wyatt: Thomas Wyatt, *Collected Poems*. Ed. K. Muir and P. Thomson. Liverpool: Liverpool University Press, 1969.

Commentary

1–7. The opening lines of the *MV* may owe something to the beginning of Skelton's *Garland of Laurel*. There are at least sufficient coincidences between the beginnings of the two works to suggest the possibility: both open with an astronomical allusion involving a "retrogradaunt" sign (cf. *Garland*, vv. 1–3), a solitary narrator (cf. *Garland*, v. 8) musing on fortune's mutability (cf. *Garland*, vv. 9–14) near an oak tree (or in the case of *Garland*, its stump—cf. vv. 17–21). In addition there are occasional Skeltonic echoes in the *MV* (see e.g. Commentary vv. 379–80, 510–11, 1434–73), which, together with Cavendish's known tendency to plagiarize, reinforce such a hypothesis.

3. Gemynye] *E* reads *Gemynys*, a form printed without comment by Hammond. I have followed the *D* reading, since the *E* form seems without warrant.

4. a sygne retrogradaunt] Cf. Skelton, *Garland of Laurel*, 3: "When Mars retrogradant reuersyd his bak." Hammond notes that "This means that the constellation or 'sign' was on the western or descending side of the meridian line" (p. 527).

5. In a mean measure] i.e. "at an indeterminate point."

22. Whan] Some appositive word or phrase (e.g. "But") clearly has to be understood before the beginning of this stanza.

24–28. idelnes] See Hammond's note (p. 527) for other expressions of a concern with idleness (a cardinal sin) in medieval literature.

50–53. I onworthe] Cavendish here adopts the rhetorical device of the modesty *topos*, a device he uses elsewhere in the *MV* (see e.g. vv. 1364–67, 1838–41, 2391–404).

61. colours haue I none to paynt] i.e. the "colours" of rhetorical skill; cf. Lydgate's reference in *FP* VI, 2993, to "the colours and crafft of elloquence" and Hammond's authoritative note on this phrase (pp. 452–53) which concisely outlines the history of the "colours of rhetoric."

63. An . . . style] Hammond draws attention (p. 528) to a number of earlier illustrations of this view, including *FP* VI, 3144–50.

64–67. This is a borrowing from *FP* I, 240–41: "Or onto whom shal I for helpe calle? / Calliope my callyng will refuse." Hammond (p. 528) notes only the borrowing of the second line. Calliope is the muse of epic poetry.

69. musis . . . syng] Cf. *FP* I, 458: "the Muses that on Parnaso synge."

85–259. Cavendish's verse treatment of his former patron, Wolsey, stands in contrast to the balanced portrayal in his later prose *Life of Wolsey*. Indeed, in his unrelenting focus on Wolsey's deficiencies Cavendish places himself within a developed tradition of attacks on the cardinal. For a survey of this tradition see P. L. Wiley, "Renaissance Exploitation of Cavendish's *Life of Wolsey*," *Studies in Philology*, 43 (1946), 121–46. Cavendish rehearses traditional criticisms of Wolsey's secular and religious abuses with no attempt to qualify them, as in *LW*, from the viewpoint of his own intimate personal knowledge of Wolsey. It is difficult to account for the striking divergence both in tone and in viewpoint between the two treatments.

92. pouertie to plentie] The history of Wolsey's rise to power is detailed in *LW* 6/20–28/35.

93. Cardynall] Wolsey was created cardinal on September 10, 1515 (Pollard, p. 55); see *LW* 16/12–36 for an account of Wolsey's elaborate preparations for the reception of his papal hat.

93. legate de latere] Wolsey was not created legate until May 17, 1518 (Pollard, p. 170), considerably after the other honors detailed in this stanza. Here, however, as in *LW* 16/13, Cavendish implies that the legacy was closely linked in time with his cardinalate. Wolsey was made legate first for a period of three years and later for life. For a discussion of the office and the difficulties in reconciling it with Wolsey's role as agent of Henry's secular authority, see Pollard, p. 169.

94. bysshope] Wolsey received his first bishopric, that of Tournai, in 1513 (cf. *LW* 15/14), but he never took possession of the see. He was

consecrated bishop of Lincoln on March 26, 1514 (cf. *LW* 15/12–24 and note).

94. archebysshope] Wolsey was created archbishop of York in succession to Christopher Bainbridge, who died on or near July 13, 1514. Wolsey first received the temporalities of this office on August 5, 1514 (Pollard, p. 21); cf. *LW* 15/19–22.

95–97. Chauncelor of Englond] Wolsey became chancellor of England on December 24, 1515 (Pollard, p. 58). For an examination of Wolsey's power and influence as chancellor, see Scarisbrick, pp. 66–70.

96. suche auctorytie] Cf. the contemporary observation of Guistiniani, the Venetian ambassador, who in 1519 observed that "This Cardinal . . . is the person who rules both the king and the entire kingdom" (quoted in Pollard, p. 103). For an examination of Wolsey's role as "prime minister" see Pollard, pp. 99–111.

99–105. I gathered me Riches] For a detailed account of Wolsey's lavish style of living see *LW* 18/26–28/32. His wealth and its sources are discussed by Pollard (pp. 320–28), who concludes that "the papal legate became the richest man in England save the king, and even that exception has to be qualified" (p. 320).

106–12. byldynges somptious] Cavendish appears to have in mind particularly Hampton Court, Wolsey's most magnificent residence.

106–10. gold and byse] Law discusses one of the original ceilings in the Clock Court at Hampton Court: "[It] was very beautiful, being of pure cinquecento design in octagonal panels, with decorative scroll-work and other ornaments in relief. The ribs are of moulded wood, with balls and leaden leaves at their intersections; these, and the ornamental work with the panels, are gilt, the ground being of light blue [i.e. 'byse']" (I, 53).

107. Shone lyke the Sone] Proverbial; cf. Whiting S 897, where examples are cited from *FP* IV, 3281, and VIII, 875, 2533.

110. expertest artificers] Cf. Law, I, 50:

For the execution of the ornamental work about the buildings and for the internal decoration of the rooms [Wolsey] employed the best carvers, painters and guilders in London, many of them being Italians who had come over to this country attracted by his liberal patronage of the arts. Sometimes he sent directly to Italy for decorative work [as in the case of his terra cotta busts of the Roman Emperors, done by Joannes Maiano].

113. My Galleryes] On the galleries at Hampton Court see Law, I, 49, who notes their existence in the Clock Court and First Court at Hampton.

115. My Gardens] On the gardens at Hampton Court in Henry VIII's time, see Law, I, 206–8. The various gardens were divided by low brick walls, the "walles strong" to which Cavendish refers here.

118. arbors and alyes] "Arbours" were bowers or shady retreats within a garden; see D. Pearsall's useful note in his edition of *The Flower and the Leafe and The Assembly of Ladies* (London, 1962), pp. 132–33. "Alleys" were paths "usually bordered with a low rail and covered with sand" (Pearsall, p. 153).

119. The pestylent ayers] As Hammond points out, "It was the general medieval belief that disease and pestilence were caused and spread by bad air" (p. 529). See also the references she gives, pp. 529–30.

120–22. arras fynne / Importyng personages . . .] These lines appear to refer to the tapestries at Hampton Court; for a more detailed description of these, see Skelton's *Colyn Clout* (ll. 942–70).

123–26. clothe of estate] Cf. *LW* 69/24–26: "the clothe of estate [was borne] towardes the myddes of the chamber couered w^t lynnen clothes of dammaske worke swetly perfumed." As Hammond notes, the cloth of estate was "the canopy over the seat of honor" (p. 530).

127–28. Plate . . . Of facions newe] *LW* 69/28–29 records preparations for a banquet of Wolsey's in November 1527 which included a cupboard "full of gilt plate very somptious & of the most newest facions." Law, however, points out (I, 81) that Cavendish is not quite correct in representing Wolsey as indifferent to old plate, for the inventories made at his fall (*L&P* IV, 30, 42–48) "prove that he owned much in the antique style."

130. dayntes vyaundes] As it stands *dayntes* must be a substantive, and its conjunction with *vyaundes* makes at best awkward sense, an omitted or understood conjunction having to be assumed. It seems arguable that *dayntes* should be emended to an adjectival form *daynte[e]* (cf. *MED*, s.v. "deynte" 3). Such an emendation gains obvious support from the possibility of palaeographic confusion between *e* and *s*. *D*, however, agrees with *E*.

133. worshipfull] *E* reads *worshpfull*, an instance of Cavendish's tendency to omit letters. I have adopted the *D* form.

134–40. crossis twayn] Cavendish seems to echo parts of *LW*; cf. 23/25–23/3:

thus passyng forthe w^t ij great Crossis of Syluer borne byfore hyme w^t also ij great pillers of syluer . . . And whan he came to the hall doore ther was attendaunt for hyme his mewle trapped all to gether in Crymmosyn velvett and gylt Stirropes whan he was mounted w^t his crosse berers and Piller berers also vppon great horsis trapped w^t red skarlett Than marched he forward w^t his trayn & furnyture in maner as I haue declared hauyng abought hyme iiij^{or} footmen w^t gylt pollaxes in ther handes.

Wolsey's elaborate progresses seem to have been a popular target for contemporary satire. See Skelton's contemptuous allusion in *Speak Parrot* to "Suche pollaxis and pyllers, suche mvlys trapte withe golde" (v. 510). A contemporary ballad also exhorts Wolsey to "let downe thi pyllers, pollaxis, & crosses / By the whiche this lande hathe had grete lossys" (*Ballads from MSS*., p. 360, vv. 256–57).

141–47. My legantyn prerogatyve . . .] Cf. *LW* 17/13–24: "endowed w^t the promocion of an archebysshop and Cardynall legatte allso de latere . . . visited also all sprituall howsis and presentyd by prevencyon whome he listed to ther benyfices." As Sylvester notes, *prevencyon* (cf. 145) refers to

"the privilege in Canon Law possessed or claimed by an ecclesiastical superior of taking precedence of or forestalling an inferior in the execution of an official act regularly pertaining to the latter" (*OED*). The seventh of the articles against Wolsey in 1530 specifically mentions his abuse of this power. [p. 199]

See Pollard, pp. 198–202, for discussion of Wolsey's treatment of vacant benefices.

144. Presentyng than my Clarke] The reference is presumably to Wolsey's chaplain, John Allen, "who accompanied with a great Train, and riding in a kind of perpetuall progress from one religious House to another, is said to have drawn large Sums for his Master's service from them" (Richard Fiddes, *The Life of Cardinal Wolsey* [London, 1724], p. 372).

153–54. Somme oon . . . at large] Sylvester in *LW* (p. 258) points to the parallel between these lines and the concluding lines of *LW* 188/16–18: "an other person who parauenture he hated in his lyfe shall spend it owt & consume it." The "somme oon" Cavendish has in mind is of course Henry VIII.

155–61. parcyall ware my domes] Cf. the accusations made against Wolsey by Skelton, *Why Come Ye Nat to Court*:

> All iustyce he pretended
> All thynges sholde be amended,
> All wronges he wolde redresse,
> All iniuris he wolde represse,
> All periuris he wolde oppresse
> And yet this graceless elfe,
> He is periured himselfe,
> As playnly it dothe appere . . . [vv. 1107–14]

156. I spared non estate] This is probably an allusion to Wolsey's strengthening of the power of the Court of Requests, designed specifically to deal with the pleas of poor men; see Pollard, pp. 82–85, for details of Wolsey's association with this court. His involvement with it and with the judicial process provoked contemporary literary responses; cf. John Heywood's interlude, *The Play of Love* (probably produced c. 1528 or 1529 for one of the Inns of Court), which satirizes Wolsey from a legal viewpoint; see R. J. Schoeck, "Satire of Wolsey in Heywood's 'Play of Love,'" *Notes and Queries*, 196 (1951), 112–14.

157. I preferred whome me lyst] There is evidence of Wolsey's independent attitude to preferment. The most famous instance of this was his appointment of his own nominee as abbess of Wilton against the wishes of Henry. For an account of this episode, placing it within the context of Wolsey's attitude on this question, see D. Knowles, "'The Matter of Wilton' in 1528," *Bulletin of the Institute of Historical Research*, 31 (1958), 92–96.

157–58. exaltyng symple gromes] According to Cavendish, one of the complaints of the "great lordes of the Councell" against Wolsey was that he "kept them lowe and rewled theme as well as other meane subiectes" (*LW* 35/27–28). This antifeudal policy expressed itself in such acts as the execution of Edward Stafford, Duke of Buckingham, in 1521 and in the increased power of those like Thomas Cromwell, who although of humble birth were able to forge careers of enormous influence from their beginnings under Wolsey's patronage.

158. Above . . . spiritualitie] Wolsey was rather less lenient toward the church than Cavendish allows here. Pollard, after a careful examination of this aspect of Wolsey's administration (pp. 26–54), concludes that he "wanted as much practical reform of the church as would at least render possible the continuance of ecclesiastical autonomy. He wanted the church to be reformed by itself or rather by himself" (p. 54).

161. say chekmate] A popular phrase of Cavendish's occurring in various forms elsewhere at vv. 641, 1092, 1237, 1267, 1912; the phrase probably derives from Lydgate, e.g. *FP* I, 182; I, 1526.

165–66. in Fraunce] Wolsey journeyed to France in August 1527, but rumors of his possible fall from power were circulating as early as May of that year (cf. Pollard, p. 221). It was during his absence that Anne Boleyn and the Court faction supporting her began to gain a decisive ascendancy, prevailing upon Henry to make his first independent efforts to obtain a divorce. See Scarisbrick, pp. 212–15, for an examination of this aspect of Wolsey's fall.

167–68. This is a borrowing from *FP* II, 4437–38: "For who with fraude fraudulent is founde, / To a diffraudere fraude will ay rebounde."

169–72. These lines are probably based on *FP* II, 4432–35:

> Deceit deceyueth and shal be deceyued,
> For be deceit[e] who is deceyuable,
> Thouh his deceitis be nat out parceyued,
> To a deceyuour deceit is retournable

Such wordplay is not uncommon in the *MV*, and may be a development of Lydgatean diction of the kind quoted above; see below, e.g. vv. 222–24, 348–50, 421–41.

176–77. The sense of these lines is obscure, chiefly because the subject of *Cheafely disdayned* (v. 177) has been omitted. I understand them to read: "It came about that because of my 'subtill dealyng' [my enemies] 'cheafely disdayned' [me] for [i.e. on account of] whom I suffered ('toke') pain."

181–82. Venus the goddesse] Cf. *LW* 29/3–4: "[Fortune] procured Venus the Insaciat goddesse to be hir Instrument to worke hir purpose." The reference is of course to Henry VIII's love for Anne Boleyn, mentioned in the following lines (*LW* 29/4–8), which "wrought the Cardynall myche displeasure" (7–8).

186–87. folowed myn owen] Cf. Wolsey's famous dying words as reported by Cavendish; *LW* 178/34–179/4: "But if I had serued god as dyligently as I haue don the kyng he wold not haue gevyn me ouer in my gray heares howbeit thys is the Iust reward that I must Receyve for my worldly dyligence & paynnes that I haue had to do hyme seruyce oonly to satysfie his vayn pleasures not regardyng my godly dewtye."

188. Proverbial; cf. Whiting F300, Tilley F378. This is a favorite Lydgatean metaphor (as Hammond points out, p. 449); see e.g. *FP* I, 4424, 6079; III, 355–58; IX, 3348–51.

190–203. all sodenly] Wolsey's fall from power did not come as "all sodenly" or so totally as Cavendish suggests here. *LW* provides the clearest indication of this. Wolsey surrendered his great seal of office on October 22, 1529. But Henry continued to show him evidence of favor (cf. *LW* 101/27–104/12 recounting the messages of comfort Henry sent to Wolsey through Norris). Immediately after this, however, Wolsey found himself virtually destitute (104/13–25). He was deprived of the bishopric of Winchester, his various colleges and buildings, and the abbey of St. Albans. Yet subsequent to this, when Wolsey fell ill in December, Henry sent him his personal physician and a ring as tokens of his favor (120/8–32) and later (122/13–18) "iii^{re} or iiij^{or} Cartloodes of Stuffe." Later with the king's permission he removed to Richmond (127/13–22) and then at the beginning of Lent to the Charterhouse there (130/5–7). On April 5 he began his journey to his diocese of York with Henry's encouragement and a grant of £ 1000 (132/3–5). It was not until November 1, 1530 that a warrant was finally issued for his arrest.

204–10. my corage was so hault] After his fall Wolsey appealed for protection and support from abroad. Both Albrecht the German elector and the Duke of Saxony sent envoys to Henry on Wolsey's behalf in the winter of 1529/30 (Pollard, p. 282). He also appealed for help to the pope and to the emperor (see Pollard, pp. 283–86, 289–92, for details). It was the arrest of his chaplain with letters bound for the Continent which precipitated Wolsey's arrest. Curiously there is no mention in *LW* that Wolsey was seeking foreign aid at this time.

207. without triall] Wolsey maintained that if he were brought to trial he would be able to prove himself innocent; cf. *LW* 159/28–34: "if I may come to myn answere I feare no man a lyve ffor he lyvyth not vppon the

yerthe that shall loke vppon this face . . . shall be able to accuse me of any ontrouthe And that knowyth myn ennemyes full well w^{che} woll be an occasion that I shall not haue Indifferent Iustice but woll rather seke some other synyster wayes to distroy me."

211–14. Accused me of treason] Wolsey was arrested at Cawood Castle on November 4, 1530, on charges of treason.

215–17. Deathe . . . In Leycester] Wolsey died on November 29, 1530, at Leicester Abbey, on his way back to London; his death is described in *LW* 177/15–182/3.

216. Deathe with his dart] The image of death bearing a dart is a commonplace one in sixteenth-century literature; cf. e.g. Hawes, *Pastime of Pleasure*, "Dethe with his darte a rest me sodaynly" (5384) and Thomas Spooner, "Whan ragyng dethe doth draw his darte" (T. Wright, ed., *Songs and Ballads . . . Chiefly of the Reign of Philip and Mary* [London, 1860], p. 105).

219. wordly] Cavendish uses this form at a number of points (e.g. vv. 333, 1113, 1647, 1662), as well as the form "worldly" (e.g. v. 724). Sylvester emends the form "wordly" in *LW* (e.g. 179/2, 182/7), but the form is sanctioned by *OED* (s.v. "wordly, -lyche"), as an obsolete variant spelling of "worldly." I have therefore allowed it to stand as a preferred spelling, rather than emend it.

222. mynd] Cavendish originally wrote *memory* here, presumably owing to an initially erroneous attempt to make the rhyme conform with that of the following rather than preceding lines. The error provides one of the infrequent indications of revision in the course of the transcription of *E*.

225–31. my Tombe] "Wolsey had planned an elaborate mausoleum for himself, the work of the Florentine artist Rovezzano, who came to England about 1520. It was not complete at the time of Wolsey's fall, and the king seized it for himself. . . . The work however was never finished" (Hammond, pp. 532–33). Wolsey was in fact buried in a "Coffen of bordes" (*LW* 182/29) in the "tyrant's grave" at Leicester, where Richard III had been interred.

232–36. Ffarewell] Anaphora is one of the few rhetorical devices employed by Cavendish; cf. e.g. below, vv. 393–96, 477–80 (the latter in imitation of Lydgate), 1385–91, 1399–405, 1698–703.

232. Hampton Court] Wolsey had begun work on Hampton Court in 1515. According to Hall, it had already passed into Henry's possession by

1525/26: "At this tyme, the saied Cardinall gaue to the kyng, the lease of the Manor of Hampton Court. . . . Therefore the kyng of his gentle nature, licensed hym to lie in his Manor of Richmond" (p. 703). Cavendish's account of this transaction in *LW* is ambiguous as to its date (123/26–27). Together with York Place (see below, v. 233), Hampton Court seems to have been a target for contemporary criticism of Wolsey; cf. Skelton, *Why Come Ye Nat to Court*:

> The kynges courte
> Shuld haue the excellence;
> But Hampton Court
> Hath the preemynence
> And Yorkes Place
> With my lordes Grace [403–8]

233. Westmynster Place] It was "the kynges pleasure . . . to haue [Wolsey's] howesse at westminster (than called yorke Place)" (*LW* 117/13–14) in late 1529. It was formally vested in the Crown in early 1530 (Scarisbrick, p. 647).

234. the Moore] Wolsey's palace between Rickmandsworth and Northwood, now Moor Park, Hertfordshire. Pollard describes it as Wolsey's "favourite country house" (p. 325).

234. Tynnynainger] Tyttenhanger belonged with the Moor to St. Alban's abbey, which Wolsey received on December 17, 1521 (Pollard, p. 321). Henry, according to Hall (p. 750), repaired there in 1528 to avoid the sweating sickness. Wolsey was deprived of the abbey in 1529.

235. my Colege Cardynall] Wolsey founded Cardinal College and his Ipswich school in 1524 with funds from suppressed monastery lands. Cf. Hall, p. 694: "with these landes he endewed with all his Colleges, which he began so sumpteous and the Scholers were so proude that euery persone iudged, that thende would not be good, as you shall heare fiue yeares hereafter." The college passed to the king on January 15, 1531. In January 1547 it became Christ Church College.

236–38. my Scole gramaticall] Wolsey's school in Ipswich was among his possessions which "the kyng toke into his owen handes" (*LW* 125/4–5) by November 22, 1529, whereupon it was suppressed.

241–42. dompe in the daunce] The dance of death was an iconographic commonplace in late medieval English literature and art; for a useful survey, with special emphasis on Lydgatean connections, see R. H. Bowers, "Iconography in Lydgate's *Dance of Death*," *Southern Folklore Quarterly*, 12 (1948), 111–28.

242. tryppe on the trace] Cf. v. 840 for the same phrase. The conjunction of "dance" and "trip" is a common one in medieval verse; for examples see *OED* (s.v. "trip" v. I. 1).

246–52. This is a borrowing from *FP* III, 3760–66:

> What may auaille hem ther fethirbeddis softe,
> Shetis of Reynys, longe, large & wide,
> Duyers deuises or clothes chaunged ofte
> Or vicious mene walking be ther side,—
> Void of vertu, ambicious in ther pride,
> Which causeth princis, be report of swich fame
> For ther mysleuyng to han an heuy name.

This indebtedness was first noted by Hammond (p. 534).

247. Shettes of Raynes] "A fine linen was made at Rennes in Brittany" (Hammond, p. 534).

249. vicious chapleyns] Cf. *LW* 106/28 where Cromwell complains of Wolsey's "Idell chapleyns" and concludes that "all the world woll haue them in Indignacion & hatred for ther abhomynable Ingratytude to ther m^r & lord" (106/32–33).

253–59. seruaunt] Cavendish was Wolsey's gentleman usher and an eyewitness to his death. See *LW*, xix–xxi, for fuller details of this period of Cavendish's life.

254. Cf. Wolsey's praise of Cavendish's fidelity in *LW* 159/2–5: "howe faythfull howe diligent And howe paynfull synce the begynneng of my troble he hathe serued me Abandonyng his owen contrie his wyfe & childerne his howsse & famelye his rest & quyotnes only to serue me."

264–65. I did not departe] See *LW* 132/19–182/10 passim for a fuller account of Cavendish's relationship with Wolsey during his final days.

274–630. These lines deal with a closely related group of tragedies, the executions of Anne Boleyn's brother, George, Viscount Rochford, a group of Henry VIII's courtiers, Sir Henry Norris, Sir Francis Weston, Sir William Brereton, Mark Smeaton, and Anne Boleyn herself, all of whom were executed in 1536. The crucial factor in all their deaths was almost certainly Anne's inability either to provide Henry with a male heir or to retain a firm hold on his affections. As early as September 1534 the king had begun to show an interest in Jane Seymour and a few months later took Margaret Shelton as a new mistress. The desire to rid himself of Anne was doubtless decisively strengthened by her miscarriage in January 1536, which once again robbed Henry of the desired son. On April 24 a commission was set up to find grounds for Henry to rid himself of his queen. Within ten days all those named above were in the Tower, arrested on Smeaton's confession which alleged Boleyn's incestuous and the others' adulterous relationships with the queen. Modern historians have tended to be skeptical about the validity of the charges. Most implausible of all perhaps is the charge of incest against George Boleyn, which was, as K. Muir observes, "such a convenient way of getting rid of [Anne's] brother . . . one is bound to be sceptical" (*The Life and Letters of Sir Thomas Wyatt* [Liverpool, 1963], p. 28). Almost as difficult to credit are the charges against such members of the court as Norris and Brereton, both long-established intimates of Henry. Their fall provides some indication of the urgency of Henry's desire to take a new wife. For a recent argument that all these deaths were caused by faction within the court, see E. W. Ives, "Faction at the Court of Henry VIII: The Fall of Anne Boleyn," *History*, 57 (1972), 169–88.

This group of tragedies is celebrated elsewhere in contemporary verse in a poem in the Blage manuscript attributed to Thomas Wyatt; see Wyatt CXLVI.

277. vicount honorable] Boleyn appears to have been knighted by October 8, 1529, when he is referred to as "Sir George Boulayn, gentleman of the Chamber" (*L&P* IV, pt. 3, 6513).

282. gyftes of naturall qualities] Cf. Wyatt, CXLVI, 21–22, for similar praise of Boleyn.

283–84. meter and prose . . . plesaunt dities] Later writers also testify to Boleyn's talents as a versifier; cf. Bale, *Scriptorum Maioris Britanniae* (Basle, 1557), p. 103: "Georgius Bulleyn, comes Rocheferdiae et Annae reginae frater, diuersi generis in anglico sermone edidit *Rhythmos elegantissimos*. Lib. 1," and Holinshed (p. 1613): "George Bulleyn, lorde Rochforde, brother to Quene Anne, wrote dyuers Songs and Sonettes." But no poems survive that can be attributed confidently to Rochford. I know of no evidence that Rochford wrote prose works. Singer in his edition altered *prose* to *verse* (p. 20).

285–87. highe dignytes] Rochford received numerous honors as a consequence of his sister's rise in Henry's favor. The list of his lands and offices is recorded in *L&P* X, 878. These posts held a total yearly value of £441.10s.9d. See also above, v. 277, and below, vv. 288–90.

288–90. to the prevy councell] I have been unable to discover any record of when Boleyn became a member of the Privy Council. He is not mentioned in such a capacity in *L&P*.

291. in his chamber] The reference is presumably to Rochford's appointment as esquire of the body to Henry VIII, which had taken place by June 1528; see Bapst, pp. 8–9.

292. Or yeres thryes nyne] Cavendish provides the only evidence for the date of Rochford's birth, which must therefore be c. 1507.

293. thyng] *E* reads *thynges*, but the context clearly requires a singular form. I have adopted the *D* reading. Cavendish seems to have had a tendency to write plural for singular forms, cf. v. 1099 and e.g. *LW* 93/16, 100/30.

295–308. My lyfe not chast] In general terms the assertion of Boleyn's lechery is questionable. He undoubtedly lived in a licentious court, and Cavendish may have had opportunities to observe his conduct before Wolsey's fall from favor. Certainly after 1529, however, he was engaged on frequent diplomatic missions to France, and Cavendish was no longer at court. In the absence of supporting evidence, the charge of Rochford's "sensuall apetyte" is perhaps best seen as an indication of Cavendish's antipathy to the Boleyn family.

309–15. This is a borrowing from *FP* III, 3711–17:

> Noble Pryncis, that seen so moche and reede,
> Remembryng stories of antiquite,
> Afforn prouidyng that tresoun nat proceede
> Beth ay most dreedful in hih prosperite,
> Lat othris fallyng a merour to you bee.
> The tourn of Fortune al auctours reprehende,
> Wher who sit hiest is rediest to descende.

316–22. This is a borrowing from *FP* V, 1142–88:

> Loo, how Fortune chaunge can hir tides!
> To oon this day she can be fauorable,
> Make capteyns & thes grete guides,

Which wende ha founde hir wheel ferme & stable.
But that she is ay froward & chaungable,
Freendli today, to-morwe at discord,—
Yiff this be trewe, Siphax can ber record.

323–27. This is a borrowing from *FP* III, 1457–61:

For wher that God list punshe a man off riht
Bi mortall suerd, farweel al resistence:
Whan grace faileth, awey goth force & myht,
Feblith off pryncis the magnyficence
Chaungeth ther power into impotence

330–36. This is a borrowing from *FP* IV, 1996–2002:

Noble Princis, with hool hert & enteer
Lefft up your corages, holdeth this no fable:
Thouh ye sit hih, conceyueth with good cheer
No worldli lordshipe in erthe is perdurable;
And sithe ye been of nature resonable,
Among remembreth, as thyng most necessarie,
Al stant on chaung; record upon kyng Darie.

336. all standythe on ffortune] A medieval commonplace; cf. Whiting F 523, Tilley F 606.

337–42. Rochford was arrested on May 2, "more than six houres after the others" (*L&P* X, 782). He was tried on May 15 with Anne Boleyn. It was charged that he "violated and carnally knew the . . . Queen, his own sister, at Westminster; which he also did on divers other days before and after at the same place, sometimes by his own procurement and sometimes by the Queen's" (*L&P* X, 876). He pleaded not guilty but was condemned.

337–40. Alas . . . expresse] Cf. Rochford's dying words as reported by Wriothesley: "As for myne offences, it can not prevayle you to heare them that I dye here for, but I beseche God that I may be an example to you all, and that all you may be wayre by me" (I, 40).

343. lost my hed] Boleyn was beheaded on May 17, 1536.

345. chaunce] Cavendish appears to have had difficulty with forms of this word, which he here writes as *chauance*. Elsewhere he incorrectly copies it as *chamce* (v. 434) and *perchauaunce* (v. 922).

351ff. Sir Henry Norris seems to have been a trusted and long-standing member of Henry's inner circle of courtiers. Apparently a member of the Royal Household from the early years of the reign, he is first listed among the gentlemen of the Privy Chamber in 1516 (*L&P* II, pt. 1, 2735) and received numerous honors during the following years. The most significant of these were perhaps his appointments as Esquire for the Body, chief of the king's Privy Chamber, and Chamberlain of North Wales.

It is difficult to determine with certainty the factors that led to the downfall of this hitherto highly trusted and apparently faithful courtier. Scarisbrick's suggestion, that there may have been a "psychosexual motivation" (p. 455) to Henry's sudden disfavor, deriving from Norris's involvement with Henry's former mistress, Margaret Shelton, remains a tempting one, although the hypothesis cannot be substantiated. Certainly, as is indicated below, Henry seems to have attached a particular weight to Norris's alleged role.

Cavendish's attitude toward Norris is doubtless colored by personal antipathy. It was Norris who conducted him to the king after Wolsey's death (*LW* 184/4ff.), and there are several passages in the *LW* which testify to his role as an intermediary between Wolsey and the king after Wolsey's fall (e.g. 93/4ff., 101/34ff.).

353. be] Both *E* and *D* agree in reading *me* for *be*. But the transcription of this line seems to have posed problems for Cavendish; *me* has been cancelled later in the line before *highly* (interl.). As it stands the line makes no sense. The cancelled *me* perhaps gives a clue to Cavendish's original intentions. He possibly intended *me* to be placed after *dyd*, but was led by a form of dittographic error to place it incorrectly instead of *be* after *To*. *Me* must be understood following *dyd*.

353. Grome of his stoole] I have been unable to discover any record of Norris's having held such a position. He is not so designated anywhere in *L&P*. Cavendish, however, also refers to him by this title in *LW* 93/4.

354. prevye chamber] Norris was "chief of the king's Privy Chamber" by July 1533, when he is so designated in *L&P* VII, 790.

355–60. Offices and Romes] Norris's lands and offices at the time of his death are detailed in *L&P* X, 878; they had a total yearly value of £1327/15s/7d.

359. On Cavendish's personal acquaintance with Norris, see Commentary vv. 351ff.

361–64. Current rumor gives some support to Cavendish's assertion of Norris's ambition. Cromwell on May 14 links all the arrests to "a certain conspiracy of the king's death" (*L&P* X, 873). And Chapuys in a dispatch of May 19 particularizes Norris's role in this alleged conspiracy: "there was a promise between her [Anne Boleyn] to marry [Norris] after the king's death, which it thus appeared they hoped for" (*L&P* X, 808). Norris had been charged, however, on May 12 with "violation and carnal knowledge of the Queen" (*L&P* X, 848), to which he pleaded not guilty. It may be that the rumors of conspiracy were part of a belated attempt to lend credibility to Norris's condemnation.

369. This line seems to have been initially omitted and subsequently squeezed in after the transcription of the following line(s).

372–78. Contemporary accounts confirm the reported offer of clemency to Norris in return for a confession implicating Anne Boleyn. Cf. Constantyne, p. 64: "Apon May daye Mr. Noryce justed. And after justinge the Kynge rode sodenly to Westminster, and all the waye as I heard saye, had Mr. Noryce in examinacyon and promised hym his pardon in case he wolde utter the trewth. But what so euer cowld be sayed or done, Mr. Norice wold confess no thinge to the kynge, where vpon he was committed to the Tower in the mornynge." Cf. also the "Histoire de Anne Boleyn," p. 186.

379–80. To sighe . . . lament] These lines may echo the opening line from Skelton's "Dolorouse Dethe . . . of the most Honourable Erle of Northumberland": "I wayle, I wepe, I sobbe, I sigh ful sore."

379–99. Cf. the lament on Norris's fall in Wyatt, CXLVI, 25–32:

> A! Norrys, Norres, my teares begyne to Rune
> To thynk what hap dyd the so led or gyd,
> Wherby thou haste bothe the and thyn vndone.
> That ys bewaylyd in court of euery syde;
> In place also wher thou hast neuer bene
> Both man and chyld doth petusly the mone.
> They say: "Alas, thou art ffar ouer seene
> By there offences to be thus ded and gonne.

396. led to the barre] Norris was tried on May 12 (see Commentary vv. 361–64). He pleaded not guilty but was condemned for treason.

399. hedlesse here I lye] Norris was beheaded on May 17, 1536.

401. pale as leade] Proverbial; cf. v. 1482 and Whiting, L 126, Tilley, L 135.

402. the wanton] Evidence of Weston's vice does not survive. He is, however, reported at his death to have said: "I had thoght to have lyved in abhominacion yet this twenty or thrittie yeres" (Constantyne, p. 65).

414–20. Weston is first recorded as a member of Henry's entourage in January 1526, when the articles for the Royal Household declare that "young Weston [is] to be the King's page" (L&P IV, 863). The Privy Purse expenses for the next few years record a number of payments to him in this capacity. He is listed among the gentlemen of the Privy Chamber for January 1532 (L&P V, 686). Other honors followed. He was a Knight of the Bath at Anne Boleyn's coronation on May 31, 1533 (L&P VI, 562), and in November of the same year he was, with his father, made captain, warden, and governor of the Channel Islands (ibid., 1481 [6]). He was still a gentleman of the Privy Chamber in January 1534 (L&P VII, 1534). Henceforward his name virtually disappears from the records until his arrest in 1536.

425. kyndeled] *in* must be understood

427. Spared] *I* must be understood preceding this word.

428–34. Weston was arrested on May 2 and tried with the other alleged conspirators on May 12, when he pleaded not guilty. At Anne Boleyn's trial it was alleged that "the Queen, 8 May 26 Hen. VIII and at other times before and since, procured Sir Fras. Weston . . . whereby he did so on the 20 May &c." (L&P X, 876).

It would seem that Cavendish's evident hostility did not necessarily reflect the contemporary view. Indeed, of those condemned he appears to have been the most likely to escape death. Only four days before his execution it was reported that "If any escape, it will be young Weston, for whom importunate suit is made" (L&P X, 865). And Chapuys reports that he died "notwithstanding the intercession of the bishop of Tarbes, the French ambassador resident, and the sieur de Tinteville" (L&P X, 908). The "Histoire de Anne Boleyn" (p. 195) reports that Weston's wife made suit on his behalf to Henry "offrait entierement / Rentes et biens pour son delivrement." Cf. also the praise of Weston by Wyatt, CXLVI, 33–40:

> A! Weston, Weston, that pleasant was and yonge;
> In actyve thynges who myght with the compayre?
> All wordis exsept that thou dydyst speake with tonge;
> So well estemyd with eche wher thou dydyst fare.
> And we that now in court doth led our lyffe
> Most part in mynd doth the lament and mone;
> But that thy ffaultis we dayly here so Ryffe
> All we shuld weppe that thou art dead and gone.

and the "Histoire de Anne Boleyn" (p. 195), which describes him thus:

> . . . pauvre Waston qui estoit de jeune aage,
> Yssu de hault et très ancien lignaige,
> De bonnes meurs et graces tous passant,
> En lisse, en bal à saulter effaçant,
> En jeu de paulme en grand perfection
> Les plus adroictz de ceste nation,
> Et de tous biens en luy tant abondoit
> Que le pays tout honoré rendoit.

441. losse of my hed] Weston was beheaded on May 17.

442. approched] *E* reads *approced* as at v. 1256; the emendation appears justified by the lack of any record of this form elsewhere and by Cavendish's use of the form *approched* at e.g. v. 1270.

447–48. loo . . . lust] Proverbial; cf. Whiting F 546.

449ff. There is no biography of Brereton. He does seem to have been associated with the Royal Household from the early years of Henry's reign. He is first mentioned in 1516 as one of the Esquires to the Body Extraordinary (*L&P* II, pt. 1, 2735), and from 1524 seems to have received a variety of grants from the king. In January 1526 he is designated as groom of the Privy Chamber (*L&P* IV, pt. 1, 1939). A full list of his lands and offices at the time of his death is included in *L&P* X, 878, possessing a total value of £1236.12s.6 1/4d. It would seem that, as with Norris, he was a trusted and long-serving member of the King's court circle, and as such was probably personally known to Cavendish. The tone of Wyatt's lament for him is somewhat cool:

> Brewton, ffarwell, as one that lest I knewe.
> Great was thy love with dyuers as I here;
> But common voyce dothe not so sore the Rewe,
> As other twayne that dothe beffore appere.
> But yet no dobt but thy ffrendes thee lament,
> And other her ther petus crye and mone.
> So dothe eche hart ffor the lykwyse Relent,
> That thou gevyst cause thus to be ded and gonne.
>
> [CXLVI, 41–48]

456. Furnysshed with Romes] Grants made to Brereton include one of 200 acres in part of Cheshire (*L&P* IV, pt. 2, 3087 [26]) in April 1527; in the following month he received further grants of manors in Chester and Flint (ibid., 3142 [30]). He was also granted the keepership of Merseley Park in Wales in August 1529 (*L&P* IV, pt. 3, 5906 [20]), and in June 1530 the chamberlainship of the county palatine of Chester (ibid., 6490 [11]), and, in survivorship, the manor of Longendale, Chester. In March 1534 he was granted the late abbey of St. Thomas the Martyr in Kent (*L&P* VII, 419 [6]).

457–62. In November 1527 Brereton was made "chief and master steward and receiver of the castles of Lyons or Holt and Chirke" (*L&P* IV, pt. 2, 3622 [15]).

465. Eton] Eton is presumably the John Eton described as a gentleman usher extraordinary of the Royal Household in 1516, when Brereton is first mentioned (*L&P* II, pt. 1, 2735). The circumstances of Brereton's relationship with and responsibility for the death of Eton have resisted examination. That Brereton had a significant role in his downfall does, however, seem clear. A list of the "escriptes and writings" in Cromwell's possession in July 1534 includes: "A roll of the displeasures between Wm. Brereton and John Eton" (*L&P* VII, 923, xxxvi). An undated petition of the previous year from Eton himself throws little more light on this affair. Eton states that: "Whereas he had been gentleman usher to the king more than six years: on some evil surmises he had been committed to the Tower of London, 12 weeks last past . . . where, by the surmises of his enemies, he has since been restrained" (*L&P* VI, 1648). I have been unable to discover the date or circumstances of his death; but he may have been dead by March 4, 1535, when Magdalen College replied to a request

by Cromwell for the preferment of one of his servants to the receivership of Manby, described as previously held by Eton (*L&P* VIII, 331).

470–76. Brereton was arrested and indicted with the others, pleaded not guilty, but was condemned. No record of the precise indictment against him survives, but at Anne Boleyn's trial it was alleged that "Also the Queen, 3 Dec. 25 Hen. VIII, and divers days before and after, at Westminster, procured one Will. Bryerton, late of Westminster, gentleman of the privy chamber, to violate her, whereby he did so on 8 Dec. 25 Hen. VIII. at Hampton Court . . . and on several other days before and after, sometimes by his own procurement and sometimes by the Queen's" (*L&P* X, 876). He was beheaded and afterward quartered (*L&P* X, 911) on May 17, 1536.

As with the others there must be substantial doubt about the justice of Brereton's death. George Constantyne's comments are of interest as those of a personal acquaintance of Brereton's:

By my troeth, yf any of hem was innocent, it was he [i.e. Brereton]. For other he was innocente, or els he dyed worst of them all . . . Apon Thursdaye afore Maye daye in the mornynge I spake with hym about nyne of the clocke. And he tolde me that there was no waye but one with any matter . . . But at his death these were his wordes: I haue deserued to dye if it were a thousande deathes, But the cause wherefore I dye judge not: But yf ye judge, judge the best. . . . If he were gyltie, I saye therefore that he dyed worst of them all. [p. 65]

472. Who . . . ouerthrowe] Proverbial; cf. Whiting S 978; not in Tilley. The source is biblical; cf. Matthew 26:52: "all they that take the sword shall perish with the sword."

477–83. This is a borrowing from *FP* II, 1856–62:

> Loo, heer the eende off moordre and tirannye;
> Loo, heer the eende off vsurpacioun;
> Loo, heer the eende off fals conspiracye;
> Loo, heer the eende off fals presumpcioun!
> Born rihtful heires, wrongli to put hem doun.
> O noble Pryncis, thouh God hath maad you strong,
> To rihtful heires be war ye do no wrong!

484ff. Biographical details of Mark Smeaton are scanty. He is not entered in *DNB*, and there are no certain references to him in *L&P* before 1536. He is very probably the same "Mark" who is mentioned on a number of occasions in the Privy Purse expenses between 1529 and 1532 (cf. N. H. Nicolas, *The Privy Purse Expenses of King Henry the Eighth* . . . [London, 1827], passim). If Smeaton became a member of Henry's household c. 1529 it would accord chronologically with Cavendish's assertion that he was a "syngyng boy" (v. 486) of Wolsey's. Possibly he joined Henry's court (as Cavendish himself was invited to do) after Wolsey's fall. At any rate, he seems to have gained royal favor and become one of Henry's inner circle of courtiers. The indictment of Anne Boleyn describes him as "groom of the privy chamber" (*L&P* X, 876).

Smeaton was the only one of those accused to admit to adultery with Anne Boleyn. In late April he was interrogated by Cromwell, and implicated himself and others. Constantyne reports that "the trewth he confessed it, but yet the saying was that he was first greuously racked" (p. 64). Other contemporary reports stress the weakness of a case based on his confession alone; cf. Edward Baynton's report: "noman will confesse any thyng agaynst her [i.e. Anne Boleyn], but all only Marke of any actuell thynge. Wherfore (in my folishe conceyte) it shulde myche toche the kings hono^r if it shulde no farther appeere" (*L&P* X, 799). And it was also reported (*L&P* X, 956) that Smeaton may have been influenced in his confession by jealousy of his fellow courtiers. Certainly Smeaton seems to have been an unpopular figure. Cavendish's own hostility toward him may be compared with that of a member of the court; cf. Wyatt, CXLVI, 49–56:

>   A! Mark what mone shuld I ffor the mak more?
>   Syns that thy dethe thou hast deseruyd best,
>   Save only that myn eye ys fforsyd sore
>   With petus playnt to mone the with the Rest.
>   A tym thou haddyst aboue thy poore degre,
>   The ffall wherof thy frendis may well bemone.
>   A Rottyn twygge apon so hyghe a tree
>   Hathe slepyd thy hold and thou art dead and goonn.

486. Chaple] *E* reads *Chapleyn*; I have adopted the *D* reading. It is noteworthy that Cavendish makes a comparable error in *LW* 54/8, where he initially had written *Chapley* before altering it to the correct *Chappell*.

486. a syngyng boy] Wolsey's entourage included "xij syngyng Childerne" (*LW* 19/29).

491–95. My ffather . . . My mother . . .] Cavendish's account, though scanty, provides the fullest surviving account of Smeaton's antecedents and early years. Cavendish's position as a fellow member of Wolsey's household tends to give credibility to his assertions here. The fact that Smeaton's father was a carpenter is confirmed by the *Spanish Chronicle*: "They told her [Anne Boleyn] that he [Smeaton] was the son of a poor carpenter" (p. 55).

497. de stercore et erigens pauperem] Cf. Psalms 112:7: "de stercore erigens pauperem."

498. hyghe] *E* reads *hyght*, an adjectival form not recorded in *OED* or *MED* except as a rare late medieval northern or Scottish dialectal form (cf. *OED* s.v. "height" *a*.). Palaeographic confusion of *t* and *e* seems possible. I have adopted the *D* reading.

500. Knewe not myself] On this phrase see Edward E. Lowinsky, "A Music Book for Anne Boleyn," in *Florilegium Historiale, Essays Presented to Wallace K. Ferguson*, ed. J. H. Rowe and W. H. Stockdale (Toronto: University of Toronto Press 1971), pp. 195–77. Lowinsky interprets these lines in the light of a motto in Royal College of Music MS. 1070 (a manuscript possibly compiled and edited by Smeaton) reading (p. 232): *Tuo te pede metire. Nosce teipsum ut noris quam sit tibi curta supellex*. Lowinsky sees these lines as a contemporary epitaph on Smeaton. Quoting Cavendish (vv. 491–504), he observes: "The contemporaneous accounts reflect what must have been the common opinion of the time: that Mark, of humble origins, aspiring to the court of the king, overreached himself and came to fall through his own *hubris*" (p. 196). See also the *Spanish Chronicle*, pp. 56–58, for a detailed (if not reliable) account of Mark's extravagance and arrogance; it reports that: "There was much jealousy of him, and many murmured to see him so smart and lavish."

504. to dye lyke a wretche] Smeaton pleaded guilty to violation and carnal knowledge of the queen and threw himself on the king's mercy (*L&P* X, 848). He was sentenced with the other alleged conspirators.

COMMENTARY   173

510–11. These lines may contain echoes from Skelton's *Why Come Ye Nat to Court*:

> Wherfore he suffred payn,
> Was headyd, drawen and quarterd
> And dyed stynkingly marterd. [736–38]

Of those condemned Smeaton was the only one to confess his guilt, perhaps after torture. Constantyne reports that at his execution he said: "Masters I pray you all praye for me, for I haue deserued the death" (p. 65).

519ff. Cavendish's comments on Anne Boleyn must, of course, be seen in the context of his known antipathy toward her because of her role in Wolsey's downfall (cf. *LW* 43/32–44/24 for Cavendish's account of this).

538. Curse and ban] A common medieval collocation; cf. *MED*, s.v. "banne" 2 (b); its continuing use in the sixteenth century can be demonstrated elsewhere; cf. Wyatt CVII, 63: "The gold is good, and tho she curse or ban."

540–45. Cf. *LW* 29/4–7: "[Venus] brought the kyng in love w^t a gentillwoman that after she perceyved and felt the kynges good wyll towardes hir And howe dilygent he was bothe to please hir And to graunt all hir requestes."

546. "Trust" and "treason" are proverbially associated; cf. Whiting T 492.

547–49. Henry married Anne on January 25, 1533. He had not in fact encountered her first "At home with . . . ffather" (v. 549) but when she became one of Catherine of Aragon's maids of honor.

551–53. To an Erele] On Boleyn's rise cf. *LW* 29/9–20. Boleyn became Earl of Wiltshire and Ormond on December 8, 1529.

561–67. Cf. Lydgate's account of Athaliah, *FP* II, 1884–90:

> Gathalia with hir duplicitees
> And conspired fals intrusiouns
> Slouh Dauides seed, tentre ther dignitees,
> And to possede ther domynaciouns;
> But for hir hatful fals collusiouns

Onwarly slayn, for hir gret couetise,
Had off God warnyng, & list nat for to rise.

565. murder . . . murder] Probably proverbial; not in Whiting or Tilley.

568–71. It is not at all clear what legislation Cavendish has in mind here; I have not been able to discover any specific statutes relating to "spekyng ayenst" Queen Anne. It does, however, seem clear that efforts were made to suppress such criticism and to punish those involved. H. Ellis in his *Original Letters* (London, 1824) prints a letter of Edward, Earl of Derby, and Sir Henry Faryngton to Henry reporting an interrogation in Lancashire of a "lewde and noghty preist" who was promulgating "unfittyng and sklaunderous reports and sayings" against Anne (II, pp. 42–45). Such resentment seems to have been general; cf. the account in Forrest's *History of Griseld the Second*, pp. 70–73. Cavendish is probably here identifying Anne with the totality of the Reformation legislation rather than with any specific piece of it.

572–73. My sede to auaunce] No such allegation was made against Anne at her trial or elsewhere that I have been able to discover. Cavendish may have in mind the allegation that she planned to marry Norris after Henry's death; see Commentary vv. 361–64.

582–88. Cf. the praise of chastity and examples of chaste women employed by Anne Boleyn's sister-in-law, Viscountess Rochford, vv. 1000–1006.

599. for bast] i.e. "as a bastard." The reference is to Elizabeth Tudor, born September 7, 1533. After Anne's death she was declared the illegitimate daughter of Henry Norris (*L&P* X, 909).

600. swett . . . tast] Proverbial; cf. Whiting S 65; Tilley S 97.

603–5. quen Iane] Henry married Jane Seymour on May 30, 1536.

606. thou art deade] Jane died on October 24, 1537, twelve days after giving birth to Edward VI.

623. no smoke . . . eschewe] Proverbial; cf. Tilley S 569.

624–30. Cf. the praise of Henry attributed to Anne by Hall (p. 819) in her dying speech from the scaffold on May 19, 1536: "I pray God save the king and send him long to reygn ouer you, for a gentler nor a more merciful prince was there neuer; and to me he was euer a good, a gentle and souerayne lord."

630. This line is a borrowing from *FP* V, 89: "Sharp mortal suord

made the recompense." According to contemporary reports Anne was "beheaded according to the manner and custom of Paris, that is to say, with a sword, which thing had not before been seen in this land of England" (F. Michel, ed., *Lettre d'un Gentilhomme Portugais . . . sur l'execution d'Anne Boleyn* [Paris, 1832], p. 12). This is confirmed by the *Spanish Chronicle* (p. 170), which reports that Henry "had to send a week before to St. Omer for a headsman."

631–72. This group of tragedies is puzzling in its apparent randomness. It brings together a number of groups and individuals executed during the period 1537–41 (with the exceptions of More, v. 664, executed in 1535, and possibly Fisher, see v. 667). Of those mentioned, Aske, Bygott, Bulmer, Percy, Tempest, Hussey, Darcy, and Constable were all executed in 1537 for their association with the Pilgrimage of Grace. Neville and Carew died because of their association with Exeter and Montague (see vv. 750–819). Dacres, Mauntell, Frowdes, and Roydon were charged together in 1541 with murder. Gray was executed for treason in Ireland. Fortescue died probably because of his close relationship with Anne Boleyn. And Hungerford was executed on a variety of charges. There seems to be no unifying principle of selection. It may be noted, however, that Hussey, Darcy, Constable, Aske, Bygott, Bulmer, Percy, Neville, Lumley, Tempest, Fortescue, Dingley, and Carew were included in the bill of attainder passed retroactively by Parliament on April 28, 1539 (*L&P* XIV, pt. 1, 867).

638–42. fortunes mutabylitie . . . late] Proverbial; cf. Whiting F 523, Tilley F 606.

650. not all of oon affecte] i.e. "not all to do with the same matter."

654. lord Husy] Sir John, Baron Hussey (?1466–1537), one of the leaders of the Pilgrimage of Grace. It was charged on May 15, 1537 that, with others, he "traitorously assembled, [to] conspire to deprive the King of his title of Supreme Head of the English Church, and to subvert and annul divers salutary laws made in the time of the said king and to depose the king by force" (*L&P* XII, pt. 1, 1537). He pleaded not guilty but was condemned to execution at Lincoln (Hall, p. 825) at some point after June 29 (*L&P* XII, pt. 2, 166) and before July 8, when Cromwell announced his death to Wyatt (*L&P* XII, pt. 2, 228). There are brief biographies in *DNB* and Dodds passim, especially I, 21–25.

lord Darcy] Thomas, Lord Darcy (1467–1537), one of the leaders of the Pilgrimage of Grace. Darcy was tried on May 17, 1537. It was charged that together with Constable, Bigod, Percy, Bulmer, Lumley, Aske and Tempest and others, he did "conspire to deprive the king of his title of Supreme Head of the English Church, and to compel him to hold a certain Parliament and convocation of the clergy of the realm and did commit divers insurrections &c. at Pountefret" and that in spite of the King's pardon they "again falsely conspired for the above said purposes and to annul divers wholesome laws made for the common weal and to depose the king" (*L&P* XII, pt. 2, 166). He pleaded not guilty but was condemned and executed at Tyburn on June 30 (*L&P* XII, pt. 2, 1207). There are brief biographies in *DNB* and Dodds passim; see especially II, 185–95, for an account of the dubious nature of the charges brought against him and of his trial.

Constable] Sir Robert Constable (?1478–1537), one of the leaders of the Pilgrimage of Grace. For details of the charges against him see above, v. 654 (s.v. "lord Darcy"). He was tried on May 17 with Bigod, Percy, Bulmer, and Aske. He pleaded not guilty but was sentenced to execution at Tyburn (*L&P* XII, pt. 1, 1227). He was "hanged in chaynes on Beuerley Gate at Hull" (Hall, p. 825) sometime after June 27, 1537. Cromwell reports his death in a dispatch to Wyatt on July 8 (*L&P* XII, pt. 2, 228). There is a brief biography in *DNB*.

655. Lord Hungerford] Walter Hungerford, first baron Hungerford of Heytesbury (1503–40). Hungerford was attainted in April 1540. The summary of legislation before Parliament charges that (among other things) he "procured Sir Hugh Woods, chaplain, and Dr. Mawdelyn, and one mother Roche to conjure and show how long the king whould live; and moreover has practised the abominable vice of buggery with Wm. Maister, Thos. Smith and other of his servants" (*L&P* XV, 498). He was executed on July 28, 1540 with Cromwell.

656. lord Leonard Gray] Lord Leonard Grey, Viscount Grane (d. 1541). Grey was appointed deputy governor in Ireland in January 1536. There were numerous complaints about his conduct, and Henry appointed a commission to investigate his activities in 1537. It was not until his return to London in 1540 that he was arrested on charges of treason. (*L&P* XVI, 304, contains a lengthy series of depositions against him.) The most salient of the charges are summarized by Stow: "The lord Leonard Gray being indited of certaine points of treason by him committed, as was alleged against him during the season that he was the kings lieutenant in Ireland, to wit, for deliuering his nephew Girald fitz

Gerard . . . and also for he caused certaine Irishmen to inuade the lands of the kings friends, whom he fauored not" (*Annales*, p. 981). On December 15, 1540 the Privy Council concluded "unless Lord Leonard could make better answer he was in great danger" (*L&P* XVI, 320). No record of his trial survives, but it is reported (*L&P* XVI, 941) that he was tried on June 25. Holinshed reports that "he discharged the Jury and confessed thenditement" (p. 1581). He was beheaded on June 28 (*Grey Friars Chronicle*, p. 44), not as the *DNB* has it on July 28. Although there seems to be little evidence to support Cavendish's conviction of his innocence, Stow does describe him as a "right valiant and hardie personage, hauing in his time done his prince and countrey good seruice" (*Annales*, p. 981).

659. Aske] Robert Aske (d. 1537); for details of the charges against Aske, one of the key figures in the Pilgrimage of Grace, see above, v. 654 (s.v. "lord Darcy"). He was "hanged upon the dungeon of York Castle" (*L&P* XII, pt. 2, 228) on July 5, 1537. See *DNB* and Dodds, passim, for his biography.

660. Bygott] Sir Francis Bigod (1508–1537). On the terms of his indictment see above, v. 654 (s.v. "lord Darcy"). The charge was also made that he, together with George Lumly, "with a great multitude in arms did make divers traitorous proclamations to call men to them to make war against the king, and having thereby assembled 500 persons, did, 22 Jan. 28 Hen. VIII., levy war against the king" (*L&P* XII, pt. 2, 1207). He was hanged at Tyburn on June 2. For details of his biography see *DNB* and Dodds, passim, especially II, 55–98.

Bulmer] Sir John Bulmer (d. 1537). A Yorkshire landowner, Bulmer was tried on May 17, 1537, with Constable and the others, pleaded guilty, and was sentenced to execution at Tyburn (*L&P* XII, pt. 1, 1227). It is reported (*L&P* XII, pt. 1, 1285) on May 26 that he was executed on "Friday in Whitsun week." Hall reports that he was "brent at Smithfelde" (p. 825), but Wriothesley (I, 63) maintains that he was "hanged and heddyd" with Nicholas Tempest on May 25.

Percy] Sir Thomas Percy (d. 1537); for the terms of his indictment see above, v. 654 (s.v. "lord Darcy"). He was beheaded at Tyburn on June 2 (*Grey Friars Chronicle*, p. 41). For a brief biography see *DNB* (s.v. "Percy, Henry Algernon, sixth earl of Northumberland").

Nevell] Sir Edward Neville (d. 1538). He was arrested for his alleged part in the Montague/Exeter conspiracy (see vv. 750ff.). He was tried on December 4, 1538 with Geoffrey Pole, George Croftes, John Collins, and

Hugh Holland on charges of treason, to which he alone pleaded not guilty. For an account of his trial see *L&P* XIII, pt. 2, 986. He was beheaded on December 8, with Exeter and Montague.

661. Lumly] George Lumley, son of John, fifth baron Lumley (d. 1537). Hall (p. 824) erroneously gives his Christian name as William. For the indictments against him stemming from his involvement in the Pilgrimage of Grace see above, v. 654 (s.v. "lord Darcy") and v. 660 (s.v. "Bygott"). He was "hongyd, heddyd and qwarterd" on June 2 (*Grey Friars Chronicle*, p. 41). For brief biographies see *DNB* (s.v. "John Lumley, fifth baron Lumley") and Dodds, especially II, 66–72.

lord Dacres] Thomas Fiennes, ninth baron Dacres (1517–41). The charge was made on June 27, 1541 that with Mantell, Frowdes, and George Roydon they did on

20 April 32 Hen. VIII assemble at Hurst Monneseux, in the mansion of the said Thomas lord Dacre and illegally conspire how they might best hunt the park of Nic. Pelham at Lawghton, Suss., with dogs and nets called "bukstalles" and other engines, and bound themselves to slay any of the King's lieges who might resist them in their illegal purpose. Then, on 30 April 33 Hen. VIII they met again in the same house. . . . On the way thither to a place called Pykehey in the parish of Hellyngleigh John and James Busebrygge and Ric. Somener were standing, and, fearing lest they should be recognized and hindered by them, Thos. lord Dacre and those with him attacked them and mortally wounded John Busebrygge, who died on the 2nd of May following. [*L&P* XVI, 931]

They were all sentenced to death and hanged on June 29.

662. Tempest] Nicholas Tempest (d. 1537). There is no biography. On the charges against him arising from his part in the Northern risings see above, v. 654 (s.v. "lord Darcy"). It was alleged that he was a "setter forth of the first musters and principal doer of the second insurrection" (*L&P* XII, pt. 1, 1020). He was executed with Bulmer (q.v. v. 660) probably on May 25.

663. Ffortescue] Sir Adrian Fortescue (?1476–1539). He was arrested for treason in February 1539, and charged with having "refused his duty of allegiance" (*L&P* XIV, pt. 1, 867). He was executed with Thomas Dingley on July 9, 1539 (*Grey Friars Chronicle*, p. 43).

Dyngley] Sir Thomas Dingley. There is no biography. Dingley's attainder, which describes him as "one of the freers of the order of St. John of Jerusalem," charged that with Robert Braunceter he was guilty of "devising the king's destruction, who having knowledge of the late rebellion made by Darcy and others, moved divers outward princes to levy war against the king" (*L&P* XIV, pt. 1, 867). He was executed on July 9, 1539.

Roydon] George Roydon. There is no biography. He was indicted with Dacres (see v. 661) and the others for murder and executed on June 29, 1541. In a dispatch just after his death Marillac refers to him as "one Reddyn, of a Kentish family" (*L&P* XIV, pt. 1, 941).

Froudes] There is no biography. For his indictment see above, v. 661.

Mantell] John Mauntell. There is no biography. For details of the charges against him and his execution see above, v. 661. Marillac describes him as "one of the kings 50 gentlemen, whom he calles his Pensioners." Immediately after his sentence Paget reported to Wriothesley that at his trial Mauntell "acted very temperately and christianly" (*L&P* XIV, pt. 1, 932). Hall reports that "Great mone was made . . . most especially for Mantell, who was as wittie, and as towarde a gentleman, as any was in the realme, and a manne able to haue dooen good service" (p. 842).

664. Carowe] Sir Nicholas Carew (d. 1539). By virtue of his association with the Marquis of Exeter, Carew was tried on February 14, 1539, on charges that "knowing the said Marquis to be a traitor [he] did . . . falsely abet the said Marquis . . . and . . . had conversation with him about the change of the world [and received] divers traitorous letters [from the Marquis]" (*L&P* XIV, pt. 1, 290). He was executed on March 3, 1539 (Hall, p. 827). For his biography see *DNB*; for an account of his trial see Dodds, II, 319–21.

Moore] A marginal note in *E*, in a contemporary hand (which is not Cavendish's own), identifies "Sʳ Thomas Moore" who was executed on July 6, 1535. Although Cavendish was related by marriage to More's family, this is the only mention of him in either the *MV* or *LW*. For discussion of this curious silence, see *LW*, pp. xx–xxi.

666–67. prestes and prelattes] A number of clergy were executed as a consequence of their parts in the Northern risings (which presumably Cavendish has in mind here). For a full account of these executions see Dodds, II, 141–81, 211–16.

667. a bysshope] A note in *E* in a contemporary hand (not Cavendish's) identifies the bishop as "Ffisher the bishop of Ruff" (i.e. John

Fisher, bishop of Rochester, executed on June 22, 1535). Cavendish alludes to Fisher's death in *LW* 79/30–33.

670. sayd] "They" must be understood before this word.

673–74. knewe as well as I] Cavendish knew Cromwell personally; they had been members of Wolsey's household.

677. kynges secretarye] See below, v. 690. For a contemporary account of Cromwell's rise in Henry's favor, derived from *LW*, see *Revue de l'Université d'Ottawa*, 43 (1973), 292–96.

679. lord prevye seale] Cromwell was created Lord Privy Seal on July 2, 1536 (*L&P* IX, 202 [3]).

680–86. This is a borrowing from *FP* IV, 2948–54:

> Sum man forthred of sodeyn auenture,
> Set in a chaier of roial dignite,
> Wenyng his empire euer shold endure,
> Neuer to be troubled with non aduersity:
> With roial egles a kite may nat flee,
> A iay may chatre in a goldene cage,
> Yit euer sum tech mut folwe of his lynage.

684–86. a kight . . . disdayn hys parentage] According to Holinshed (pp. 1578–79) Cromwell's father was a blacksmith ("in his later dayes a bruer"). In his dying speech, Holinshed reports, Cromwell reiterated his humble origins: "I haue been a great traueyler in the worlde & being but of a base degree was called to high estate."

687–88. assendyng the degrees] There are numerous accounts of Cromwell's rise to power; see for example R. B. Merriman, *Life and Letters of Thomas Cromwell* (Oxford: Clarendon Press, 1902), I, pp. 77–88, and A. G. Dickens, *Thomas Cromwell and the English Reformation* (London: English University Press, 1959), pp. 11–73 passim. For a discussion of Cromwell's various offices and an evaluation of the significance of his tenure of them see G. Elton, *The Tudor Revolution in Government* (Cambridge, 1953), pp. 98–139.

689. privye councell] Cromwell was certainly a privy councillor by January 10, 1531, when he is addressed in a letter as a councillor (*L&P* V, 38).

690. cheafe secretory] Cromwell appears to have been secretary of state by April 1534. In a letter of April 7, 1534 (*L&P* VII, 446), the Mar-

quis of Exeter addresses him as "master secretary," the earliest direct reference known to me.

694. vicegerent] Cromwell became vicegerent in spirituals in mid 1535.

695. Gouernor of the prelacye] Cromwell became vicar-general on January 21, 1535 (see *L&P* VIII, 75).

696. master of the Rolles] Cromwell became Master of the Rolls on October 8, 1534 (*L&P* VII, 1352[3]).

699. thestate of baron] Cromwell became Lord Cromwell on July 9, 1536 (*L&P* X, 202 [4]).

700. an Erle] Cromwell became Earl of Essex on April 18, 1540 (Wriothesley, I, 115).

701–7. Much mystery surrounds Cromwell's sudden and dramatic fall from favor in mid 1540. The standard account is G. Elton, "Thomas Cromwell's Decline and Fall," *Cambridge Historical Journal*, 10 (1951), 150–85. The chief factors, as Elton enumerates them, were: his lack of support within the Council and the particular antipathy of Gardiner and the Duke of Norfolk; the failure of the marriage treaty with Anne of Cleves and the rise to power of Katherine Howard, and consequently of the Norfolk faction; and the heretical activities of Friar Barnes, a reformist protégé of Cromwell's, in March 1540.

707–14. A man the Agagite] Hamon's fate is recounted in *FP* III, 4761–851. The detail of the "fyvetye cubyttes" is not in Lydgate but is biblical; see the Book of Esther, 5:14.

715–21. the lawes of this land] The reference is to Cromwell's frequent use of the Act of Attainder to condemn Henry's enemies without trial (cf. e.g. the complaint of the Countess of Salisbury, v. 1094 below, that she was "condempned withowt examynacion"). Cromwell was himself condemned by attainder, as v. 721 implies.

715. land] The rhyme scheme at this point is defective in *E* and *D*, the *a* rhyme *realme* not according with v. 717, *understand*. The emendation to *land* seems justified by the possibility of an error having been made by Cavendish in the course of transcription caused by collocation of *lawes* with *realme* or *land* in stock phrases.

721. Cf. Matthew 7:2: "What measure ye mete, it shall be measured to you again." Cf. also v. 1200 below.

729–35. Cromwell was arrested on June 10 on charges of heresy and of secretly opposing Henry's religious policies. A bill of attainder was introduced into the House of Lords on June 17 and sent to the House of Commons on the nineteenth. A second bill was introduced "for heresie, treason and fellonie, and extortion" (Wriothesley, I, 120). This bill passed both Lords and Commons on June 29; see Elton, "Thomas Cromwell's Decline and Fall," 177–78.

734. All . . . end] Proverbial; cf. Tilley E 120.
737. the chayer] i.e. "the chair of fame," cf. v. 994.
738. Cf. Whiting B 31.
744. Ffordulled with writyng] Cf. v. 1219, "My penne was fordulled."

750ff. The executions of Henry Courtenay, Marquis of Exeter (?1496–1538) and Henry Pole, Baron Montague (?1492–1538) were probably due to a complex of factors. It would seem from the available evidence that the prime target was Montague. The reasons for this are succinctly summarized by Castillon in a dispatch of November 5, 1538, immediately after the arrest of the pair: "Il y a bien longtemps que ce Roy m'avoit dict qu'il vouloit exterminer ceste maison de Montagu, qui est encore de la Rose Blanche, et de la maison de Polle dont est le Cardinal [Cardinal Reginald Pole]. Je ne scay encore qu'on veult faire du dit Marquis" (*L&P* XIII, pt. 2, 753). This in turn echoes the earlier perception of Martin de Cornoca in a dispatch to Charles V in 1534: "The king is suspicious of [the] Pole family on account of their title and their wealth (although the Crown has usurped the greater part of the latter), their fidelity to the Queen [Catherine of Aragon] and on account of Pole's absence" (*L&P* VII, 1040).

Clearly there were many reasons that Montague would excite Henry's displeasure in the late 1530s. Apart from his obvious power and influence and his claims to Plantagenet blood, he became particularly vulnerable to Henry's disfavor after his brother Reginald fled from England in 1534 to support the papal cause against Henry. Henry never succeeded in presenting any substantial evidence of Montague's guilt. The chief witness against him was his brother, who attempted suicide immediately after his confession (see below, vv. 785–819).

The evidence against the Marquis of Exeter appears to possess even less weight. His chief fault seems to have been (in the words of John Rylande, a servant of Montague's), that Montague "had great trust" in him and "often did resort" to him (*L&P* XIII, pt. 2, 702). In the end, as

Dodds notes (II, 313), the prosecution proceeded against him largely on the basis of two inconclusive scraps of conversation. His personal popularity also may have influenced Henry to destroy him. A conservative Catholic, he was, in the words of a contemporary document, "lusty and strong of power, specially beloved . . . and next unto the Crown of any man within England" (*L&P* XIII, pt. 2, 732). Certainly together Montague and Exeter provided a potential rallying point for Catholic, anti-Reformation opinion. This was sufficient to ensure their executions. See Dodds, II, 297–328, which remains the best general account of the deaths of Exeter and Montague.

752. lynne imperyall] Exeter was the grandson of Edward IV, his father, William Courtenay, having married Edward's youngest daughter, Catherine. Montague was the grandson of the Duke of Clarence, Edward IV's brother. Together with Montague's mother, the Countess of Salisbury (see vv. 1042–104), they were the last surviving members of the Plantagenet line.

753. hathe] "We suffered" or some such phrase should be understood after this word.

755–56. ffortune . . . violence] Proverbial; cf. Whiting F 505.

757–58. a marques of late creacion] Henry Courtenay was created Marquis of Exeter on June 18, 1525; see *L&P* IV, pt. 2, 1431 (14).

758–59. Erldome of Devonshyre] Courtenay's father, Sir William Courtenay, was created Earl of Devonshire by Henry VII on October 26, 1485. Courtenay succeeded to his father's title on May 10, 1511; see *L&P* I, pt. 1, 784 (16).

764–84. Montague and Exeter were arrested on November 4, 1538, and brought to trial on December 3. For details of the charges against them, see *L&P* XIII, pt. 2, 979. Both were sentenced to death and executed on December 9 at Tyburn.

785–819. The most significant factor in the condemnation of Montague and Exeter was undoubtedly the confession of Montague's brother, Sir Geoffrey Pole. He confessed on October 26, 1538, that

> he and many other with whom he had conferred have wished a change in this world without meaning any hurt to the king. . . . Also the lord Montacute his brother was of the same opinion before the death of his wife, but since that time he has found him more indifferent. Also the Marquis of Exeter was at first of the

same mind, but he had not spoken with him for nearly two years; but by his communication with lord Montacute during these two years he knows that the Marquis and his said brother were of one opinion. [*L&P* XIII, pt. 2, 695]

It seems reasonable to assume that Pole had been placed under considerable pressure to provide evidence against his brother. He had been arrested on August 29, 1538 [*L&P* XIII, pt. 2, 232), and the time lag between arrest and confession is suggestive. A highly colored account of the circumstances surrounding his confession occurs in Richard Morison's *An Invective Ayenste . . . Treason* (1539), sigs. E ii^v–vi^v. If Morison's account can be credited, Pole tried to stab himself rather than incriminate his brother. He succeeded only in wounding himself, and, overcome with guilt, "disclosed all the hole treasons" (Ev). The chronology of his attempted suicide is not clear. Two days after his confession it was reported that "Sir Jeffrey Pooll was examined in the Tower by my Lord Admiral. They say he was so in despair that he would have murdered himself, and has hurt himself sore" (*L&P* XIII, pt. 2, 986). This account leaves it uncertain whether the suicide attempt preceded or followed confession.

Pole was tried on December 4, 1538 (*L&P* XIII, pt. 2, 986), pleaded guilty, and was condemned to death. But he was pardoned on January 4, 1539 (*L&P* XIV, pt. 1, 18) after apparently attempting suicide again (ibid., 19). For an evaluation of Sir Geoffrey's character and his role in the demise of Montague and Exeter, see Dodds, II, 306–10. After his pardon he went abroad. He died in 1558.

806–10. This is a borrowing from *FP* VI, 1660–64:

> Be sleihte & meede whan he was maade strong,
> He beseged his fadir round aboute,—
> Vnto nature, me seemeth, he dide wrong
> To putte his fadir in so gret a doute
> Kyndenesse was ferr shet withoute.

811–12. This is a borrowing from *FP* VI, 1651–52: "For of al vicis, shortli to conclude / Werst of all is ingratitude."

848–1041. These lines comprise another related group of tragedies, those of Catherine Howard, Thomas Culpeper, and Viscountess Rochford, whose deaths were interlinked in 1541. By March of that year

Catherine was beginning to show considerable favor to Culpeper (see below, vv. 937–64). Lady Rochford, one of Catherine's ladies of the Privy Chamber, appears to have acted as intermediary between them, organizing a number of illicit meetings, where, as she subsequently confessed, "Culpeper hath known the queen carnally" (*L&P* XVI, 1939). There can be little doubt that the trio were at least guilty of criminal folly in their pursuit of an illicit relationship within the confines of the court and even during Henry's progress through the North in the summer of 1541.

The exact nature of the relationship between Catherine and Culpeper cannot be determined. Much depends on the confession of Lady Rochford, who lost her reason during the course of the investigation. Certainly the one letter that survives from Catherine to Culpeper is at best indiscreet (*L&P* XVI, 1134). It was, however, reported that he "had not passed beyond words" with her (*L&P* XVI, 1426). Still, this was sufficient under the Treason Act of 1534 to justify condemnation, even though much of the evidence was acquired either under torture or the threat of it, or was based on unsubstantiated hearsay. For a full discussion of Catherine's possible guilt and the circumstances surrounding her trial, see Smith, pp. 190–96.

Catherine herself had first gained the king's favor in 1540. Originally appointed as one of the maids of honor to Anne of Cleves, she seems immediately to have attracted the king. It is reported that the "King's Highness did cast a fantasy to Catherine Howard the first time that ever his Grace saw her" (*L&P* XVI, 1409 [i] sec. 4; quoted in Smith, p. 103). The best account of her rise is in Smith, pp. 102–22.

854. was] *E* at this point originally read *is*. This provides the only hint that parts of *E* could have been composed contemporaneous with the events they describe.

858. as I hir last . . . of late] The reference is interesting in its possible biographical implications. The likelihood that Cavendish may have been a member of Catherine Howard's household cannot be discounted. He reveals elsewhere a specialized knowledge of her entourage (see below, vv. 1775–76), as well as an acquaintance with Viscountess Rochford (cf. v. 971). In addition, he offers extended praise of Surrey, Catherine's cousin (cf. vv. 1105–88). But the matter cannot be conclusively resolved. There is, however, nothing in the known albeit scanty facts of Cavendish's biography during the 1530s and 1540s (cf. *LW*, xxii–iii) to invalidate such a hypothesis.

186   COMMENTARY

863. Cf. Whiting B 32.
869. To be a quen] Henry married Catherine on July 28, 1540. She was proclaimed Queen of England on August 15 (*L&P* XV, 976), although Holinshed reports that she was "shewed openly as Queene at Hampton Court" (p. 1580) on August 8. Smith rightly points out that she was never crowned, remaining a queen consort (p. 154).
Following this line in *E*, v. 877 (i.e. the corresponding line of the next stanza) was initially written and then deleted. This provides evidence that Cavendish was copying from another manuscript.
870. Fflorysshyng in youthe] Catherine's age at the time of her marriage cannot be determined with any certainty. She may possibly have been born "some time between 1518 and 1524" (Smith, p. 210).
870–71. with beawtie] Catherine's appearance is described in a dispatch by Marillac the French ambassador on September 3, 1540. She is said to be "rather graceful than beautiful, of short stature &c. The king is so amourous of her that he cannot treat her well enough and caresses her more than he did the others" (*L&P* XVI, 12).
871. Cf. Whiting S 685.
873–75. Wantyng no thyng] Catherine received lavish demonstrations of Henry's affection. She was granted on her marriage the lands of Jane Seymour, Thomas Cromwell, Lord Hungerford, and the Abbot of Reading, as well as large numbers of jewels (detailed in *L&P* XVI, 1389) and a large retinue and household. For further details, see Smith, pp. 147–48, and the references cited there.
883–89. On Catherine's amours both before and during her marriage, see below, vv. 904–10.
887. youthe . . . sighte] Probably proverbial, but not in Whiting or Tilley.
889. her] Both *E* and *D* read *ther*, which makes no sense, the referent of *ther* having to be *shame*. The error is doubtless due to some carry-over in Cavendish's mind during transcription from the preceding words in the line.
901. Cupydes fier] From classical times Cupid was frequently depicted carrying a flaming brand. The tradition seems to have been familiar to Cavendish's contemporaries; cf. *Mirror for Magistrates*, p. 433, v. 38: "the shot of Cupids firy shafte"; cf. also *Tottel's Miscellany*, I, 139, v. 20.
904–6. Culpeper yong] When Catherine began her affair with Culpeper is uncertain. At her trial she was charged with adultery "on the 29

August, 33 Hen. VIII and at other times and places before and after, with Thos. Culpeper" (*L&P* XVI, 1395).

907–10. With Dereham first] Francis Dereham was a gentleman pensioner of the Duke of Norfolk. There is no doubt that he and Catherine were lovers before her arrival at Court, while they were both resident in the Duke of Norfolk's household at Lambeth (see *L&P* XVI, 1320, 1321, 1339, 1385, for various confessions as to their relationship). The length of their affair is not known. Marillac reports that Dereham was condemned "for having not only kept the lady from the time he violated her at the age of 13 until 18 but having since been of her Chamber" (*L&P* XVI, 1426). Catherine herself subsequently maintained that they were lovers for only "a quarter of a year or a little above" (HMC, *Marquis of Bath*, II, 8–9, quoted in Smith, p. 185). It certainly seems to have been the case that their relationship was discontinued after Catherine went to Court in December 1539. But after Catherine's marriage, in August 1541, Dereham was appointed her private secretary and usher of the chamber in her household. It was subsequently alleged that an actual precontract of marriage had existed between them, but the charge was never pressed. Dereham was tried with Culpeper on December 1, 1540. The charges relating to him were that "before the marriage between the king and her [i.e. Catherine] [she] led an abhominable, base, carnal, voluptouous and vicious life, like a common harlot, with divers persons, as with Francis Dereham" (*L&P* XVI, 1395). He was executed with Culpeper on December 10. Holinshed reports that he was "hanged, dismembred and headed" (p. 1583). For full biographical details, see Smith, pp. 57–64, 178–87.

911–17. Henry was presented with evidence of Catherine's infidelity on November 1, 1540. Possibly on the seventh she confessed to Cranmer her relationship with Dereham (*L&P* XVI, 1325). It was no earlier than the eleventh that suspicion was also attached to Culpeper (*L&P* XVI, 1333).

919. the day of my dekaye] A bill of attainder was introduced into the Lords on January 21, 1542; it received its second reading on January 28 and third on February 8. She was executed on February 13, 1542, on charges of high treason.

925–31. In fact the Howard "Bretherne and frendes" suffered surprisingly little hardship after Catherine's fall. The whole family, with the exception of the Duke of Norfolk, forfeited all their lands on grounds of misprision on December 22, 1541. But restoration of favor followed quickly. Those members of the Howard family who were condemned to the Tower—Margaret, wife of Lord William Howard, and Anne, wife of Catherine's brother Henry—were pardoned and released in February 1542; the Duchess of Norfolk was released in May 1542, and Lord William himself in August of that year. Indeed, the Earl of Surrey received a royal grant of £10 within a month of Catherine's execution. Only Lady Rochford, Catherine's accomplice, died with her; see Smith, p. 200, to whom I am indebted for these points.

930–31. pray ye to God] It was reported that in their final moments Catherine and Jane Rochford "desired all Christian people to take regard unto their worthy and just punishment with death, for their offences against God heinously from their youth upward, in breaking of his commandments . . . commending their souls to God and earnestly calling for mercy upon Him" (*L&P* XVII, 106).

932–36. There is no compelling reason to assume this deviation from Cavendish's usual rhyme royal implies that *E* is incomplete or defective at this point. The two portions of the main body of the work (i.e. excluding the later *Ephitaphe to . . . Marye*) headed *Ephitaphe* (here and vv. 1434–73) provide the only points at which Cavendish departs from rhyme royal. It seems probable that he wished to make these epitaphs metrically distinctive from the rest of the work.

933. beawtie . . . chastitie] Proverbial; cf. Whiting B 150, Tilley B 165.

937–43. For the history of the Culpeper family, see M. F. Lloyd Prichard, "The Significant Background of the Stuart Culpepers," *Notes and Queries*, 205 (1960), 408–16. Culpeper's own career can only be scantly documented from contemporary sources. It is further complicated by the confusion existing between him and his elder brother of the same name, a servant of Thomas Cromwell's. There is little reason to doubt Cavendish's assertion that he was "Admyttyd ffrome a boy to be the kynges page" (938). He can be identified with some confidence as the "Culpepir of the privy chamber" first recorded in June 1535 (*L&P* VIII, 937). He is listed among the gentlemen of the Privy Chamber in 1538 (*L&P* XIII, pt. 2, 1), and became Keeper of the Armoury for the King's Body in that year (ibid., 1309 [36]). He received several grants in 1539 (e.g. *L&P* XIV, 1056 [28], 1192 [25]; pt. 2, 264 [16]).

944–57. There are indications before Culpeper's affair with Catherine of his "vyce"; a contemporary rumor maintained that he "had violated the wife of a certain parkkeeper in a woody thicket, while, horrid to relate! three or four of his most profligate attendants were holding her at his bidding. For this act of wickedness he was, notwithstanding, pardoned by the King, after he had been delivered into custody by the villagers on account of this crime, and likewise a murder which he committed in his resistence to them, when they first endeavoured to apprehend him" (*Original Letters Relative to the Reformation*, ed. H. Robinson [Cambridge, 1846], I, 226–27; quoted in Smith, p. 166).

946. All is but vanytie] Proverbial; Whiting A 92.

958–64. Culpeper was tried with Dereham on December 1, 1540. He was sentenced to be hanged, drawn and quartered on charges of high treason (*L&P* XVI, 1395). The sentence was subsequently changed to beheading (ibid., 1434). He was executed on December 10.

965–66. towardes thend of my boke] Cavendish makes similar announcements of the imminent conclusion of his work elsewhere in the *MV*; see e.g. vv. 1217–18 and 1914. It seems probable that such announcements are attempts at literary artifice rather than genuine statements of intent.

968. a wydowe] Jane, Viscountess Rochford, was the widow of George Boleyn, executed in 1536 (see above, vv. 274–343).

969. This line is omitted in *E*, although space is left for it there. *D* provides the sole, dubious authority for it.

971. Whome I oons knewe] Cavendish presumably met Viscountess Rochford while serving as Wolsey's gentleman usher.

972. father . . . of the Morlas lynne] Jane was the daughter of Henry Parker, eighth baron Morley (1476–1556).

973. My mother of the Seynt Iohns] Jane's mother was Alice St. John, daughter of Sir John St. John; the St. Johns were connected to the royal family by the marriage of Margaret Beauchamp, grandmother of Henry VIII.

976–81. Little is known about Viscountess Rochford's early life. She married George Boleyn before 1526 (Bapst, p. 20), and apparently remained in the Court until his death, when she withdrew. She returned as one of Catherine Howard's ladies of the Privy Chamber. It is difficult to know how much to credit the assertions of vice that Cavendish puts into her mouth. Certainly, after her arrest she confessed that she had sinned "against God heinously from [her] youth upward in breaking all his commandments" (H. Ellis, *Original Letters* . . . 1st series [1824], II, pp. 128–29).

982. whan my beawtie began for to be spent] Lady Rochford's age at the time of her death is unknown. Marillac, in a dispatch to Francis I of November 22, 1541, refers to her role in Catherine's fall, observing that "she . . . in her old age [has] shown little amendment" (*L&P* XVI, 1366).

985. others I entised] Lady Rochford's role was that of go-between for Catherine and Culpeper; it is discussed by Smith, pp. 189–90.

994. chayer of ffame] Cf. vv. 736–37: "you all / That formost ride a loft in the chayer."

1000. Sara, Rebecca and Racell] None of these examples occurs in *FP*; they are of course all biblical—see the Book of Tobit, and Genesis 34 and 39.

1001. For Judith, see *FP* III, 1555–61; for Hesther, see *FP* III, 4782–851; for Penelope, see *FP* I, 6032–34.

1002–4. Cornelia] Presumably Cornelia Gracchus, see *FP* V, 2593–99.

1007–8. sturdy Silla] Cf. *FP* I, 6673: "Scilla was sturdi & vengable"; see also *FP* I, 2483–646. Silla's father, Nisus, king of Megara, possessed a hair that rendered him invincible. She stole it and gave it to her lover, Minos, who then killed her father.

1009. Cleopatra] For Cleopatra see *FP* VI, 3632–68.

1010. Pasiua] For Pasiphae see *FP* I, 2668–709. The legendary Minotaur of Crete was the offspring of Pasiphae and a bull.

1011. Messalyn] For Messalina see *FP* VII, 320–592.

1021–27. Viscountess Rochford was condemned on charges of high treason. Included in Catherine's Act of Attainder, she was executed with her on February 13, 1542. A description of their deaths occurs in *L&P* XVII, 106 (see Commentary v. 930–31).

1035. ffortune . . . estate] Proverbial (?); not in Whiting or Tilley.

1042ff. The death of Margaret Pole, Countess of Salisbury (1473–1541) is linked to the deaths of Lord Montague and the Marquis of Exeter (see above, vv. 750–819 and Commentary). To a large degree the same factors operated in determining her destruction as in theirs: she was the last surviving member of the Plantagenet line, and she was Reginald Pole's mother. In her case an additional factor was probably her close friendship with Catherine of Aragon, to whom she had been first governess and then friend for many years. Henry certainly seems to have felt a strong antipathy; as early as February 1535 he had spoken of her as an "old fool" (*L&P* VIII, 263). For accounts of her career and destruction see Dodds, II, 316–17, 323–25 and J. E. Paul, *Catherine of Aragon and Her Friends* (London: Burns & Oates, 1966), especially pp. 246–52.

1045. all . . . ballaunce] Proverbial; Whiting B 17.

1048–50. doughter of a kynges brother] Margaret Pole was the daughter of George, Duke of Clarence (1449–1478), brother to Edward IV.

1051–55. Who was condempned] The story of the death of the Duke of Clarence is recounted in Holinshed:

one of the dukes seruantes was sodeinly accused . . . of poysoning, sorcerie or inchauntemente, and therof condemned, & put to execution for the same, the Duke whiche might not suffer the wrongfull condemnation of his man . . . nor yet forbeare but to murmure and reproue the doyng therof, moued the kyng with his dayely exclamation to take suche displeasure with hym that finally the Duke was cast into the Tower, and therwith adiudged for a traytour, and priuily drowned in a butte of Malmesey. [p. 1350]

1056–59. A brother] Margaret Pole's brother, Edward Pole, Earl of Warwick, was executed by Henry VII in 1499. Margaret was twenty-six at the time of his execution.

1059. bought and sold] Proverbial; Whiting B 637.

1060–62. Restored me agayn] Margaret was created Countess of Salisbury on October 14, 1513 (*L&P* I, pt. 2, 2422 [11]). Her lands were restored in December 1515 (*L&P* II, pt. 1, 1363, ii).

1063–67. The countess seems to have earned a contemporary reputation for probity and decorum. In a dispatch Chapuys describes her as "a lady of virtue and honor if there be one in England" (*L&P* VI, 1528).

1068–76. Assigned me the gouernaunce] I have been unable to discover the date of the Countess of Salisbury's appointment as governess to Mary Tudor. It was certainly no later than June 28, 1520, on which date she is described as "lady-governess" (*L&P* III, pt. 1, 896).

1077–83. The countess was not in fact as docile as Cavendish has her maintain here. At times her stubbornness in matters of principle and doctrine led her into direct conflict with the king's wishes. For example, in 1533 she declined to deliver up Princess Mary's jewels without "the king's letters . . . in that behalf" (*L&P* VI, 1009), a position she subsequently reiterated (ibid., 1041). After most of Mary's servants had been dismissed, the countess "offered to follow and serve her at her own expense with an honourable train" (*L&P* VI, 1528), against the king's evident wishes. Later, in 1535, her name is mentioned as one of the leading dissuaders of the Prior of Bissame from resignation (*L&P* VIII, 596). This intransigence was doubtless an additional factor in her demise.

1077–79. offend . . . amendyd] The rhyme scheme is defective at this point, the *a* rhymes not being in agreement.

1084–90. In a deposition in November 1538, one Gervase Tyndall charged that Margaret had sent letters to the exiled Reginald Pole, and a John Ansard charged her with resistance to Henry's religious reforms (*L&P* XIII, pt. 2, 817). She was interrogated in November by the Earl of Southampton and the Bishop of Ely, the interrogations apparently continuing into the next year. But the countess remained indomitable, refusing to admit to any charges. Southampton and Ely reported ruefully: "We assure your Lordship we have dealt with such a one as men have not dealt withal to fore us; we may call her rather a strong and constant man than a woman" (*L&P* XIII, pt. 2, 855). At some point between the end of March and the end of May 1539, she was removed to the Tower.

1091–97. I saw no remedy] In fact there seems to have been some uncertainty as to what should be done with the countess. She had been attainted on April 26, 1539, on the charge that, together with Hugh Vaughan, she had been "falsely confederate with lord Montague and Reginald Poole, sons of the said Countess" (*L&P* XIV, pt. 1, 867 cap. 15). But her life remained in the balance for over two years. Cromwell's "remembrances" for May 1539 include: "To remember what shall be done with the lady of Sarum, and where she shall be kept" (*L&P* XIV, pt. 1, 1050), which implies some uncertainty about her fate. Similar uncertainty is reflected in subsequent remembrances in 1539 and 1540 (*L&P* XIV, pt. 2, 287; ibid., 427; XV, 438). She was excluded from the general pardon of April 12, 1540 (ibid., 498). but apparently it was not until the following February 23 that her case was discussed by the Privy Council (*L&P* XVI, 557). Then there is a hiatus of over three months before Marillac reported on May 29: "the countess of Saalberi, mother of Cardinal Pol and the late lord Mountaigu was yesterday morning about 7 o'clock beheaded in a corner of the Tower. . . . It was the more difficult to believe as she had been long prisoner, was of noble lineage, about 80 years old, and had been punished by the loss of one son and banishment of the other, and the total ruin of her house" (*L&P* XVI, 868).

1094. I was condempned withowt examynacion] The countess was attainted and never brought to trial. Chapuys reports that "when informed of her sentence, she found it very strange, not knowing her crime" (*L&P* XVI, 897).

1099. estate] *E* reads *estates*, *D* reads *estats*. The emendation is necessary to conform with the *b* rhyme of 1101–2.

1104. It is possible that there is a genuine lacuna following this stanza. There are only two stanzas on this page and space has been left for a third. Possibly Cavendish intended to insert an envoy to the countess's lament. Certainly the transition to the following lament is extremely abrupt.

1105–11. Surrey was heir to Thomas Howard, third duke of Norfolk. He was created Earl of Surrey on his father's accession to the title on May 21, 1524 (Casady, pp. 26–27). His early career reflects an ascent of "ffortunes whele" (v. 1109) insofar as this is synonymous with Henry's favor. Not only was Surrey the chosen companion of the king's illegitimate son, the Duke of Richmond, until his death in 1536, but he also survived the eclipse of the Howard family in 1542 without any apparent loss of the king's approbation. And his various excesses do not (before 1547) appear to have earned him any but the most short-term disapproval. See Casady, pp. 38–88 passim.

1119–25. The Duke of Norfolk was arrested on December 12, 1546 (Wriothesley, I, 176) and charged with treason, together with Surrey. Norfolk confessed to the charge on January 12, 1547 (*L&P* XXI, pt. 2, 696) and was saved from death only by Henry's own death on January 28. He remained in the Tower until Mary's accession. The assertion both in vv. 1123–24 and vv. 1159–60 of Norfolk's "perpetual presonment" may shed a little light on the chronology of the *MV*. They would seem to suggest that this portion of the work was composed some time before August 3, 1553, when Norfolk received his freedom.

1121. actes marsheall] Norfolk fought with his father at Flodden and assisted in the suppression of the Pilgrimage of Grace in 1537.

1126–32. The murder of Caesar by Brutus is recounted in *FP* VI, 2864–919.

1133. Comen] *E* reads *coen*, an error that Cavendish repeats elsewhere in *MV*; see vv. 1164, 1411, 1956. Sylvester notes that in *LW*, "Cavendish frequently omits the abbreviation mark for *m* in *comen*" (p. 207).

1152–53. oon offence] Surrey was condemned for having treasonably quartered his own arms with the royal arms (cf. *L&P* XXI, 1425, where Garter alleged that Surrey "showed me a scucheon of the arms Brotherton and St. Edmunde and Ajoye and Nowbreye quartered and said he would bear it").

But underlying the particular charge was doubtless the cumulative weight of a series of events that had done much to alienate the Council and Henry. As early as 1537, Surrey had attacked Edward Seymour within the confines of the Court (Casady, p. 61). In 1542 he had been imprisoned in the Fleet for issuing a challenge (Casady, pp. 88–89), and he was again imprisoned in the following year for eating meat in Lent and for disturbing the peace (Casady, pp. 97–98). After his return to Court in early 1546, he attempted to attack George Blage, a supporter of Edward Seymour's, and prevented a reconciliation between Norfolk and the Seymours (Casady, pp. 179–80). His highly abrasive and indiscreet nature is also indicated in the various allegations that were made against him after his arrest. It was charged among other things that he suggested to his sister that "his majesty might cast some love upon her" (*L&P* XXI, 555 [4]); it was also reported that he said "who were so meet to govern the Prince as my . . . father" (ibid., 555 [7]). There can be little doubt that the actual charge laid against Surrey was only the climax to a sequence of activities that had alienated him from the Court and rendered him a serious potential danger to the authority of the Council.

The "thousaund conquestes valyaunte" ascribed to Surrey here are hyperbolic. In fact Surrey's military career was marked in the main by lack of distinction or by folly comparable to his other offenses. He fought in Scottish border raids and in the battle of Solway Moss in 1542. In 1543 he was present at the unsuccessful siege of Landrecy. He was marshall to the English army in 1544 and in this capacity played a part in the siege of Montreuil, injuring himself on September 19 in an unsuccessful and extremely hazardous attempt to storm the walls of the town.

His final and most prestigious appointment was as Captain of Boulogne from August 31, 1545. A significant factor in his recall in March of the following year was his instigation of an unsuccessful skirmish on January 7, 1546, which led to heavy English casualties. See Casady,

COMMENTARY 195

pp. 131–74 for a detailed discussion of his tenure as Captain of Boulogne. This is modified in certain respects, especially with regard to the January 7 skirmish, by M. Bryn Davies, "Surrey at Boulogne," *Huntington Library Quarterly*, 23 (1959–60), 339–48.

1160. dethe for my desertes] Surrey was sentenced to death on January 13 and beheaded on January 19, 1547 (Wriothesley, I, 177).

1164–67. It was reported that at his trial Surrey asserted that Henry wanted "to get rid of all noble blood around him and to employ none but low people" (*Spanish Chronicle*, p. 148). Surrey doubtless had in mind those increasingly influential members of the Council, John Dudley and the Seymours, who in spite of humble birth held power in the later years of Henry's reign.

1170. worthy exaltacion] *worthy* occurs with the ellipsis of *of* from late Middle English onward; see *OED*, s.v. "worthy" II, 2.

1171. dygnyties honorable] Apart from his military appointments, Surrey does not appear to have received very many *dygnyties*. In spring 1541 he was dubbed knight (Bapst, p. 232), and he was elected knight of the Garter on April 23, 1541 (Casady, p. 82). Earlier, on September 8, 1540, he had been appointed with his father as steward of Cambridge University (Casady, p. 84). At various other times he received minor commissions or grants of land (e.g. *L&P* XII, i, 646 [48]; XIV, ii, 29; XVI, 1488 [18]; XVII, 362 [66]).

1180. An old prouerbe] Proverbial; cf. Whiting W 49.

1187–88. thend of so many noble estates] Presumably Cavendish has in mind here the executions of such members of the hereditary nobility as the Duke of Buckingham (executed in 1521) and those others who, like Montague, Exeter, and the Countess of Salisbury, had any claim to Plantagenet blood.

1200. measure . . . falle] A version of Whiting M 467.

1222. dame fame . . . trompe] Fame and her trumpet are mentioned several times in *FP*, e.g. I, 5117; IX, 3468.

1227. Deade is that Royall prynce] Henry died of fever on January 28, 1547.

1233. dethe . . . tyde] Probably proverbial; not in Whiting or Tilley. The sense seems to be: "Death will not be prevented by any circumstance."

1233–34. dethe . . . kyng or kaysier] Cf. *LW* 10/34: "Whan deathe that favoryth non Estate, kyng or Cayser" As Sylvester notes, "Kyng or

Cayser" is "a Middle-English alliterative phrase still common in the sixteenth century" (p. 196); cf. Whiting, K 46.

1259–65. Clotho . . . Lacheses . . . Attrophos] The three fates, Clotho, Lachesis, and Atrophos, here represented as cutting the thread of Henry's life, occur together in *FP* I, 5013–19.

1262. brent] Singer and Hammond both read *hent*, against the evidence of the manuscript.

1275. fffleshe is frayle] Proverbial; cf. Whiting F 272, Tilley F 363.

1276. deathe . . . mewe] Proverbial (?); not in Whiting or Tilley.

1282. brent] Singer and Hammond read *hent*, against the evidence of E.

1286. So] "Because" should be understood before this word.

1308–12. This is a borrowing from *FP* I, 5146–50:

> But O allas, that euer it sholde fall,
> So noble a knyht, so manli, so notable,
> That any spotte sholde his pris appall
> Or cause his corage for to been onstable,
> Which is a thyng doolful and lamentable.

1315–19. I brake the bond of mariage] The reference is of course to Anne Boleyn, see above, vv. 519ff.

1320–21. Making newe lawes] The legislation deriving from Henry's desire for a divorce is fully detailed in Scarisbrick, pp. 398–460, in his examination of the extensive legislation of the Reformation Parliament.

1329–33. This is a borrowing from *FP* I, 5531–35:

> Wher froward Venus hath dominacioun,
> And blynde Cupide his subiectis doth auaunce,
> And wilful lust thoruh indiscrecioun
> Is chosen iuge to holden the ballaunce,
> Ther chois onlefful hath thoruh onhappi chaunce . . .

1336–40. This is a borrowing from *FP* I, 5160–64:

> Thus Hercules, astoned and ashamed,
> Onto Bochas shewed his presence,

> Seide, "allas! my knyhthod is diffamed
> Bi a ful fals amerous pestilence,
> So sore constreyned bi mortal violence.

1343–49. This is a borrowing from *FP* I, 6252–58:

> Thouh Alisaundre was myhti off puissaunce,
> And al the worlde hadde in his demeyne,
> Yit was his resoun vnder thobeisaunce
> Off flesshli lustis fetrid in a cheyne;
> For in his persone will was souereyne,
> His resoun bridled be sensualite,
> Troublyng the fredam off riht & equite.

1350–56. The chronicle of Henry's marriages is too well known to require detailing here.

1353. some that did non ill] i.e. Anne Boleyn and Catherine Howard, on the probable degree of innocence of whom see Commentary vv. 519ff., 848ff.

1357–61. Cf. Henry's praise of Catherine of Aragon in *LW* 82/25–30: "She hathe byne to me as true obedyent & as confirmable a wyfe as I cowld in my fantzy wyshe or desier She hathe all the vertuouse qualities that owght to be in a woman of hir dignytie or in any other of basser estate Sewerly she is also a noble woman borne if nothyng ware in hir but oonly hir condicyons woll well declare the same."

1362. that I did hir devorse] Henry's marriage to Catherine of Aragon was declared null and void on May 23, 1533, by Cranmer, the archbishop of Canterbury.

1369. pacient Greseld] Cf. *LW* 35/21–22, where Catherine is described as a "perfect Grysheld." The contemporary significance of the reference is discussed in *LW*, pp. 259–62.

1370. hyr] D adds *in*, clarifying Cavendish's somewhat elliptical syntax.

1371–77. Henry fell into considerable financial difficulty during the later years of his reign. The chief reasons for this were his renewal, in 1542, of the war with France (which by the time of his death had cost over two million pounds), and his debasement of the coinage begun in

1544. For full details, see F. Dietz, *English Public Finance, 1485–1558* (Urbana: University of Illinois Press, 1921), especially pp. 146–48, 154–55, 174–77.

1383–84. nothyng . . . dethe] Proverbial; cf. Whiting D 78, Tilley D 69.

1385. all . . . end] Proverbial (?); not in Whiting or Tilley.

1406–12. Edward VI was proclaimed king in succession to his father on January 31, 1547.

1410. Prosperously] *E* reads *Properously*, a form unsanctioned by the *OED*; Cavendish uses the form *prosperously* in v. 1467 below.

1416–18. dethe . . . lyvyng . . . bootte] Proverbial; cf. Whiting D 78, Tilley D 142–43.

1422. forthe] "I" must be understood before this word.

1434–73. Here, as above, vv. 932–36, Cavendish abandons his usual rhyme royal to indicate a formal epitaph.

The tradition of linking praise of contemporaries with the great names of the past is a common medieval rhetorical convention. A version of the list of the nine worthies is often employed in the convention. But Cavendish's list seems unusual in its mingling of various of the nine worthies (e.g. Caesar and Hector [vv. 1442–43], Arthur [v. 1445], David and Alexander [vv. 1448–49] and Charlemagne and Godfrey of Boulogne [vv. 1455–56]) with various classical deities (e.g. Jupiter [v. 1438] and Mars [v. 1440]) and biblical figures as well as such relatively obscure figures as Phocion and Fabricius (vv. 1458–59). The element of confusion is indicated by the repetition of Caesar (vv. 1442 and 1464).

No model has been convincingly suggested for this passage. Singer mentions (p. 102) the *Coplas* of Jorge Manrique, the fifteenth-century Spanish poet, but acknowledges the improbability of any direct relationship between it and the *MV*. More apposite perhaps is a passage in Skelton's "Howe the Duke of Albany . . . ," of which this part of the *MV* seems reminiscent:

> . . . our royall regent,
> Our perelesse president,
> Our kyng most excellent:
>
> In merciall prowes

COMMENTARY 199

> Lyke vnto Hercules;
> In prudence and wys dom
> Lyke vnto Salamon;
> In his goodly person
> Lyke vnto Absolon;
> In loyalty and foy
> Lyke to Ector of Troy;
> And his glory to incres
> Lyke to Scipiades . . . [427–39]

1437. Tenthe worthy worthy] The view of Henry as the Tenth Worthy supplementing the existing nine (see Commentary vv. 1434–73) has some support in contemporary iconography. The *Chronicle of Queen Jane* reports a procession through London on July 25, 1554, where "aboute the winding turred was fynely portrayed the ix. worthies and King Henry the eight and Edwarde the vjth in their tabernacles" (p. 78).

1442. A Ceser] Caesar was traditionally one of the Nine Worthies.

1443. Hector] Hector was traditionally one of the Nine Worthies.

1445. Arthore] Arthur was traditionally one of the Nine Worthies.

1449. An Allexander] Alexander was traditionally one of the Nine Worthies.

1450. A Plato] The comparison is not one, so far as I can discover, made elsewhere in praise of Henry.

1455–56. A Charlmayn . . . A Godfroy] Both Charlemagne and Godfrey of Boulogne were traditionally among the Nine Worthies.

1457. A Rowlond] The French hero of the battle of Roncevalles.

1458. Phocion] Phocion (c. 402–318 B.C.) was an Athenian statesman and general, who ruled Athens from 322–318 B.C. In 318 he was deposed, tried for treason, and executed.

1459. Ffabricyus] Fabricius is mentioned briefly in *FP* IV, 3856, and V, 760.

1460. Caton] Presumably Cato the stoic, who is mentioned several times in *FP*; his virtues are praised at length at III, 1226–95.

1461. Pompeyous] Pompey's exploits are recounted in *FP* VI, 2024–464.

1462. Marcus Marcellus] He is not mentioned in *FP*. He is briefly alluded to in Skelton's *Phyllyp Sparowe*, v. 734.

1463. Cipio Affrican] Lydgate discusses the career of Scipio Africanus in *FP* V, 1643–712. Cavendish uses Scipio as an example earlier in the *MV*; cf. vv. 1133–39.

1465. Octauyon] The first emperor of Rome, Octavius Caesar. He is mentioned only briefly in *FP*, e.g. II, 4478; VI, 3523–98 passim.

1468–69. Of progeny Troiean] Singer and Hammond erroneously read *Grecean* for *Troiean*. The legend of the descent of British kings from Trojan forbears is a common one in medieval and Tudor literature. The ultimate source of the belief is Geoffrey of Monmouth's *Historia Regum Britanniae*, whose role in the development of the legend is discussed in T. D. Kendrick, *British Antiquity* (London: Methuen, 1950), pp. 4–17. Geoffrey's work was, as Kendrick shows (pp. 34–44) extensively popularized by Tudor writers.

1472. forthy] E reads *for thyn*, which destroys the rhyme scheme; D reads *far worthy*, an intelligent attempt to make sense of a difficult reading. Singer reads *thyn eie*. I have followed Hammond in emending to *forthy*, "therefore, consequently"; see her note on this line (p. 382).

1477. swetnes vnto bitter gall] Proverbial: Whiting S 948.

1488ff. Cavendish's attitude toward Thomas Seymour (?1508–1549) is one of the more puzzling features of the *MV*. Seymour had risen to power with his brother the Duke of Somerset after their sister Jane married Henry VIII. When Somerset became Lord Protector he was rewarded with a barony and made Lord High Admiral. It seems clear that Seymour was dissatisfied wih the degree of power he possessed. In 1547 he secretly married Henry's widow, Catherine Parr; after her death, he sought the hand of Elizabeth Tudor and made strenuous attempts to gain influence over Edward VI. Simultaneously he flagrantly abused his authority, indulging in acts of piracy and illegally debasing the coinage (for full details of the charges against him see *APC* II, 248–56). There can be little doubt that he was a dangerous political opportunist who made an ill-judged attempt to seize power. Cavendish's insistence (cf. vv. 1621–27) on his innocence flies in the face of the compelling weight of evidence assembled against him at the time. This insistence may in part be explained by Cavendish's evident aversion to fratricide (cf. vv. 1523–29 and above, vv. 795–98), but such an aversion scarcely accounts for the vehemence of his defense. Yet Cavendish was not alone in his admiration for Seymour and belief in his innocence. Sir John Harington in 1567 drafted an admiring sonnet in Arundel/Harington MS [2]. And Sir Nicholas Throckmorton is equally loud in his praise:

> In praise of whome [i.e. Seymour] loude peales I ought to ring;
> For he was hardie, wise, and liberall.
> His clymbing high disdayned by his peeres
> Was thought the cause he liv'd not out his yeares. [st. 66]

But Harington and Throckmorton were, of course, former servants of Seymour. For a full evaluation of Seymour and his fall, see Jordan, I, 368–82.

1488. lord Seymor . . . vncle to a kyng] Seymour was created Baron Sudeley on February 16, 1547. He was the maternal uncle to Edward VI by virtue of the marriage of his sister Jane to Henry VIII in 1536.

1492–93. I maried the Quene] Seymour secretly married Henry's widow, Catherine Parr, in April or May 1547, without the Council's knowledge.

1494. some disdayned] It ws reported that "the Lord Protector was much offended" with his brother's marriage (Edward's *Chronicle*, p. 6).

1495. groned] Both *D* and *E* read *goned*, a form unsanctioned by *OED* or *MED*. The emendation is an obvious one given Cavendish's tendency to omit single letters.

1495–99. They grudged] Seymour's secret marriage, with its obvious political implications, inevitably earned the enmity of the Council. This is reflected in certain of the charges formulated against him at his trial. Article 19 (*APC* II, 251) objects that:

not onely before you maryed the Quene [you had] attempted and gone about to marie the Kinges Majestes sister, the Ladie Elizabeth . . . [and] being than let by the Lorde Protectour and others of the Cownsell, sithens that tyme bothe in the lief of the Quene contynewed your olde labour and love, and after her deathe by secrete and craftie meanes practised to acheieve your saide purpose of marying the saide Ladie Elizabeth, to the daungier of the Kinges Majestes persone and perill of the state of the realme.

And Article 20 (*APC* II, 251–52) refers to the child of this marriage; if it had been born any sooner, it shulde have bene a great doubt whither the childe borne shuld have bene accompted the late Kinges or your, whereuppon a marvailous daungier and perill might and was like to haue ensued to the Kinges Majestes succession and quyet of the realme.

1500–501. Procured by a woman] The reference is to Anne Stanhope, Somerset's wife, who had quarrelled with Catherine Parr, Seymour's wife, over questions of precedence. The *Spanish Chronicle* reports that "there was great jealousy between the Queen and the Protector's wife, who seeing that the Queen was the wife of the younger brother, resolved not to pay the usual honour to her. . . . The Admiral was greatly grieved at this" (p. 160). Cf. also *Cooper's Chronicle*, f. 344: "[Seymour] had maryed Queene Catherine late wyfe to kynge Henrie. She vpon what occassion I know not, conceyued a stomake againste the Lorde Protectors wyfe Duchess of Somersette, and thervpon also in the behalfe of their wyfes, dyspleasure and grudge beganne betwene the two brothers . . . diuerse also reported that the Duchess of Somerset wrought his [i.e. Thomas Seymour's] death."

1501. no malice lyke thers] Proverbial; cf. Whiting M 26.

1507–8. Nero slewe his mother] Nero's murder of his mother is described in *FP* VII, 726–32.

1509–12. The sense of these lines is difficult: Somerset ("nature") behaved arrogantly toward his brother after his marriage ("natures newe estate") offering coldness ("nature to repyne") instead of affection ("nature to reioyce"); nature would think itself "unnatural" if it were to cause Somerset to behave in an unbrotherly way ("frome nature to declyne").

1516–17. I allwayes ment iustly] For an excellent analysis of the charges against Seymour, see Jordan, I, 374–81, who concludes that Seymour "undoubtedly stood guilty of numerous acts that were technically treasonable" (I, 381).

1518–19. My souerayn lord . . . I loved and obeyed] In fact Seymour attempted to win the king's favor through gifts, sought to obtain possession of his person, and tried to marry him to Lady Jane Grey, a member of his household; see Jordan, I, 372, and Tytler, I, 131.

1523–29. This is a borrowing from *FP* I, 3900–906:

> I dempte off hym as off my trewe brother,
> Wenyng he hadde feithful been to me;

> I sauh no signe, nor I kneuh non other,
> In hym supposyng no duplicite.
> But, o allas, how myhte it euer be,
> Or who dede euer in any story fynde
> Blood onto blood to be so onkynde!

1523–26. brotherly love voyed of all duplicite] In fact Somerset seems to have sought to avoid taking any action against his brother for as long as possible, and to have sought to warn him as to his conduct. See A. F. Pollard, *England under Protector Somerset* (London: Kegan Paul & Co., 1909), pp. 197–98, who, after examining Somerset's reluctant role in his brother's impeachment, concludes: "The assumption that the Protector destroyed his brother . . . is not supported by a particle of evidence. It is manifest, on the contrary, that Somerset felt considerable affection for the Admiral, and keen grief at his execution" (p. 197).

1530ff. Cavendish here reworks passages from Lydgate's account of Atreus and Thyestes in one of his most successful pieces of adaptation.

1530–36. This is a borrowing from *FP* I, 3893–99:

> But as a brother sholde his brother triste,
> I trusted hym off herte, will & thouht;
> Bi apperence non othir cause I wiste,
> For in his persone I supposid nouht
> That euer he koude so fals a thyng ha wrouht.
> But who may soner a-nother man deceyue,
> Than he in whom no malice men conceyue?

1534. hathe] *E* adds *a*, a clear instance of dittography; cf. the earlier *a* in the line.

1537–41. This is a borrowing from *FP* I, 3914–18:

> My brothir fond a fals occasioun
> Ageynes me, and gan a cause feyne
> To banyshe me out off our regioun,
> And gan at me off hatrede so disdeyne,
> Vpon me affermyng in certeyne . . .

1538–39. To condempn me of treason] Seymour was arrested on charges of treason on January 17, 1549.

1541–43. The full indictment against Seymour is printed in *APC*, II, 248–56, the charges running to thirty-three articles. The decision that Seymour was guilty, made on February 23, was a conciliar decision, rather than Somerset's own.

1544–50. This is a borrowing from *FP* I, 3921–27:

> This he compassid ful falsli off malis,
> Hymsilff weel knowyng that it was nat so,
> Ay founde onkynde, and in his auys,
> Nat lik my brother, but my dedli fo;
> And to encrece gret parcell off my wo,
> Bi long processe in his entencioun
> He ymagined my destruccioun.

1551–55. This is a borrowing from *FP* I, 3928–32:

> And his cheeff cause was false couetise,
> Touchyng this thyng which he dede on me feyne;
> And yit this kyngdam, treuli to deuise,
> Shold haue be partid of riht atwen vs tweyne:
> But a-geyn trouthe he dede so ordeyne . . .

1553–54. gouernaunce . . . vs bretherne twayne] Seymour is reported to have said that "it was neuer seen, that in the Mynorite of a king, when ther hath bene two Brethren, that thone Brother shuld have all rule, and thother none" and that "he thought yt was not the King's will that dead ys, that eny oon Man sholde have bothe the Government of the king that now ys, and also the Realme. And that in Tyme past, yf ther were two Uncles, being of the Mothers syde, thoon shulde have thoon, thother thother" (Haynes, I, 82, 90).

1558–71. the Erle of Warwyke] There is some substantiation for Seymour's implication of Warwick in his fall. De Noailles, who became the French ambassador to London in 1553, asserts that "Warvick fomentoit avec soin la division des deux freres; et en meme temps qu'il se declaroit hautement pour le parti du protecteur, il faisoit insinuer secretement a l'admiral par ses emissaires, qu'il ne devoit plus ecouter aucune proposition d'accommodement si on me lui cedoit la charge du gouveneur du prince" (*Ambassades de Messieur de Noailles en Angleterre. Redigées par*

René Aubert de Vertot d'Aubeuf [Leyden, 1763], I, 138–39). Although based on hearsay, this report does suggest that the allegation Cavendish has Seymour make was at least a current one.

1565–68. This is a borrowing from *FP* I, 3886–89:

> Allas! my brother, roote off onkyndenesse,
> Attreus callid, off tresoun sours & well,
> And fyndere out of tresoun & falsenesse,
> And all other in fraude doth precell . . .

1572–78. This is a borrowing from *FP* I, 3991–97:

> The wili wolff that cast hym to deuoure
> The celi lamb, which can no diffence,
> Nor non helpe hymseluen to socoure,
> So feeble he is to make resistence,
> Which demeth trouthe off fals apparence—
> What wonder ist the fraude nat conceyued,
> Though such lambes onwarli be deceyued?

1572. beare] The bear is the traditional crest of the Warwicks; cf. *Mirror for Magistrates*, p. 229, v. 232: "For all the broode of Warwickes geve the Beare."

1581–85. The deathe of the quen] Historically there is little to suggest such deep grief on Seymour's part for Catherine Parr (who died in childbirth in September 1548). The following reported conversation between Catherine and Seymour casts doubt on his protestations here. Catherine complained that she was "'not well handled, for those about me care not for me, but stand laughing at my grief, and the more good I will to them, the less good they will to me'. Whereunto my lord admiral answered, 'Why, sweetheart, I would you no hurt'. And she said to him again loud, 'No, my lord, I think so,' and immediately she said to him in her ear, 'But, my lord, you have given me many shrewd taunts.'" (Haynes, I, 103.)

1588–89. Whos . . . mutabylitie] The sense of these lines is somewhat awkward: "the origins ('Orygynall') of whose death ('alterasion') is caused by ('derived ffrome') etc." (cf. *OED*, s.v. "original" *sb*. 2 for comparable usages).

1593–99. Cf. Throckmorton who reports, "Thus guiltlesse he, through malice went to pott; / Not answering for himselfe, not knowing cause" (st. 76). Seymour was examined by the Council first on February 23, 1549, when the full array of charges was laid before him. On this occasion he declined to answer the charges (*APC*, II, 256). On the following day (February 24) however, Seymor made a partial and evasive answer to the first three charges laid against him (*APC*, II, 258–60) and declined to answer the others. The Council immediately began work on a bill of attainder, which was introduced into the Commons on February 25 (*APC*, II, 260).

1600–6. ther purpose . . . resolued] The bill of attainder was passed against Seymour on March 5, 1549 (*APC*, II, 260). On March 17 the Council reached final agreement on his execution (*APC*, II, 262–63). He was executed on March 20.

1607–20. a precher] Hugh Latimer, bishop of Worcester, made several attacks on Seymour in his sermons preached before the king on March 29, April 5, and April 19. The relevant passages can be found in *The Works of Hugh Latimer*, ed. G. E. Corrie (Cambridge, 1844), I, 161–65, 181–86, 228–29. I quote the last, briefest comment: "He shall be Lot's wife to me as long as I live. He was, I heard say, a covetous man, a covetous man indeed: I would there were no more in England! He was, I heard say, an ambitious man: I would there were no more in England! He was, I heard say, a seditious man, a contemner of common prayer: I would there were no more in England! Well: he is gone. I would he had left none behind him!"

1613. for] "by" must be understood following this word.

1650. O deathe oncertayn] Proverbial; based on Whiting D 96.

1653. the vre] "Of" must be understood before this phrase.

1656–57. I clame aloft] Edward Seymour (?1506–1552) first came into a position of power when Henry VIII married his sister Jane in 1536. After this marriage on June 5, he was created Viscount Beauchamp of Hache and granted extensive lands in Wiltshire. In the months following he was also made governor of Jersey and chancellor of north Wales. In 1537 he was created Earl of Hertford and, on October 16, made a member of the Privy Council. During the later years of Henry's reign his reputation and power grew. A skillful soldier, he was active in France and Scotland during the 1540s, and his increasing favor is reflected in his appointments: knight of the Garter (January 9, 1541), warden of the Scottish marches (September 1542), lord great chamberlain (January 1543), lieutenant general of the north (March 5, 1544), lieutenant of the kingdom (July 1544) and lieutenant general both of the north (May 1545) and of France (April 1546). He was created Duke of Somerset on February 16, 1547.

1665. To be than the protector] Somerset was appointed Protector of the Realm on January 31, 1547; see below, Commentary vv. 1677–83.

1666. banysshed all theme] Presumably this is a reference to the fall of Thomas Wriothesley, Earl of Southampton and Lord Chancellor since 1544. Wriothesley was dismissed from his post and lost his seat on the Privy Council on March 6, 1547 (*APC*, II, 48–59) for illegally delegating his judicial responsibilities just after Edward's coronation. For an account of his fall, see Jordan, I, 69–72.

1667. to avoyd all stryfe] Cf. *FP* III, 3175, "tauoide hem from stryves," i.e. "to keep from strife."

1668–69. lawes of this realme] Once again this may be a reference to Somerset's pro-Protestant policies, most notably the repeal of the Treason Act on December 21, 1547, during the first session of Somerset's protectorate.

1671. Cf. *FP* I, 933: "As we precelle in wisdom and resoun."

1677–83. As he left them in writyng] In accepting the appointment as Protector, Somerset undoubtedly violated the provisions of Henry's will, which had specified a conciliar form of government until Edward's majority. But modern historians have tended to view the will as practically unworkable, and as "an instrument of political control during the old king's life and of no great consequence for the new reign"; see L. B. Smith, "The Last Will and Testament of Henry VIII: A Question of Perspective," *Journal of British Studies*, 2 (1962), 26. Certainly Somerset's appointment was unanimously endorsed by the Council.

1684–90. I . . . bare a kyngly port] After his appointment as Protector, Somerset was made in quick succession on January 13 "Protector of his realmes and dominions and Governor of [the king's] person" and "our chief and principal councillor and chiefest of our Privy Council" and granted power on March 21 "to do all things which a governor of the king's person ought to do" (*APC*, II, 5, 69).

1691–92. warre and debate] *Warre and debate* were consistent features of Somerset's protectorate. He was involved in a lengthy Scottish campaign which, after the initial brilliant victory at Pinkie (September 10,

1547), gradually lost impetus and led ultimately to an inglorious English retreat. Throughout his administration there was continuous armed conflict around English-occupied Calais and Boulogne. And Somerset's first fall was directly precipitated by the risings in the West and East Anglia in the summer of 1549.

1693–97. thos ffortes] The forts Cavendish has in mind are presumably Boulogne, which Henry had successfully besieged in 1544, and, by association, England's other French stronghold, Calais. It was not Somerset, however, who was responsible directly for the loss of Boulogne, which was finally ceded to France in March 1550, before Somerset had been readmitted to the Council.

1694. Whan in his owen persone] This line poses some problems. *Whan* is Cavendish's spelling of "won" in accordance with his tendency to introduce an otiose -*h*- between *w* and a vowel; cf. e.g. vv. 58, 2260, *whofull*, and 1358, *whomanly*. But the sense requires "in" following it. I have inserted "in" since its omission seems to have been caused by eye-skip; cf. *in his* in the latter part of the line.

1698. I mynysshed . . . regall port] Somerset certainly made considerable inroads into Crown assets, redistributing them among the nobility, particularly those of recent creation. See Jordan, I, 103–24.

1699. I consumed his treasure] See Commentary v. 1698. Cavendish may also have in mind the debasement of the coinage during Somerset's protectorate. Modern historians have been more sympathetic to this aspect of Somerset's administration than Cavendish was; cf. E. C. Challis, "The Debasement of the Coinage, 1542–1551," *Economic History Review*, 2nd series, 20 (1967), 441–66.

1700–1701. no gentilmen of aunciente condicions] Cf. Jordan, I, 81: "The Edwardian Privy Council [during Seymour's Protectorate] is . . . remarkable . . . for the fact that its complexion is almost exclusively that of new men, of new families, of thrusting men whose fortunes were only being made."

1702. comens to make insurreccions] I fail to grasp Cavendish's allusion. It may be that he has in mind the rebellions in the West and in East Anglia in 1549 which were prompted by discontent over new parliamentary legislation, namely the introduction of the form of service prescribed by the Book of Common Prayer and the reinforcement of the laws against enclosures.

1703–4. the comens to haue suere ayd] After Somerset's second fall

COMMENTARY 209

from power he was denied the support of the Commons, which was prorogued by the Council. It finally met on January 23, 1552, the day after Somerset's death.

1705–18. shedyng of my brothers blood] On the death of Thomas Seymour, Baron Sudeley, Somerset's brother, see Commentary vv. 1488–627 passim. As is noted there, Somerset's culpability for his brother's death is much less great than Cavendish asserts. But there does seem to have been a general contemporary revulsion against Somerset for his brother's death; cf. Throckmorton:

> This Duke did bring
> His onlie brother to destruction;
> Wherefore our God, whoe hated much that thing,
> Did justlie send on him confusion,
> And, that noe letts might rise through policie,
> Hee turn'd man's witt to meere simplicitie. [st. 83]

1725. Twyse I was subdued] Somerset first fell from power in October in the aftermath of Kett's rebellion. He went to the Tower, but he was pardoned on February 18, 1550 and his estates were restored. By April of that year he was again a member of the Privy Council. He was rearrested on October 16, 1551, charged with treason.

1726–32. led to the barre] Somerset was tried before the Lords on December 1, 1551. A full account of his trial occurs in Cobbett, *State Trials*, I, 510–22.

1728. mak or to marre] Proverbial; cf. Whiting M 24. The same phrase occurs in *LW* 105/16.

1733–34. To hang lyke a Thefe] Hanging was the normal penalty and Somerset was so sentenced. But the sentence was subsequently altered to execution by beheading.

1745. My hed is lost] Somerset was beheaded on January 22, 1552 (Wriothesley, II, 65).

1754–67. Ffower knyghtes] The four knights who appear before Cavendish—Thomas Arundell, Michael Stanhope, Ralph Vane (or Fane), and Miles Partridge—were all charged with complicity in the alleged conspiracy of Somerset in October 1551. It was charged that Arundell, Vane, and Partridge were to assist in seizing the City and Tower of London. Stanhope, half-brother to Somerset's wife, was alleged to have been a messenger between them. All four were executed together on February 26, 1552. The evidence of their complicity is not uniformly strong, and, in Arundell's case, not even probable. For an assessment of these four and their degrees of probable guilt, see Jordan, II, 110–11. They all continued to protest their innocence to their deaths; cf. *Grey Friars Chronicle*, p. 74: "And theis iiij knyghttes confessyd that they ware never gylte for soche thynges as was layd unto their charge and dyde in that same oppinion." See also Wriothesley (II, 67) for a similar account of their deaths.

1768ff. Cavendish was personally acquainted with Arundell, who is mentioned in *LW* 104/22. After Wolsey's fall he appears to have acted as a messenger between the cardinal and the king.

1769–71. a yonger brother] Arundell was the second son of Sir John Arundell, knight baronet of Lanherne.

1772–74. Cardynall Wolsey] Arundell was brought up in Wolsey's household and became one of the gentlemen of his privy chamber. He was not however knighted until Anne Boleyn's coronation in 1533.

1775–79. Chauncylor . . . to Katheren Howard] I have been unable to find any support for Arundell's assertion that he was Catherine Howard's chancellor. Smith does describe him as "among the Howard satellites" (pp. 23–24). But *L&P* XV, 21, and XVI, 422, which list Catherine's household, describe Sir Anthony Denny as the Queen's chancellor.

1780–81. quen is dekayd] On the fall of Catherine Howard, see above, vv. 862–936.

1787–88. not . . . Gyltie] Arundell had been arrested on a charge of treason on either October 16 (Stow, *Annales*, p. 1023) or 17 (Wriothesley, II, 57), 1551. He was tried on January 28 (Wriothesley, II, 66). Clearly considerable pressure was put on the jury to return a guilty verdict. The diary of Henry Machyn gives the following account "The xxvij day of Januarij was reynyd sir Thomas Arundell knyght, and so the qwest cold nott fynd ym tyll the morrow after, and so he whent to the Towre agayn, and then the qwest wher shutt up tyll the morow with-out mett or drynke, or candylle or fyre, and on the morow he cam a-gayne, and the qwest qwytt hym of tresun, and cast hym of felony to be hangyd" (p. 15).

1789–95. The question of Arundell's treachery in the "first ouerthrowe" of Somerset appears to be based on a contemporary confusion that Singer was unable to resolve. He asserts that: "I am not aware [that] this circumstance of Sir Thomas Arundel being confederate formerly with Northumberland . . . is elsewhere recorded" (p. 126n.). *DNB*, although sceptical, quotes "Bishop Pouet": "Arundell conspired with that ambitious and subtil Alcibiades, the Earl of Warwick, after Duke of Northumberland, to pull down the good Duke of Somerset." The passage is actually from John Ponet's *A Short Treatise of Politic Power* (Strasbourg, 1556) and more accurate quotation from it clarifies matters: "& whan Wriothesley, Arundell and South=/well conspired with thambicious and subtil Alcibia=/des of England, the Erle of Warwike (afterwar=/de duke of Northumberland) to pull the good Duke of Somerset king Edwardes vncle and protectour out of his authoritie, and by forgeing a great meany of false lettres and lies to make the Protectour hated" (Sig. I iii^r). The context makes it clear that the reference must be to Henry Fitzalan, Earl of Arundel, who in conjunction with his fellow Catholics, Wriothesley and Southwell, gave Northumberland significant support in the first overthrow of Somerset.

But when the three names are again linked, Ponet, presumably through confusion, is clearly referring to Sir Thomas. After chronicling the decline of Wriothesley and Southwell he asserts: "And at therles [i.e. of Northumberland's] sute Arundel hathe his head with the axe divided from the shoulders" (Sig. I iii^v). Fitzalan actually survived Northumberland and arrested him on Mary's succession. Sir Thomas was himself in prison during Somerset's first fall, having been arrested on January 30, 1549, on suspicion of complicity in the Western rebellions of that year (*APC*, II, 376). He was not released until October 4, 1551 (*APC*, III, 378).

Clearly both Ponet and Cavendish are in error. The reason for their apparently independent confusion may lie in the fact that the Earl of Arundel was also sent to the Tower in November 1551, the date being given variously as November 6 (Wriothesley, II, 62), and November 8 (Machyn, p. 12).

1803–5. To be hanged] Although sentenced to be hanged, Arundell was beheaded, as was Stanhope (see *APC*, II, 484) on February 26, 1552. Vane and Partridge were hanged at the same time.

1810–14. a knyght] Michael Stanhope (d. 1552) was knighted in 1547 after the accession of Edward VI.

1815. prevye chamber] Stanhope is first described in surviving documents as "Chief Gentleman of the Privy Chamber" on August 15, 1549.

perhaps left inexplicit by design. The lines may be an indirect contemporaneous criticism of Northumberland's tenure of power. This possibility is strengthened by vv. 1826–27, which seem to imply a date before Mary's accession.

1828. fortunes whele] Proverbial; cf. Whiting F 506 and Tilley F 617. But his appointment may well have begun some considerable time before this, possibly from the beginning of Edward's reign. He is described on August 24 as having the "gouvernaunce" of the king (*APC*, II, 260).

1817–23. Some persons] The obliquity of this stanza is curious. The "some persons" alluded to must be Northumberland (Stanhope was himself arrested specifically on a charge of plotting Northumberland's death). The "purpose" which "did all honest hartes abhorre" (v. 1823) is perhaps left inexplicit by design. The lines may be an indirect contemporaneous criticism of Northumberland's tenure of power. This possibility is strengthened by vv. 1826–27, which seem to imply a date before Mary's accession.

1828. fortunes whele] Proverbial; cf. Whiting F 506 and Tilley F 617.

1830. hedlesse] Stanhope was arrested on either October 16 (Stow, *Annales*, p. 1023) or October 19 (Wriothesley, II, 58) and tried on February 9. He was "condempned for fellonie and had judgement to be hanged" (Wriothesley, II, 66). He was, however, beheaded (Wriothesley, II, 67).

1831–37. Too other knyghtes] Ralph Vane was knighted in 1544 and after Edward's accession was created knight banneret at Musselburgh in 1547. (The event is recorded in Edward's *Chronicle*, p. 8.) He was arrested on either October 16 (Stow, *Annales*, p. 1023; Machyn, p. 10) or October 18, 1551 (Wriothesley, II, 58), after trying to escape (Edward's *Chronicle*, pp. 88–89). On January 27, 1552 he "was condemned of felony in treason, answering like a ruffian" (ibid., p. 108) and hanged on February 26, 1552 (Wriothesley, II, 67).

Miles Partridge was knighted after Edward's accession at Roxburghe, on October 28, 1547. He was arrested on either October 16 (Stow, *Annales*, p. 1023) or October 17, 1551 (Edward's *Chronicle*, p. 89). He was hanged with Vane on February 26, 1552.

1838ff. Verse laments on the death of Edward are surprising both in number and chronological span. Cavendish's appears to be the earliest; there is an epitaph in the Arundel / Harington MS. [294]; one early broadside (*STC* 5229) survives, and possibly two other ballads from the period 1557–58, see E. Arber, *A Transcript of the Registers of the Stationers Company of London* (London, 1875), I, 75, 78. Later laments were composed by William Baldwin, *The Funeralles of King Edward the Sixth* (1560) and Thomas Churchyard in his *General Rehearsalle* (1579), Ee iij^v–iiij.

1844. in his tender age] The only other point at which Cavendish employs a refrain is vv. 2279–383. The phrase occurs in an anonymous undated broadside, "An Epitaph Vpon the Deth of Kyng Edward" (*STC* 5229).

1848–49. Sober . . . gravitie] Cf. the assessment of Hieronymus Cardano in October 1552: "when the gravity of a king was needful, he carried himself like an old man; and yet he was always affable and gentle as became his age" (quoted in Jordan, II, 409). See also below, vv. 1873ff.

1850–58. Yet deathe devoured hyme] Edward died of consumption on July 6, 1553; he was fifteen years and nine months old.

1859–61. Salomon's right heyer . . . Absolon in beawtie] The citation of worthies in part echoes Cavendish's epitaph on Henry VIII in the mention of Salomon (cf. v. 1444) and Absolon (cf. v. 1451). Bale describes Edward as "dicta plus quam Salamonice" (Nichols, *Remains*, I, cci).

1866–70. Alexander . . . Severe] The introduction of Alexander Severus in comparison to Edward is puzzling. He is briefly mentioned in *FP* VIII, 267–87, in highly uncomplimentary terms. I know of no contemporary source from which Cavendish could have derived his favorable view of Alexander.

1873–74. Wanton youthe . . . gravytie] Cf. "Epitaph": "So graue and so sage / So well learned and wittie"; and Arundel/Harington MS. [294], vv. 1–4:

> A pierlesse Prynce, of worthie weldinge witt
> Whose youthlye years, was rul'de by reasons skill
> In whome was learninge lodg'd / and knowledge fytt
> To guyd by wysdome / youthes vnconstant will.

1873–79. There are frequent contemporary testimonials to Edward's various kingly qualities; cf. the examples quoted in Nichols, *Remains*, I, cci, ccvi–vii.

1894–1900. Cavendish is here concerned to depict Edward as the embodiment of the negation of the seven deadly sins (in the order he cites them: pride, covetousness, envy, anger, gluttony, sloth, and lust).

1894. stryve] *E* reads *styve*, a form unsanctioned by the *OED*. I have adopted the *D* reading.

1904. is] *E* reads *are*. But the subject has to be *experyence*, which is unrecorded either in *OED* or *MED* as a plural form. Possibly Cavendish made the error because of confusion involving the plural form of the immediately preceding word, *matters*.

1926. Torned . . . solace] Cf. Whiting S 507.

1927–28. a mayden quene] The allusion to Mary as a *mayden quene* places this part of the *MV* before her marriage to Philip of Spain on July 25, 1554.

1929ff. A number of extant poems in praise of Mary's accession could have been known to Cavendish; e.g. William Forrest's "A New Ballad of the Marigold" (printed in *Harleian Miscellany*, X [1813], 254), John Seton's *Panegyrici in Victoriam Illustrissime D. Mariae* (1553, *STC* 22258), George Marshall's *A Compendiouse Treatise in metre declaring the first originall of Sacrifice* (1554, *STC* 17469) and Richard Beard's *A Godly Psalme of Mary Queene* (1553, *STC* 1655).

1929–36. many stormye showers] The vicissitudes of Mary's life before her accession are fully detailed in H. F. M. Prescott, *Mary Tudor*, rev. ed. (London: Eyre & Spottiswoode, 1952), especially ch. III–X passim.

1936–42. borne by iust dissent] For details of Henry VIII's will vesting the succession in Mary, and of Edward VI's *Deuise*, which was designed to frustrate this intention, see Commentary vv. 2020–34.

1937. lawfull quen] The legitimacy of Mary's claim is stressed by other contemporary versifiers who praised her accession; cf. Beard, *Godley Psalme*:

> The lawful, iust and rightuouse,
>   Of England, head, and Queene:
> To bee the true enheritoure,
>   As hathe her brother beene.
>
> Not clayming by collusion
>   Nor cloking it by sleyght

> But by her byrth, descending from
> Her godly father streight.
>
> She beeing eldest sister right
> Unto oure soueraigne Lord
> Kynge Edward late the syxt by name,
> Whose strength was gods trew word.

1942. Cf. Proverbs 21:1: "ita cor regis in manu Domini." Cavendish quotes elsewhere from Proverbs in *LW* 137/26–27.

1951. Wye dost thou rebell] The reference is to Wyatt's rebellion in January 1554; for full details of this episode see Loades, pp. 12–127, and Commentary vv. 2125–87.

1952. Maliciously abrode Scedycion to sowe] Many Protestants fled to the Continent, particularly to Germany, during Mary's reign, both to avoid persecution and to pursue their resistance to Mary's Catholic, pro-Spanish policies. These exiles printed and smuggled quantities of seditious pamphlets into England; see D. M. Loades, "The Press under the Early Tudors," *Transactions of the Cambridge Bibliographical Society*, 4, i (1964), 29–50, especially 35–42.

1953–56. To slaunder hir honor] The slanders Cavendish has in mind most probably relate to the unfavorable reaction in England to Mary's proposed marriage to Philip. On the various contemporary popular expressions of disquiet at the impending union see C. H. Firth, "Ballad History of the Later Tudors," *Transactions of the Royal Historical Society*, 3rd series, 3 (1909), 66–67.

1971–73. knyghtes . . . myght] The rhyme scheme at this point is defective: the *a* rhymes do not correspond.

1985–91. Clarkes old . . . tragedies] The reference is doubtless to Lydgate's *Fall of Princes*. Fifteenth- and sixteenth-century allusions to Lydgate often refer to him as a "clerk."

1994–98. This is a borrowing from *FP* VI, 871–75:

> His looke doun cast in tokne of sorwe & wo
> On his cheekis the salte teris lay,
> Whiche bar record off his dedli affray,—
> Wherfore, Bochas, do thi penne dresse
> To descryue his mortal heuynesse.

I am indebted to Mrs. E. Cox for drawing my attention to these lines.

2006. a duke . . . to dye] The reference is to the death of the Duke of Somerset (vv. 1642–746).

2009. for ffellony] On Somerset's condemnation on charges of felony, see vv. 1726–32.

2012. knyghtes fower . . . Tower Hyll] Sir Thomas Arundell, Sir Michael Stanhope, Sir Ralph Vane, and Sir Miles Partridge were executed on Tower Hill on February 26, 1552, on charges of complicity with the Duke of Somerset.

2013–19. Ffroward ambycyon] There is no adequate biography of John Dudley, Duke of Northumberland. For a useful account of his rise to power see B. L. Beer, "The Rise of John Dudley, Duke of Northumberland," *History Today*, 15 (1965), 269–77, which surveys his increasing influence up to the death of Henry VIII. The son of Edmund Dudley (executed by Henry VIII in 1510), he emerged as a successful soldier in the 1530s and was created Viscount Lisle in March 1542. In 1543 he became Lord Admiral and a member of the Privy Council. After Edward's accession he was created Earl of Warwick. For an assessment of his role in the first overthrow of Somerset in 1549, see Commentary vv. 1558–71. After Somerset's fall Northumberland emerged as the de facto head of the administrative structure. He was created Duke of Northumberland on October 11, 1551. His role in the final destruction of Somerset is examined in Jordan, II, 70–115. For an assessment of his later career, rebellion, and death, see W. K. Jordan and M. R. Gleason, "The Saying of John, Late Duke of Northumberland upon the Scaffold, 1553," *Harvard Library Bulletin*, 23 (1975), 139–79.

2020–33. gouerne most lykest a kyng] Henry VIII's will, in 1547, vested the succession in (in order) Mary and Elizabeth Tudor; Frances, Duchess of Suffolk, and her daughters, Jane, Catherine, and Mary Grey; and Margaret Clifford.

As Edward's health declined in early 1553, efforts were made, either by Edward himself or in collusion with Northumberland, to alter this order of succession. The result was a "Device" excluding Mary and Elizabeth from the succession, otherwise preserving the order of Henry's will, but vesting the succession in the male heirs of those named. Subsequently this was altered to bring Jane herself into direct line of succession. Meanwhile, on May 21 Northumberland had laid his claim to the succession by marrying his son Guilford Dudley to Jane. For full details of the succession documents see S. T. Bindoff, "A Kingdom at Stake, 1553," *History Today*, 3 (1953), 642–48.

2025. lond] Both *E* and *D* read *land*, destroying the rhyme scheme. The error may have been caused by catching from below to the corresponding point in the next stanza, where v. 2032 reads *land*.

2027–30. This is a borrowing from *FP* III, 4110–13:

> He hadde a douhtir yonge & tendir of age,
> Which of the peeple stood in gret fauour;
> And he hym caste to yiue hir in mariage
> To a yong kniht, sone of a senatour.

2034–39. This is a borrowing from *FP* III, 2654–59:

> For he presumed bi vsurpacioun,
> In Perse and Mede to quench the cleere liht,
> And trouble the lyne off iust successioun;
> For as he off force and nat off riht,
> Nothyng rasemblyng to a trewe knyht,
> The moordre off Xerses falsli dede ordeyne.

2039–40. To subdue the lawfull quene] Jane Grey was proclaimed queen in succession to Edward on July 10, 1553.

2041–47. Two days after the proclamation of Jane as queen, Mary Tudor was herself proclaimed in East Anglia. On July 14 Northumberland, with the support of the Council, set out to confront her. As Holinshed reports: "the longer the Duke lingered in his voyage, the ladie Marie, the more increased in puissance, the heartes of the people being mightily bent vnto hir" (p. 1718). Mary's support increased rapidly. The Council, in London, perceiving the mood of the country, proclaimed her queen on July 19, repudiating Northumberland. He retreated to Cambridge, where many of his supporters deserted him. On July 24 he surrendered to the Earl of Arundel. The following day he was committed to the Tower.

2048–54. This is a borrowing from *FP* III, 2248–54:

> But thilke Lord that can the meeke enhaunse,
> And from ther sees the proude putte doun,

> And namli them that haue no remembraunse
> To aduertise off wisdam and resoun,
> To knowe the Lord, most myhti off renoun,—
> The Lord off Lordis, which, pleynli to compile,
> Will suffre tirantis to regne but a while.

2055–61. This is a borrowing from *FP* III, 3991–97:

> For tirannye and fals oppressioun
> Causeth princis to stonde in gret hatreede.
> And what is worth ther domynacioun,
> Withoute loue lat preue it at a neede?
> Men for a tyme may suffre hem weel & dreede;
> But whan that dreed constreyned is & goone
> Than is a prince but a man allone.

2055. Cruell murder and falce oppression] Certainly Northumberland's rule, from his suppression of insurrection in the summer of 1549, was marked by an increasingly stringent attack on all those whose behaviour could be taken to imply any disagreement with those in authority. For an excellent survey of this aspect of Northumberland's administration, see Jordan, II, 427–34.

2062–68. This is a borrowing from *FP* III, 3998–4004:

> Seeth an exaumple how Malleus of Cartage,
> For al his castellis & toures maad of stonis,
> For his oppressioun, vengaunce and outrage,
> The peeple of Affrik ros on hym al attonys,
> And hew assonder his flessh & eek his bonys,
> Caste hem pleynli, on hym thei wer so wood,
> Vnto ther goddis to offren up his blood.

"Malleus" was Machaeus, Duke of Carthage.

2069–75. This is a borrowing from *FP* III, 2402–8:

> This was the first myscheeff and the dreed
> In which that Xerses the myhti prynce, stood.

COMMENTARY

> Heer men mai see, such as list take heed,
> How geri Fortune furious and wood,
> Wil nat spare, for richesse nor for good,
> Mihti pryncis, which list nat God to knowe,
> From ther estatis to brynge hem doun ful lowe.

2076–82. This is a borrowing from *FP* III, 2598–604:

> What myhte auaile the grete couetise
> Off kyng Xerses in his estaat roial?
> Or the gret peeple, which ye han herd deuise,—
> Ten hundred thousand;—the peeple was nat smal.
> But, for al that, he hadde an hidous fal,
> Whan that he was, as is toforn remembrid,
> On pecis smale pitousli dismembrid.

2083–89. My seade . . . brought to distruccion] In fact there were few reprisals against Northumberland's family. Of his *seade* only his son Guildford Dudley was executed, in the aftermath of Wyatt's rebellion, on February 12, 1554. The remaining members of his family enjoyed general prosperity in the ensuing reign. John Dudley, Earl of Warwick, died in 1554 and was succeeded by his brother Ambrose (d. 1590). Henry Dudley died in France in 1555. Robert Dudley became Earl of Leicester and the favorite of Elizabeth I.

2088. twynklyng of an eye] Proverbial; cf. Whiting T 547, Tilley T 635.

2088–89. ffortune . . . hye] Proverbial; cf. Whiting F 523, Tilley F 606.

2090–96. This is a borrowing from *FP* III, 2738–44:

> Off ther eende what sholde I mor endite,
> Nor off ther deth make a digressioun?
> God mai his vengaunce a while weel respite,
> But moordre will out, & al such fals tresoun.
> And for Artaban hadde a condicioun,
> Falsli to moordre, as ye toforn haue seyn,
> With onwar moordre he guerdonyd was ageyn.

2090. my ende] For an account of Northumberland's trial on charges of treason, see Cobbett, *State Trials*, I, 766–67.

2104–10. Northumberland was executed on August 22, 1553.

2120. betyll blynd] Proverbial; Whiting B 180a, Tilley B 219.

2125–26. a duke . . . Of Suffolke] Henry Grey (d. 1554) was created Duke of Suffolk on October 4, 1551. He came to prominence in Edward's reign as a supporter of Northumberland, becoming a member of the Privy Council and Warden of the Northern Marches. His chief importance seems not to have lain in his political abilities, which seem to have been negligible (Jordan characterizes him as "the most stupid of peers," I, 373), but in the claim of his daughter to the succession, which aroused first the interest of Thomas Seymour and then of Northumberland.

2133. quene] As Sylvester points out, "genitives without *s* are frequent in Cavendish [in *LW*]" (p. 195). This appears to be the only occurrence in *MV*.

whome she called cosyn] Grey was connected to the royal family by his marriage to Frances, elder daughter of Charles Brandon, Duke of Suffolk and Mary Tudor, Henry VIII's younger sister; see further *DNB*, s.v. "Grey, Henry, Duke of Suffolk."

2134–35. I myght . . . Delyuerd my doughter] Suffolk's daughter, Jane Grey (vv. 2209–71 and Commentary), had been condemned for treason on November 14, 1553. But before Wyatt's rebellion her reprieve remained a possibility. Grafton's *Chronicle* observes that the deaths of her and her husband "were ye rather hastened, for that the Duke of Suffolk father to this ladie, had of late . . . reysed a newe sturre and commotion in his Countrie . . . which was the shortening of her life, who else was lyke ynough to haue bene pardoned" (II, 543). Similar views are expressed in the more contemporary *Cooper's Chronicle* (f. 363) and in Stow's *Annales* (p. 1054).

2139–45. fond enterprice] Suffolk had joined the conspirators in Sir Thomas Wyatt's proposed rebellion in December 1553. His role in the rebellion was to raise Leicestershire, supplementing risings in Hertfordshire, Kent, and Devon. For details of the plan of the rising, see Loades, p. 21.

2146–49. I Claymed and proclaymed . . . the title . . . of my doughter Iane] Historically this is one of the more interesting assertions in the *MV*. It is probably the earliest account to assert that Suffolk proclaimed his daughter. It is later echoed by *Cooper's Chronicle* (f. 362^{r-v}) and in Grafton's *Chronicle* (II, 539). It would seem probable that the assertions of both Cavendish and Cooper reflect contemporary rumors circulated as government propaganda. Loades quotes a letter sent to the sheriff and justices of Gloucestershire on January 28, 1554, asserting that Suffolk "pretending upon false promises that the Prince of Spain and the Spaniards should come over to conquer this said realm while indeed [he] traytorously purpose[s] to advance Lady Jane Grey his daughter" (p. 28). The assertion is explicitly denied by Holinshed, who seems to have been aware of such rumors (p. 1733).

2150–52. my trust . . . decrease and wane] Suffolk left London on January 25 to initiate his part in the rebellion. On the following day he was proclaimed traitor. In consequence he seems to have attracted little support in his advance on Leicester and Coventry. Indeed, in Coventry, where he had some expectation of support, he found the city gates closed against him. He then retreated to his manor at Astley and disbanded his retainers. His role in the abortive rising is recounted in Holinshed (p. 1726) and *Chronicle of Queen Jane* (pp. 122–26).

2153–59. Than was I pursewed] Grafton reports that Suffolk "fledde from thence to a Manor of his called Astley sixe miles from Couentry, and committed himselfe to a man of his being keeper of his park, called Nicholas Lawrence, the which keeper bestowed the Duke his Maister in a hollow Oke within the saide parke, where he remained two or three days vndiscovered, vntill the sayde keeper . . . disclosed his case" (II, 539).

2160–62. brought to the barre] Suffolk was tried on February 17, 1553 and found guilty. For an account of his trial and execution, see Cobbett, *State Trials*, I, 762–63, and Commentary vv. 2164–66.

2164–66. I excused me] It is reported that at his trial Suffolk argued that

yt was no treason for a pere of the realme as he was to raise his power and make proclamacion onely to avoyde strangers out of the realme; and therapon he axed the sergeantes standing by whether yt was not soo or no, which they being abashed, they could not say yt was treason by eny lawe. Then ytt was laidd to his chardge he mett with CC men the quenes levetenaunt in armes, being the erle of Huntingdon, which was a treason agaynst the quene, forasmuch as the saide levetenaunt represented hir own person. To the which he made answer that he knewe not the said earle to be no such levetenant. "But," saith he, "I met him indede but with fyfty men or ther aboutes, and wolde not have shronken from him yf I had had fewer." And by theis wordes he confessed himself gilty of treason.

[*Chronicle of Queen Jane*, pp. 60–61]

2167–73. Down to the bloke] Suffolk was beheaded on February 23, 1554 on Tower Hill. For an account of his death, see *Chronicle of Queen Jane*, pp. 63–64.

2174–75. lady Ffraunces . . . of the blood Royall] Suffolk's wife, Frances, was the eldest daughter of Charles Brandon, Duke of Suffolk, and Mary Tudor, Henry VIII's younger sister.

2181–84. my bretherne] Suffolk's two brothers, Sir Thomas Grey and John Grey, joined him in Wyatt's conspiracy. Thomas was tried on charges of treason on March 9, 1554. He pleaded in his defense that "he meant none other thing but the abolyshing of strangers" (*Chronicle of Queen Jane*, p. 67). He was executed on April 27 (ibid., p. 75). John Grey was arraigned on February 20 (*Chronicle of Queen Jane*, p. 63). His trial began on May 27 (Machyn, p. 64). He pleaded guilty and was condemned on June 11; however, he was released on October 30 and pardoned in January of the following year (*Chronicle of Queen Jane*, p. 77).

2202. that tender was of age] Born in October 1537, Jane Grey was sixteen at the time of her death.

2210. As thoughe] the phrase presents some difficulty as it stands in *E*. The line invites the assumption that direct speech begins after *quod she*: "She taught me to write [what she said] by signs, *as though she spoke*." But Cavendish's practice elsewhere in the *MV* seems invariably to have been to use *quod she* (*he*, etc.) after direct speech has begun, not preceding it. Thus the phrase seems to demand to be punctuated in accordance with his habits: "As though," quod she, "Why did ye me disseyve," which does not make sense. The *D* scribe has perceived the problem and attempted to resolve it by changing *As thoughe* to *Alas*. But since the manuscript does make sense, even if at odds with Cavendish's demonstrable usage elsewhere, I have retained it with some reservations.

2218. iust enherytaunce] The basis for Jane's succession is outlined above; see Commentary vv. 2020–33.

2221–22. Me to delude] Jane insisted upon her incomprehension of the events that made her queen. In her dying speech from the scaffold, she protested that, in accepting the crown, "I consented to the thing which I was enforced unto, constraint making the law believe I did that which I never understood" (*Literary Remains*, p. 53).

2222. you] *E* reads *your*, a clear error. *D* intelligently emends to *ye*. But *you* appears likely to have been the intended form since it is homeographically closer to the incorrect reading.

not worthe a strawe] Proverbial; cf. Whiting S 805, Tilley S 917.

2223–29. poor innocent] Certainly rumor seems to have maintained that Jane in accepting the crown was acting under the influence of others; cf. e.g. *Ballads from MSS*, pp. 427, 430. Jane herself contended that she acted in unwitting innocence; cf. *Literary Remains*, pp. 47–48.

2239. haue] *E* omits this word, which has been supplied from *D*. There is no precedent in *MV* for allowing the past participle to stand as the main verb, and such an omission is in any case characteristic of Cavendish's tendencies to scribal error.

2244–50. your pride and . . . presumpcion] The reference is to Northumberland's efforts to secure the succession as designated in Edward's "Device."

2253. my father] On the death of Jane's father, the Duke of Suffolk, see Commentary vv. 2125–87.

my hosbond] Jane's husband, Guilford Dudley, was executed with her on February 12, 1554.

2258–64. lord of lordes] Jane's final days do seem to have been marked by piety and Christian devotions; cf. e.g. the prayer she composed shortly before her execution (*Literary Remains*, pp. 49–51).

2265. lady mother] Frances Grey, Duchess of Suffolk, died on November 20, 1559.

2266. my systers] Catherine and Mary Grey. Catherine died on January 27, 1568, and Mary on June 1, 1578.

2279ff. Following v. 2278 in *E* occur two cancelled stanzas, the beginnings of a discontinued addition. It is difficult to be certain what "rowt" Cavendish intended to present. But assuming the abortive addition to be coterminous with the preceding tragedies, it would seem probable that he intended to recount the fates of others executed as a consequence of Wyatt's rebellion.

The epitaph on Queen Mary was written some months after the main body of the text of the *MV* had been transcribed into *E*, and probably some years after it had been originally composed. It seems likely that it was composed as an immediate response to the event and copied directly into *E*, perhaps after the text had been bound.

Melpomene] The classical muse of tragedy; she is not mentioned in *FP*.

2280. thy Systers all] i.e. the other eight muses.

2281. Niobe] Niobe was traditionally a stock figure of bereavement.

2283. Blake be your habettes dyme and ffunerall] Cf. *FP* VI, 869: "Blak his weed & his habite also." Cavendish borrows from this stanza earlier in the *MV*; cf. vv. 1994–98.

2287. doughter of tyme] The motto *veritas filia temporis* was the personal motto of Mary Tudor. For a discussion of this motto (which does not, however, mention its use by Cavendish), see D. J. Gordon, "*Veritas Filia Temporis*: Hadrianus Junius and Geoffrey Whitney," *Journal of the Warburg Institute*, 3 (1939–40), 228–40.

2289. a virgyn cleare] *Cleare* may perhaps be an error for *cleane*; cf. v. 1927, *a virgyn clean*.

2293–96. hir vasselles rebelles] Cavendish presumably has in mind the rebellions of Wyatt in 1554 and Sir Henry Dudley and John Throgmorton in 1556.

2294. The qualities Cavendish here ascribes to Mary seem to be his version of the four cardinal virtues (justice, prudence, courage, temperance). Stress on these virtues suggests a rhetorical influence on Cavendish's elegy; see A. L. Bennett, "The Rhetorical Conventions of the Renaissance Personal Elegy," *Studies in Philology*, 51 (1954), 107–26, especially 114–16, where a number of instances of this convention are cited.

2297–98. With losse of fewe] Wyatt's rebellion resulted in probably "well under a 100" executions (Loades, p. 114). In the rebellion of Dudley and Throgmorton there were only thirteen trials, resulting in eight executions (ibid., pp. 227–31).

2300–306. Cavendish's account of the reasons for Mary's marriage to Philip is more fulsome than factual. Actually, Mary was always inordinately eager for the marriage; see Prescott, *Mary Tudor*, pp. 219–25, for details.

2307–8. The Roos and pomgranatt] The rose and pomegranate are the royal flowers of England and Spain; cf. Forrest's *History of Griseld the Second*, which links the image of these flowers specifically to Mary:

> O Mary mayden, By lyneall descent
> spronge of the fresche and sweete Rose rubycounde,
> In florischinge yeares when hee was content
> withe the Pomegarnet on stawlke to bee founde . . .

2309–10. blossomes came non] The sterility of the union is scarcely surprising since Mary was over forty at the time of her marriage to Philip. She did experience one false pregnancy.

2311–12. a Comyt envied] The comet appeared in March 1556. Accounts of its appearance occur (among other places) in *Cooper's Chronicle*, f. 372^v, and Machyn, p. 101. Mary did not die, however, until two years later.

2314–20. faded the flower] Mary died on November 17, 1558.

2338–40. gratuyte] Cavendish presumably has in mind such evidence of Mary's *gratuyte* as the release of Thomas Howard, Earl of Norfolk, and the restoration of his rank and lands immediately after her accession. He may also be alluding to the release from the Tower and elevation to the rank of earl, of the imprisoned Edward Courtenay, grandson of Edward IV. A contemporary "Epitaph upon . : . Quene Marie" echoes Cavendish's praise of this aspect of Mary's reign: "How many noble men restorde, and other states also, / Well shewd her princely liberall hart, which gaue both frend and fo" (*Harleian Miscellany*, X [1813], 259).

2342. Paule appostolike] Pope Paul IV, who died August 18, 1559.

2342–62. These lines were omitted in D, doubtless because their pro-Catholic sympathies were felt to be too vehement for the prevailing religious climate of Elizabeth's reign.

2349–55. restored the right Religion] Mary's reestablishment of Catholicism was far less conclusive than Cavendish allows. Her first Parliament repealed the religious reformations of Edward's reign and all the treason laws associated with them. She was unable to obtain parliamentary consent for the restoration of church lands or of papal authority. The Protestant persecutions began a month after the dissolution of Parliament in February 1555.

2356–62. Cf. the similar description of the state of England on Mary's accession in George Marshall, *A Compendious Treatise* (1554):

> The Churche, the aulter & Gods sacred bodye
> They robbed & spoiled, and their faith did denie

> Lyke desperate wretches, thus played they their parte
> All was forlorne, tyll good Queen Mary
> Restored them agayne to gods honour & glorye
>
> The sacramentes of ye churche was new to begin
> Adulterie & sacrilege was counted for no sinne
> Nor ye telling of offices, to mayntayne briberye
> The belles they plucked downe by subtill pretence
> To coyn therof testers, grotes and eke pence,
> Thus al came to nought, til good quene Mary
> Began to raygne . . . [C iii^v]

2367. Deathe is . . . vnyuersall] Proverbial; not in Whiting; cf. Tilley D 142, and *MV* v. 1416.

2368. The world is but vayn] Proverbial; cf. Whiting W 664; not in Tilley.

2384–90. Crepe forthe my boke] This is Cavendish's variation on the "Go little book" conceit that occurs frequently in medieval poetry. The most famous English example is perhaps the epilogue to Chaucer's *Troilus and Criseyde*, V, 1786ff. For a useful survey of post-Chaucerian uses of this conceit, see R. J. Schoeck, "'Go Little Book'—A Conceit from Chaucer to William Meredith," *Notes and Queries*, 197 (1952), 370–72.

2393. quakyng hand] A recurrent image in Lydgate; see the examples cited in D. Pearsall, *John Lydgate* (London: Routledge & Kegan Paul, 1970), p. 145.

2398–404. These lines are omitted in *D*.

2413. sugred eloquence] Cf. *FP* I, 461, which refers to "sugred aureat licour" as the proper language of tragedy.

2419. commest in to the prease] The phrase to "put in press" (i.e. "join the throng") is a common one in medieval literature; cf. D. Pearsall, *The Flower and the Leaf and The Assembly of Ladies* (London: Thomas Nelson 1962), p. 152, for references.

APPENDIX

Appendix: Variant Readings in MS Dugdale 28

The list printed below comprises all the substantive variant readings in *D*, together with those variants that are orthographically significant (i.e. where change in spelling affects rhyme and/or may affect meaning). All contractions have been expanded.

3. Gemynys] Gemini
6. Lion] Leo
   in] *adds* my
22. thyng] thynges
25. spend] spent
29. to] or
33. attise] entyse
36. shall] should
42. dothe] doe
47. Ociosite] occassion
57. toke] take
60. made] maketh
63. An^1] A
    an^2] a
69. that] which
70. tempor] set to
71. Nowe] Then
    that] the
72. thyng] thinges
75. mervell] mervals
88. begynnyng] begynn
94. crease] increase
96. avaumced] advance
105. me] *om.*
114. that] *om.*
118. so^2] *om.*
119. flauours] savors
133. worshpfull] worshipfull
137. masse] massye
140. in^2] *om.*
141. legantyn] legatyve
147. so] *om.*
150. rathest] soonest
151. blent] blynd
154. hate] hated
170. ye] youe
188. and] an
198. quykly] quyetlye
211. caught] tooke
226. that] which
249. Or] Our
253. you] *om.*
254. seruaunt] servantes
265. wond] wound

APPENDIX

293. thynges] thing
297. in] *om.*
298. eschewe] exthwe
307. it] *om.*
313. to you be] be to youe
330. hart] their
331. fable] fall
341. the] *om.*
345. chauance] chance
    cryng] crying
353. be] me *with* be *written above line*
    highly] me *written above line*
362. myddes] mydd
365. thyng] thynges
368. of] *adds* my
371. that I] my
374. dissimulaunce] dissimulacoun
381. woll] wyll
398. that] *om.*
407. not fearyng] *om.*
412. and²] nowe
416. loved] soved
427. lust] *adds* but
434. chamce] chance
436. restrayn] refrayne
441. w^t i] with
442. approced] approched
443. hathe] had
455. commiythe] cometh
486. Chapleyn] chappell
487. lowted] looked
498. hyght] highe
513. fortossed] sore tossed
546. and] *om.*
552. all them] them all
588. wold] will
589. well] wayle
599. bast] best
608. sides] sedes
621. a] or
652. playn] *om.*
676. insacyat] vnsaciat
703. as] at
714. theme] *adds* the
734. hathe] *adds* an
735. ye] yowe
744. Ffordulled] sore dulled
754. lyst] lust
759. To] of
763. therfore] therof

765. ye] yowe
767. can it not] cannot yt
772. bryttell] brickle
776. ffame] shame
784. least] best
803. nowe] *om.*
829. flykkeryng] fickering
835. in] *om.*
842. ye] youe
844. for] *om.*
846. ye] youe
857. me] my
860. Whiche] who
877. bryttill] brickle
884. appetites] appetite
896. cause and ground] ground and cause
914. sote] swet
918. quod she] *om.*
920. ne] can
921. my²] the
    shall] will
922. perchauance] perchance
930. that] *om.*
950. folowed] followe
    woll] will
969. *om.*] Who praid me in most
    lamentable mone
972. Morlas] Molayes
975. my] myne
977. Withoutten] without any
990. ne] never
994. ride] rode
995. whiche] who
1004. or] and
1006. Ne] Never
1010. Pasiua] Pasiphane
1014. flowryng] florisshing
1027. Ne] Do not
1035. ye] yowe
1036. list] lust
1039. you] ye
1041. nowther] either
1053. Ffor] of
1063. thus] this
1067. non] no
    ne] nor
1087. it] *om.*
1088. shoke] tooke
1090. not] never
1096. that] the

APPENDIX

1100. dissimuled] dissembled
1110. in myn] *om.*
1111. tourne] *adds* she (*deleted in E*)
1132. the not] not the
1133. of] *om.*
     coen] comon
1139. lyst] lust
1142. or] nor
1145. nobles] noblenes
1147. somme] *om.*
1153. make] to
1157. ye] youe
1160. and²] or
1162. endowed] indewed
1164. coen] comon
1167. and] *adds* had
1170. exaltacion] estymacoun
1174. them] suche
1187. Ye] youe
1191. them] *om.*
1202. will] woll
1221. shake] quake
1224. trome] trompe
     shyrll] shryll
1239. ye] youe
1256. approced] approched
1262. brent] bent
1268. renome] renowne
1277. there is nothyng] nothyng is
1281. Whiche] Wherof
1282. brent] bent
1286. so long shold] should so long
1291. cannot] canne no
1293. that²] which
1296. faynted] faynting
1299. Thoughe] thou
1304. woll] will
1315. bond] band
1334. my] myne
1344. thyng] thinges
1349. and] or
1367. a stile to wright] *deleted and replaced by* wordes to resyte
1370. hyr] *adds* in
     there] *om.*
1392. thyng] thinges
1400. Ffarwell] *adds* my
1402. wont] *adds* to
1410. Properously] prosperously
1411. Coen] comon

1418. none] no
1434. didest] dyd
1435. viii^th] viii
1437. Tenthe] Truth
1439. Herculus] Hercules
1445. Arthore] Arthure
1452. An] in
1460. Caton] Cato
1468. progeny] *adds* a
1472. for thyn] far worthy
1475. within] with
1485. non other stede] reade
1517. or] nor
     nother] neither
1525. non²] no
1534. hathe a] haue
1539. me] *adds* to
1544. pretenced] pretended
1568. precell] excell
1572. beare] bore
1576. mystruttyng] mistrusting
1583. full] *om.*
1585. derayn] to rayne
1587. see] skye
1588. Whos] Of whos
1595. thyng] thinges
1602. treu] then
1609. Ye] yowe
1649. momentany] momentarye
1652. world] wold
1653. the²] in
     ye] yowe
1654. a] *om.*
1661. an] a
1681. thes] those
1689. the] *om.*
1705. must] most
1708. for] *om.*
1727. raygned] areigned
1758. whilest] while
1759. ye] yowe
1760. or] before
1779. I than] then I
1786. right wyse] righteous
1791. ye] youe
1799. Thought] thoughe
1800. Ye] youe
1809. ye] youe
1826. woll] will
1829. ye] youe

1831. knyghtes] knyges
1835. gate] gave
1840. to] *om.*
1894. styve] stryve
1898. Gloteny] envy
1904. are] ys
1913. ye] youe
1926. to] into
1938. it] as
1943. ordened hyr] her ordeyned
1946. is] *adds* a
1956. Ffor] far
    Coen] comon
1960. nobles] noblenes
1963. commyt] omyt
1990. lyst] lust
1998. playnt] playntes
2004. stade] stoode
2009. convented] convicted
2015. gouernnce] governance
2062. Mallions] Mallios
2065. on hyme all at oons] all on hym at once
2071. lyst] lust
2074. lyst] lust
2113. seage] stage
2132. nedyd] moved
2137. All that] alas
2140. byng] bring
2157. no lenger myght] might no longer
2159. errant] arrant
2177. Whiche] who
2182. of] if

2197. so^2] and
2210. As thoughe] Alas
2222. yo^2] ye
2229. woll] will
2237. dynyties] dignityes
2239. To] *adds* haue
    the] *om.*
2243. no] any
2259. ihearcheyes] sterry skyes
2268. allmyght] Almighty
    Lord] God
2274. haue made] make
2276. cowld] can
2278. beyng so late] of so many
2294. hyghe] *om.*
2299. O^2] and
2304. Virginites] virgynes
2331. ioyntes] poyntes
2334. honououre] honor
2342–62. *om.*
2368. your] thy
2372. send] make
2373. contynaunce] contynewance
2375. O^2] our
2376. Haue mercy on Marie] Save Elyzabeth
2377–83. *om.*
2393. vnnethe can] can scarsely
2396. sathe] saieth
2397. well] good
2398–404. *om.*
2405. my] *om.*
2406. that^2] which

GLOSSARY

Glossary

This glossary is not an exhaustive word-list. It seeks only to record words or forms likely to present particular difficulty to the modern reader. No attempt has been made to record typical sixteenth-century orthographic variations. Initial *ff* has been treated as *f*.

abasshed   *adj*. ashamed (2390)
above   *n*. superior position (1110)
abusion   *n*. corrupt action (942)
aduert   *v*. contemplate, consider (263)
affare   *adv*. afar (394)
allyaunce   *n. pl*. allies (1389)
alyes   *n. pl*. paths (118)
appall   *v*. lessen, impair (1310)
arowe   *n*. a row (925)
arras   *n*. tapestry (120)
atchyved   *pp*. achieved (1138)
attaynt   *ppl. a*. attainted (2106)
attise   *v*. entice (33)
auctier   *n*. author, cause (568)
avoultrie   *n*. adultery (329)
avoyd   *v*. depart (198)
ayed   *n*. aid (1389)

bankettyng   *pp. a*. banquetting (1379)
basse   *adj*. base (1165)
bast   *n*. bastard (599)
baudye   *adj*. coarse (44)
bayle   *n*. affliction (12)
beatyfie   *v*. beautify (111)
bedropped   *adj*. tear-stained (1251)

behavor   *n*. behavior (828)
behove   *n*. need (18)
benyng   *adj*. benign (2388)
berd   *n*. beard (1237)
besen   *ppl. a*. regarded (450)
besspraynt   *ppl. a*. stained (401)
bewepte   *ppl. a*. disfigured by tears (859)
blase   *v*. to emblazon (2334)
blent   *ppl. a*. brought low (151)
blount   *a*. blunt (1841)
blowen (owt)   *v*. spread abroad (810)
boote, bootte   *n*. remedy, alternative (617, 915, 1418)
boote   *n*. boat (2399)
boted, botyth(e)   *ppl. & v*. availed, helped (756, 1093, 1265, 2169)
brake   *n*. snare, trap (1220)
brayd   *v*. utter a loud cry (517)
brent   *v*. brandished (1282)
brewte   *n*. reputation (996)
byse   *n*. light-blue paint (106)
bytt   *n*. bite (1854)

caier   *n*. care (1072)
cepture   *n*. scepter (2364)

235

chekemate, chekmate *n.* (say, sayd, saythe, gave, byd chekmate) to call a stop to life (161, 641, 1092, 1237, 1267, 1912)
chere *n.* understanding (332), expression (702), cheerfulness (1379)
cloos *adv.* hidden (1947)
color, coloure *n.* pretense (465), appearance (1322)
colored *v.* misrepresented (1320), disguised (1322)
coloure *v.* conceal (1320)
combred *ppl. a.* rendered incapable (286)
confuse *adj.* confused (2361)
congruence *n.* (of congruence) as is fitting, appropriate (1961)
connyng *n.* skill (108)
contrariaunt *adj.* irreconcilable (1277)
contrarious *adj.* hostile, opposed to (1007), perverse (1714)
contynaunce *n.* continuity (2373)
convented *ppl. a.* summoned on a charge (2009)
cooper *adj.* copper (226)
couert *adj.* deceitful (704, 2231)
couetous *n.* covetousness (1895, 2018)

dalyaunce *n.* leisure (1388)
date *n.* (torned hir date) proceeded to a new phase of time (350)
daynger *v.* to endanger (569)
deface, defaced, defaces, defacyth *v. & ppl.* mar, spoil (1328), stained (909), impairs (1204), destroy (326)
defamed *ppl. a.* disgraced (1338)
defuse *a.* obscure (1975)
degest, degested *v. & pp.* recover from (1243), reflected upon (1427)
dekay, dekayes *n.* ruin (488, 1499, 1630, 2181), disrepute (928)
dele, dell *n.* part (1135), whit (768)
deprave *v.* to stain (1149)
derayn *v.* to pour (1585)
deryved *v.* caused (1588)
detecte *v.* accuse (1522), divulge (651)
detected *ppl. a.* stained (776)
devysis *n. pl.* fashions (248)
discharge *v.* deprive of (153)
discommendable *a.* worthy of censure (1012)

dispight *n.* envy (205), malice (1659)
disport *n.* amusement (357)
dissimuled *ppl. a.* false (1100)
dities, dyties *n. pl.* songs (66, 67)
dobbyd *ppl. a.* invested with knighthood (1811)
doble *a.* duplicitous (87)
dole, doole *n.* lament (58, 631, 2208)
dombpe, dompe *n.* amazement (1223), reverie (1481)
dompe *v.* to be downcast (241)
dought *n.* fear (212)
doughtyd, doughtyng *pr. & pp.* afraid of (147, 212)
druge *n.* simpling (1672)
dulce *adj.* sweet (118)
duskyth *v. pr.* dims (223)
dynne *v.* to dine (122)

egere *adj.* bitter (600)
empier *n.* empire (1134)
enbanked *ppl. a.* surrounded (116)
endewed *v. pt.* endowed (282)
enknotted *ppl. a.* laid out in elaborate designs (117)
ensewe *v.* follow (296), follow behind (1746)
entaylled *ppl. a.* carved (108)
eterne *adj.* eternal (2323)
extort *adj.* extortionate (676)

fact, factes *n. & n. pl.* action(s) (1607, 1717)
fare *adv.* far (1373)
farre *n.* fare (2400)
feoble *adj.* feeble (905)
ferme *adj.* firm (2353)
fillt *pp.* felt (1375)
flee *v. pt.* flie (684)
fflees *n.* thread (1303)
force *n.* physical strength (1454)
ffordulled *pp. a.* very dulled (744), spiritless (1219)
forthy *conj.* therefore (1472)
forthynke *v. pt.* regret (361)
fortossed *ppl. a.* very tired (513)
fulfilled *adj.* full of (250)
fulfyll *v. pt.* occupy (367)
fyble *adj.* feeble (1890)

GLOSSARY 237

fyne, fynne *v.* to come to an end, die (565, 1513)
fyned *ppl. a.* completed (1303)
fynne *adj.* fine (120)

gall *n.* sensitive spot (205)
garnysht *pp.* decorated (120)
gery *adj.* fickle (2072)
gratuyte *n.* graciousness (2338)
graved *pp.* buried (2187)
greave, greves *n. & n. pl.* grief, griefs (1426, 1712)

hard *pp.* heard (1735)
hatfull *adj.* hateful (531)
hault *adj.* haughty (204)
heares *n. pl.* hairs (1120)
here *n.* heir (1406)
hewked *ppl.* clad (2333)

ihearcheyes *n. pl.* hierarchies (2259)
impe *n.* scion (1406)
importyng *pr. ppl.* signifying (121)
indyfferent *adj.* impartial (1416)
intendement *n.* understanding (1947)
intentyfe *adj.* diligent, assiduous (1143)
intier *adj.* complete (1460)
ioyell, ioyelles *n. & n. pl.* jewel (876), jewels (1387)
ioyntes *n. pl.* interrelationships of ancestry (2331)

kaysier *n.* emperor (1234)
kight *n.* kite (684)
knottes *n. pl.* beds of flowers laid out in intricate designs (117)
knytt *pp.* tied (245)
kynd *n.* nature (7)

laft *v.* left (1305)
lake *n.* lack (151)
lake *v.* to lack (38)
lowted *pp.* bowed (487)
lurke *v.* to wander, become idle (1219)
lynne *n.* line (1302)
lyvely *adj.* of life (1262)
lyvelyest *adj.* lifelike (121)

male *adj.* evil (1976)
masse *adj.* weighty (137)

mattes *n. pl.* friends, associates (1188)
meade, mede *n.* reward (475, 1353, 2271)
mean *adj.* intermediate (5), indifferent (14)
mendycitie *n.* humility of mind and body (91)
mere *adv.* entirely (1714)
met *adj.* suitable, appropriate (172)
mewe *n.* confinement (1276)
momentany *adj.* momentary (1649)
mon *v. pt.* moan (1980)
mondayn *adj.* mundane, of the world (1844)
moons *n. pl.* moans, laments (1765)
mornyng *adj.* mourning (66)
mutall *adj.* mutable (1982)
myrror *n.* warning, admonition (1177)
mysse *v.* to falter (75)

nere *prep.* near (1382)
nobles *n.* nobleness (1145)

obeysaunce *n.* obedience (1345)
ociosite *n.* idleness (47)
onlefull *adj.* unlawful (1325, 1333)
onsavery *adj.* distasteful (1218), inept (2395)
ontwynd *ppl. a.* destroyed (411)
opteyn *v.* obtain (2102)
orignyall *n.* cause, origin (1588)
owltrage *n.* outrage (975)

passing *pr. p.* caring (159)
past *v. pt.* cared (128)
pasturall *adj.* pastoral (1399)
pattes *n. pl.* pates (847)
paynfull *adj.* inflicting pain (1441)
perdurable *adj.* permanent (333)
pieusaunce *n.* authority, power (825, 1343)
pieuselles *n. pl.* maidens (1400)
poore blynd *adj.* purblind, obtuse (1205)
precell *v.* excel (1162), surpass (1568, 1671)
prerogatyfe *n.* control (948)
presse *n.* battle (1452)
prest *adj.* ready (514, 1271)
preventid *pp.* anticipated (145)

quyt, quytt *v.* & *pt.* paid back (475), requite (2397)

raced *pp.* eradicated, destroyed (910)
rathest *adv.* most readily (150)
ravyn *n.* violence, force (2003)
raygn *v.* reign (1907)
raygned *pp.* arreigned (1727)
raynes *adj.* of Rennes, Rhenish (247)
rebound *v.* redound (604)
redresse *v.* take up again (1997)
refell *v.* disprove (767)
reformyng *pr. p.* resharpening (743)
regally *n.* royalty (625), kingdom (1943)
released *ppl. a.* relieved, alleviated (1580)
relyke *adj.* surviving (1406)
remord *pp.* rebuked (1494)
remyse *n.* remission (1160)
renome *n.* renown (1268, 1651)
repayer *v.* supply (1107)
reprefe *v.* to be reproved (895)
repugne *v.* resist, deny (1505)
reputyng *pr. p.* imputing (53)
retaylle *v.* acquire (143)
retrogradaunt *adj.* descending on the western or declining side of the meridian line (4)
reuert *pp.* return back to (1431)
rewyn *n.* ruin (1317)
reyng *v.* reign (872)
roffes *n. pl.* roofs (106)
roue *v.* break in pieces (846)
rowte *n.* assemblage (666)
rusty *adj.* evilly motivated (464)
ryconyng, rykconyng *n.* expectation (1235), reckoning (1417)

sad *adj.* serious, sober (1068, 1360)
sary *adj.* sorry (1225)
sauor *n.* liking (831)
scedycion *n.* sedition (1952)
seage *n.* throne (2113)
sect *n.* class (1175)
sewe *v.* beg, request (1274)
sewer, sewere *adj.* & *adv.* sure (1515, 1911)
sewerties *n. pl.* collective security (1555)
shamfastnes *n.* shame (906)
smert *n.* smart, injury (848)
socyatt *adj.* associated (837)

sote *adj.* sweet (914)
sotiltie *n.* subtlety, cunning (2044)
sowced *pp.* plunged into (444)
speere, spere *n.* sphere (107, 1659)
spendell *n.* spindle (1284)
sporned *pp.* spurned, rejected (2359)
spot *v.* to stain, sully (595)
spotted *ppl. a.* marked (598)
stade *pp.* stood (2004)
stakeryng *pr. p.* staggering, uncertain (2395)
staye *n.* muse, reverie (1993)
stellefied *ppl. a.* placed among the stars (610)
straytly *adv.* strictly, legalistically (719)
superfluous *adj.* extravagant (101)
superfluyte *n.* promiscuity (1004)
supernall *adj.* dwelling in heaven (2268)
swer *adv.* sure (293)

tempor *v.* to tune (70)
tewned *pp.* tuned (669)
throne *n.* the pieces of thread left on a spindle (1283)
titile *n.* title (2019)
too *adj.* two (745)
torne *v.* turn (2282)
trace *n.* a measure in dancing (242, 840)
traced *pp.* led (1646)
trade, tradyth *v.* follow (945, 1015)
travayll *n.* task (2397)
travelled *pp.* worked, contrived (207, 1141)
travelles *n. pl.* labors (1148)
trayn *n.* outcome (87)
trype, tryppe *v.* (to trype on the trace) dance (242, 840)
twound *v.* twined (1291)
twyn *v.* to twine (1305)
twyst *n.* virginity (907)

vmber *n.* shadow (2)
vnnethe *adv.* scarcely (2393)
vre *n.* practice (28), habit (703), evidence (917), trend, tendency (1653)

vaylled *pp.* availed (145)
vere *n.* spring (2325)
verteus *n. pl.* virtues (1169)
voydyth *v.* disappears (219)

GLOSSARY

warbeled *pp. a.* quivering, undulating (1284)
waytie *adj.* serious (82)
wenyng *n.* self-esteem (941)
wether *v.* wither (2315)
whan *pp.* won (1694)
whele *n.* weal (1141)
whether *adv.* whither (1189)
whiles *n. pl.* wiles, stratagems (165)
whomanly *adj.* womanly (1358)

wight *adj.* white (1408)
wond *n.* wound (265)
wordly *adj.* worldly (219, 1113, 1647, 1662)
wrake *n.* wraith (856)
wye *adv.* why (1721)
wytt *n.* whit (358, 858)

yerthe *n.* earth (2345)

INDEX OF NAMES

Index of Names

Absolon (Absolom), 1451, 1861
Achilles, 1452
Affrike (Africa), 2065
Alexander Severe (Alexander Severus) 1866
Allexander (Alexander the Great), 1449
Aman (Hamon), 708
Anthonyous (Mark Anthony), 1009
Anyballe (Hannibal), 1136
Arthore (King Arthur), 1445
Arundell, Sir Thomas, 1768–809
Aske, Robert, 659
Attrophos (Atrophos), 1258, 1262, 1271, 1273, 1282, 1287, 1294, 1301

Boleyn, Queen Anne, 519–630
Breerton (William Brereton), 449–83
Brewtus Casseus (Brutus Cassius), 1130
Britayn (Britain), 1466
Bulmer (Sir John Bulmer), 660
Bygott (Sir Francis Bigod), 660

Caliope, Caliopie, 65, 67
Carowe (Sir Nicholas Carew), 664
Caton (Cato), 1460
Ceaser, Ceser, Cesare (Julius Caesar), 1126, 1442, 1464
Charlmayn (Charlemagne), 1455
Cicero, 1446
Cipio Affrican (Scipio Africanus), 1463
Claraunce (Duke of Clarence), 1049
Cleopatra, 1009

Clotho, 1259, 1280
Colege Cardynall (Cardinal College, later Christ Church College), 235
Constable, Sir Robert, 654
Cornelia, 1002
Cromwell, Thomas, 680–735
Culpeper, Thomas, 904, 937–64
Cupydes, Cupydo (Cupid), 901, 1330

Dacres, Thomas Fiennes, Baron, 661
Darcy, Thomas, Lord, 654
Davyd, Davythes (King David), 562, 1448
Dereham, Francis, 908
Devonshyre, 759
Dyngley (Sir Thomas Dingley), 663

Edward IV of England, 1050
Edward VI of England, 1407, 1813, 1838–907
Elizabeth I of England, 2363
Eton, John, 465
Europa, 2329
Exeter, Marquis of, Henry Courtenay, 750–819

Ffabricyus (Fabricius), 1459
Ffortescue (Sir Adrian Fortescue), 663
Froudes, John, 663

Gatholia (Athalia), 562
Godfroy of Bulloyn (Godfrey of Boulogne), 1456

INDEX OF NAMES

Gray, Lord Leonard, 656
Greseld (Griselda), 1369
Grey, Lady Jane, 2209–71

Hampton Court, 232
Hector, 1443
Henry VIII of England, 1227, 1273–473, 1493
Herculus (Hercules), 1439
Hester (Esther), 1001
Howard, Katherine, 854, 862–936
Hungerford, Walter (Baron Hungerford of Heytesbury), 655
Husy (Sir John, Baron Hussey), 654

Ipsewiche, 236
Irelond, (Ireland), 657

Iane (Jane, Queen of England), 603
Iudythe (Judith), 1001
Iupiter (Jupiter), 1438

Lacheses (Lachesis), 1261, 1281, 1303
Lumly (George Lumley), 661

Mallios (Machaeus), 2062
Mantell (John Mauntell), 663
Marcus Marcellus, 1462
Mardocheus, 710, 713
Mary, Queen of England, 1929–70, 2279–2383
Melpomene, 2279
Messalyn (Messalina), 1011
Montagewe (Henry Pole, Baron Montague), 750–819
The Moore (Wolsey's palace), 234
Moore (Thomas More), 664
Morlas (Morley's), 972
Morpheus, 1242, 1422

Nero, 1507
Nevell (Sir Edward Neville), 660
Niobe, 2281
Norris, Henry, 351–99
Northumberland, John Dudley, Duke of, 1566, 1792, 1999–2110

Octauyon (Octavius Caesar), 1465
Oxford, 235

Parnassus, 69
Parteryg (Sir Miles Partridge), 1831–37
Pasiua (Pasiphae), 1010
Paule (Pope Paul IV), 2342
Pennolopie (Penelope), 1001
Percy, Sir Thomas, 660
Phocion, 1458
Pirrus, 1441
Plato, 1450
Pompeyous (Pompey), 1461

Racell (Rachel), 1000
Rebecca, 1000
Rocheford (George Boleyn, Viscount Rochford), 274–343
Rocheford (Jane Boleyn, Viscountess Rochford), 972–1027
Rome, 1128, 1134, 1867, 2342
Rowlond (Roland), 1457
Roydon, George, 663

Salesburye (Margaret Pole, Countess of Salisbury), 1042–104
Salomon (Solomon), 1444, 1859
Sampson, 1454
Sara, 1000
Scipio of Affrican (Scipio Africanus), 1133
Semore (Sir John Seymour), 1632
Seymour, Lady Frances, 2174
Seymour, Lord Thomas, 1488–627
Seynt Iohns (St. John's), 973
Silla, 1007
Smeaton, Mark, 491–511
Somerset, Edward Seymour, Duke of, 1642–746, 1793, 1795
Stanhope, Sir Michael, 1810–30
Suffolk, Henry Grey, Duke of, 2125–87
Surrey, Henry Howard, Earl of, 1105–88

Tempest, Nicholas, 662
Troiean (Trojan), 1468
Tynnynainger (Tyttenhanger, Wolsey's palace), 234

Vane, Sir Ralph a, 1831–37
Venus, 181, 1329, 1346

Warwyke (Earl of Warwick), *See* Northumberland, 1566

Westmynster Place (Wolsey's palace), 233
Weston, Francis, 407–41
Wollsey (Thomas Wolsey), 85–259, 1772

Zerses (Xerxes), 2077

# THE RENAISSANCE ENGLISH TEXT SOCIETY

The Renaissance English Text Society

COUNCIL
PRESIDENT, *David M. Bevington*, University of Chicago
VICE-PRESIDENT, *Elizabeth S. Donno*, Columbia University
SECRETARY, *A. S. G. Edwards*, University of Victoria
TREASURER, *James M. Wells*, The Newberry Library

J. Leeds Barroll, University of Pittsburgh
Thomas Clayton, University of Minnesota
Richard Harrier, New York University
Robert Kinsman, University of California, at Los Angeles
Robert K. Turner, Jr., University of Wisconsin-Milwaukee

EDITORIAL COMMITTEE FOR *Metrical Visions*
David M. Bevington, University of Chicago
Robert Kinsman, University of California, at Los Angeles

THE RENAISSANCE ENGLISH TEXT SOCIETY was founded to publish scarce literary texts, chiefly nondramatic, of the period 1475–1660. Originally during each subscription period two single volumes, or one double volume, were distributed to members, who may purchase previous publications, while supplies last, at membership rates. The subscription rates are $10 each for Series 1 and 2, and $15 for Series 3, 4, and 5; student memberships are available, to persons providing proof of student status, at

$10 for all series. Prices for each series are based upon cost of printing and publication. Beginning in 1978, with the publication of Series IV, members are billed $15 annual dues (student members, $10) regardless of whether there is a volume published during the year; all subscriptions are used for printing and publishing costs, and members will be credited with the amount they have paid toward each series when it appears.

Subscriptions should be sent to James M. Wells at The Newberry Library, 60 West Walton Street, Chicago, Illinois 60610. Institutional members are requested to provide, at the time of enrollment, any order numbers or other information required for their billing records; the Society cannot provide multiple invoices or other complex forms for their needs. Non-members may buy copies, at higher rates, of past publications as follows: Volume I, from Mr. Wells; Volumes II, III, and IV from the University of Chicago Press, 5801 Ellis Avenue, Chicago, Illinois 60637; and of Volumes V–VI, VII–VIII, and IX from the University of South Carolina Press, Columbia, South Carolina 29208.

FIRST SERIES

Vol. I. *Merie Tales of the Mad Men of Gotam*, by A. B., edited by Stanley J. Kahrl, and *The History of Tom Thumbe*, by R. I., edited by Curt F. Bühler, 1965.

Vol. II. Thomas Watson's Latin *Amyntas*, edited by Walter F. Staton, Jr., and Abraham Fraunce's translation, *The Lamentations of Amyntas*, edited by Franklin M. Dickey, 1967.

SECOND SERIES

Vol. III. *The Dyaloge Called Funus*, a translation of Erasmus's colloquy (1534), and *A Very Pleasant and Fruitful Diologe called The Epicure*, Gerrard's translation of Erasmus's colloquy (1545), edited by Robert R. Allen, 1969.

Vol. IV. *Leicester's Ghost*, by Thomas Rogers, edited by Franklin B. Williams, Jr., 1972.

THIRD SERIES

Vol. V–VI. *A Collection of Emblemes, Ancient and Moderne*, by George Wither, with introduction by Rosemary Freeman and bibliographical notes by Charles S. Hensley, 1975.

FOURTH SERIES
Vol. VII–VIII. *Tom a Lincolne*, by R. I., edited by Richard S. M. Hirsch, 1978.

FIFTH SERIES
Vol. IX. *Metrical Visions*, by George Cavendish, edited by A. S. G. Edwards, 1980.